The Essence of Mergers and Acquisitions

The Essence of Management Series

Published titles

The Essence of Total Quality Management
The Essence of Strategic Management
The Essence of International Money
The Essence of Management Accounting
The Essence of Financial Accounting
The Essence of Marketing Research
The Essence of Information Systems
The Essence of Personal Microcomputing
The Essence of Successful Staff Selection
The Essence of Effective Communication
The Essence of Statistics for Business
The Essence of Business Taxation
The Essence of the Economy
The Essence of Mathematics for Business
The Essence of Organizational Behaviour
The Essence of Small Business
The Essence of Business Economics
The Essence of Operations Management
The Essence of Services Marketing
The Essence of International Business
The Essence of Marketing
The Essence of Financial Management

Forthcoming titles

The Essence of Public Relations
The Essence of Business Law
The Essence of International Marketing
The Essence of Women in Management
The Essence of Industrial Relations and Personnel Management
The Essence of Influencing Skills
The Essence of Services Management
The Essence of Industrial Marketing
The Essence of Venture Capital and New Ventures

The Essence of Mergers and Acquisitions

Dr P. S. Sudarsanam

Senior Lecturer in Finance and Accounting
City University Business School
London

FINANCIAL TIMES

Prentice Hall

An imprint of **Pearson Education**

Harlow, England · London · New York · Reading, Massachusetts · San Francisco
Toronto · Don Mills, Ontario · Sydney · Tokyo · Singapore · Hong Kong · Seoul
Taipei · Cape Town · Madrid · Mexico City · Amsterdam · Munich · Paris · Milan

First published 1995 by
Prentice Hall Europe

Pearson Education Limited
Edinburgh Gate
Harlow
Essex CM20 2JE
England

and Associated Companies around the world

Visit us on the World Wide Web at:
http://www.pearsoneduc.com

© **Prentice Hall Europe 1995**

Typeset in 10/12pt Palatino by
Keyset Composition, Colchester, Essex

Printed and bound in Great Britain by
Ashford Colour Press Ltd, Gosport, Hampshire

Library of Congress Cataloging-in-Publication Data

Sudarsanam, Sudi.
    The essence of mergers and acquisitions / Sudi
Sudarsanam.
        p. cm. – (The Essence of management series)
    Includes bibliographical references and index.
    ISBN 0-13-310889-9 (pbk.)
    1. Consolidation and merger of corporations–Great Britain.
    2. Consolidation and merger of corporations–Law and
        legislation–Great Britain.   I. Title.   II. Series
    HD2746.55.G7S83   1995
    338.8'3'0941–dc20   95-6960
                                                              CIP

British Library Cataloguing in Publication Data

A catalogue record for this book is available from
the British Library

ISBN 0-13-310889-9

---

10 9 8 7 6 5 4 3
04 03 02 01 00

To my late father, Srinivas,
and my mother, Rangam

Contents

Preface

Mergers and acquisitions are undertaken by companies to achieve certain strategic and financial objectives. They involve the bringing together of two organisations with often disparate corporate personalities, cultures and value systems. Success of mergers may, therefore, depend on how well the organisations are integrated. There is a variety of stakeholders in the merging companies who have an interest in the success of mergers. Shareholders and managers are two of the most important stakeholders, but others include employees, consumers, local communities and the economy at large. Mergers can have anticompetitive implications, and hence in many countries they attract rigorous antitrust scrutiny.

The actual conduct of takeover bids is in some countries highly regulated by statutory or non-statutory authorities. Such a regulation is particularly important in the case of hostile takeover bids, which represent a phenomenon seen almost entirely in the Anglo-Saxon countries.

Increasingly, mergers have assumed an international dimension due to global economic integration and the dismantling of barriers to trade and investment. Competition is becoming global and companies have to compete not only in their domestic markets, but also in foreign markets in order to maintain their competitive edge. This trend has caused not only higher levels of cross-border takeover activity, but also organisational innovations such as strategic alliances to achieve the same competition objectives. The move away from the cosy familiarity of domestic acquisitions and into foreign ones is full of hazards.

There is a widely held perception that companies making acquisitions and merging with other companies are unable to create value for their shareholders. In some cases, the feverish atmosphere, the inexorable momentum and thrill of the chase of a hostile bid may drive managers to foolish excess in the bid premium they pay. The causes of failure may, in other cases, stem from the fragmented perspective that managers and other players in the acquisition game have of the merger and acquisition process.

This book has evolved out of a specialist MBA elective course on Mergers, Acquisitions and Divestments (MAD) which I have been teaching at the City University Business School, London, for the last few years. It aims to provide a unified view of the organisational, legal, regulatory and financial aspects of mergers and acquisitions. It provides a framework for evaluating the strategic and financial aspects of merger proposals. The regulatory and stock market environment in which mergers take place is described. The book examines the evidence for the failure of acquisitions and the likely causes of failure.

One consequence of failure is restructuring in the form of corporate divestments. Different types and effects of such divestments are described. The book discusses cross-border mergers, the rationale behind them, the recent trend in and the barriers to such mergers. Some survey evidence on the success of cross-border mergers is provided. The book ends with an introduction to strategic alliances, which have become increasingly important as an alternative to acquisitions and mergers especially in international business.

The primary focus of this book so far as the legal, regulatory and accounting aspects are concerned is the UK, but an outline of other jurisdictions is given by way of comparison. The treatment of other aspects of mergers is of more universal relevance. Discussion of cross-border mergers and strategic alliances enhances this relevance.

The style of the book is to a large extent non-technical, and the accent is on the practical aspects of mergers and acquisitions. This practical orientation is strengthened by the copious use of illustrative examples from actual acquisitions and mergers carried out in the last few years. Quantitative areas of the subject such as valuation are explained with worked examples.

In keeping with the spirit of the Essence series, the book provides an easy and comprehensive introduction to the intriguing subject of mergers and acquisitions. The book is intended to be used by MBA students and managers who are or might become involved in mergers and acquisitions. At the MBA level, the book may be used in courses in finance, business policy, corporate strategy and industrial economics. It may also be used in similar courses at the undergraduate level.

Acknowledgements

I wish to thank a number of my colleagues and friends who have helped me in the writing of this book. Professor Alfred Kenyon, Professor Chong Choi, Dr Shiv Mathur, Dr Peter Holl, Dylan Thomas, David Citron, Dr Mez Lasfer, Dr Ayo Salami and Jimmy Lai, my colleagues at the City University Business School, London, and Paul Ryan of the University College, Dublin, offered critical and helpful comments on the earlier drafts of the book. I am particularly grateful to Alfred Kenyon for his patient and enthusiastic reading of the entire book. His vigorous comments have greatly improved the clarity and quality of presentation. Professor Julian Franks of the London Business School made valuable suggestions for enhancing the rigour of the book. Professor Patrick Hutchinson of the University of New England, Australia, helped me improve the style of presentation. Ash Mahate of the University of Greenwich not only provided detailed and perceptive comments on the text but, along with Ayo Salami and Jimmy Lai, also helped me with data collection and graphs. Peter Hall of Chase Investment Bank, Nicola Stanhope of Clifford Chance the law firm and Leslie Warman, formerly a director of Lloyds Merchant Bank, kindly scrutinised the regulatory aspects dealt with in the book. Martyn Jones of Touche Ross helped me with the tax aspects of valuation and payment methods. Professor Adrian Buckley of Cranfield School of Management, who is the Essence series editor, and Andy Goss, the Acquisitions Editor at Prentice Hall, offered me support and encouragement for which I am thankful. Finally, my wife, Padhma, deserves my most profound thanks for her patience and understanding during all the time that I was perspiring in front of my word processor, desperately awaiting inspiration for the right idea, word or turn of phrase.

1

Introduction

Mergers and acquisitions are a means of corporate expansion and growth. They are not the only means of corporate growth, but are an alternative to growth by internal or organic capital investment. From time to time, companies have preferred the external means of growth through acquisitions to internal growth. Indeed, mergers and acquisitions have tended to follow a historic pattern of 'waves', with periods of frenetic takeover activity punctuating periods of relative sedateness. Thus in the UK we have observed peaks of takeover activity in 1968, 1972 and 1989. A similar wave pattern has been observed in other countries, notably in the USA. Why do companies 'get high' on takeover fever at certain times, whereas at other times they prefer internal growth? This is a phenomenon which as yet is not completely understood.

The terms 'merger', 'acquisition' and 'takeover' are all part of the mergers and acquisitions parlance. In a merger, the corporations come together to combine and share their resources to achieve common objectives. The shareholders of the combining firms often remain as joint owners of the combined entity. An acquisition resembles more of an arm's-length deal, with one firm purchasing the assets or shares of another, and with the acquired firm's shareholders ceasing to be owners of that firm. In a merger a new entity may be formed subsuming the merging firms, whereas in an acquisition the acquired firm becomes the subsidiary of the acquirer.

A 'takeover' is similar to an acquisition and also implies that the acquirer is much larger than the acquired. Where the acquired firm is larger than the acquirer, the acquisition is referred to as a 'reverse takeover'. Although the terms 'merger' and 'acquisition' are often

1

used interchangeably, they have precise connotations in certain contexts, such as when acquirers choose which accounting rules to apply in consolidating the accounts of the two firms involved. While the distinction is important for specific contexts, we shall, in general, use the terms interchangeably.

Historical pattern of UK takeover activity

Table 1.1 presents the number and value of takeovers in the UK from 1964 to 1992. There are clearly peaks of takeover activity in 1968, 1972 and 1989 in terms of value and in terms of average size of a takeover. When allowance is made for the inflationary increase in company values, the peaks in those three years are unmistakable. Figure 1.1 shows the 1968, 1972 and 1989 peaks in total value of acquisitions at 1990 prices.

The most recent upsurge in takeovers was in the period 1984 to 1989. During that period the average size of an acquisition increased from £9.64 million to £20.38 million. While the increase in average acquisition was substantial, it conceals some megabids unthinkable in earlier periods. The second half of the 1980s thus represents a qualitatively different period from the earlier periods of high takeover activity.

The reasons for the enormous volume of acquisitions in the 1980s were manifold. The stock market in the UK, in harmony with markets in other countries, experienced a strong bull phase which culminated in the October Crash of 1987. There was a more relaxed, *laissez-faire* governmental attitude to mergers and acquisitions embodied in the new vision of Thatcherism. Many of the megamergers would, however, not have been possible but for innovations in the financing of takeovers, such as leveraged buyouts.

The 1980s also witnessed divestments on a large scale. Divestments are the flip side of acquisitions, with companies selling off divisions or subsidiaries to other corporations or to managers of the divested parts in a management buyout (MBO). As Table 1.2 shows, the value of payments for intercorporate acquisitions of subsidiaries dramatically increased after 1985. Divestments were about 31 per cent of all acquisitions and mergers in 1992, and around 25 per cent in the period 1986–92.

The simultaneous increase in acquisitions and divestments suggests a considerable amount of corporate restructuring in the UK economy in recent years. Such a restructuring has been made

Table 1.1 Acquisitions and mergers in the UK, 1964–92

Year	Number acquired	Nominal value (£m)	Average value (£m)	Value (£m in 1990 prices)
1964	940	505	0.54	45.01
1965	1000	517	0.52	44.19
1966	807	500	0.62	41.12
1967	763	822	1.08	65.76
1968	946	1946	2.06	150.97
1969	906	935	1.03	70.04
1970	793	1122	1.41	77.97
1971	884	911	1.03	56.97
1972	1210	2532	2.09	143.78
1973	1205	1304	1.08	68.63
1974	504	508	1.01	22.91
1975	315	291	0.92	10.29
1976	353	448	1.27	13.82
1977	481	824	1.71	22.66
1978	567	1140	2.01	27.90
1979	534	1656	3.10	35.96
1980	469	1475	3.14	27.01
1981	452	1144	2.53	19.03
1982	463	2206	4.76	34.29
1983	447	2343	5.24	34.48
1984	568	5474	9.64	76.47
1985	474	7090	14.96	93.92
1986	842	15 370	18.25	198.63
1987	1528	16 539	10.82	203.56
1988	1499	22 839	15.24	265.05
1989	1337	27 250	20.38	293.77
1990	779	8329	10.69	83.28
1991	506	10 434	20.62	98.66
1992	433	5939	13.72	53.70

Note: Data up to 1969 include only quoted companies. After 1969, figures include all industrial and commercial companies. The GDP price deflator has been used to restate the value of bids in 1990 prices.
Sources: 'Acquisitions and Mergers within the UK', *Central Statistical Office Bulletin*, London, May 1993, and Datastream for GDP price deflator.

possible by new organisational innovations such as management buyouts and management buyins, as well as by financial innovations like high-leverage buyouts and mezzanine finance.

There is a variety of motivations for divestments. One of the themes of the 1980s was deconglomeration and sticking to the core businesses. The divestor, on this view, was getting rid of under- or

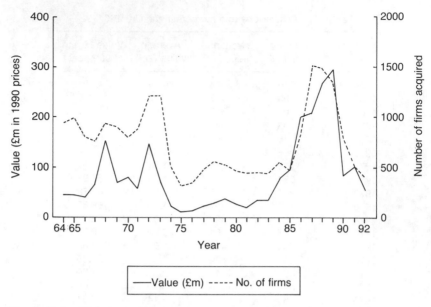

Figure 1.1 Historical pattern of UK mergers and acquisitions: value and number of firms acquired, 1964–92.

non-performing businesses so as to concentrate its resources on high-value activities. Some divestments were sometimes motivated by the need to avoid corporate financial distress or outright liquidation. We will discuss these possible motivations and the impact of various forms of divestment on the performance of both divestors and acquirers of divested assets.

Objectives of mergers and acquisitions

The immediate objective of an acquisition is self-evidently growth and expansion of the acquirer's assets, sales and market share. However, this merely represents an intermediate objective. A more fundamental objective may be the enhancement of shareholders' wealth through acquisitions aimed at accessing or creating sustainable competitive advantage for the acquirer. In modern finance theory, shareholder wealth maximisation is posited as a rational criterion for investment and financing decisions made by managers.

Shareholder wealth maximisation may, however, be supplanted

Table 1.2 Acquisitions, mergers and intercorporate divestments in the UK, 1972–92

Year	Total of acquisitions		Divestments		Divest./ total (%)
	Number	Value (£m)	Number	Value (£m)	
1972	1210	2532	272	185	7.31
1973	1205	1304	254	247	18.94
1974	504	508	137	49	9.64
1975	315	291	115	70	24.05
1976	353	448	111	100	22.32
1977	481	824	109	94	11.41
1978	567	1140	126	163	14.30
1979	534	1656	117	186	11.23
1980	469	1475	101	210	14.24
1981	452	1144	125	262	22.90
1982	463	2206	164	804	36.45
1983	447	2343	142	436	18.61
1984	568	5474	170	1121	20.47
1985	474	7090	134	793	11.18
1986	842	15 370	221	3093	20.12
1987	1528	16 486	340	4667	28.31
1988	1499	22 839	376	5532	24.22
1989	1337	27 250	441	5677	20.83
1990	779	8329	342	2941	35.31
1991	506	10 434	214	2945	28.23
1992	433	5803	199	1832	31.57

Note: The last column is based on values of acquisitions and divestments.
Source: 'Acquisitions and Mergers within the UK', *Central Statistical Office Bulletin*, London, May 1993

by the self-interest pursuit of managers making those decisions. According to the managerial utility theory, acquisitions may be driven by managerial ego or desire for power, empire building or perquisites that go with the size of the firm. Empirical evidence which we shall discuss is inconclusive as to what fundamentally drives acquisitions.

Mergers and acquisitions and business strategy

Whatever the fundamental objective of the managers in acquiring other companies, such acquisitions must form part of the business and corporate strategies of the acquirer. Business strategy is aimed at creating a sustainable competitive advantage for the firm. Such an advantage may stem from economies of scale and scope, or market power, or access to unique strengths which the acquired company may possess.

Often the acquirer may aim to transfer its 'superior' management skills to the target of acquisition and thereby enhance the earning power of the target's assets. Here the added value can be created even when the target remains a stand-alone entity, and does not depend upon any possible synergy between the acquirer and the acquired. The acquirer is pursuing a corporate strategy of value creation through efficiency improvements in the target.

An acquisition may also fulfil the acquirer's corporate strategy of building a portfolio of unrelated businesses. The aim here may be risk reduction if the earnings streams of the different businesses in the portfolio are not highly positively correlated. In an efficient capital market framework, the ability of this strategy to create value for shareholders is open to doubt.

Indeed, whether acquisitions can create value for the acquirer's shareholders is a question which has been empirically addressed by a number of researchers. Earlier evidence suggests that acquisitions, from the acquirer shareholders' perspective, are at best neutral and at worst value destroying to a small degree. These tests are, however, sensitive to the methodology adopted, and more recent evidence lends some support to the view that acquisitions can add value to the acquirer shareholders. There is almost universal agreement that target shareholders earn substantial bid premia, often amounting to 30 per cent in a matter of days surrounding the bids.

This paradox of target shareholders gaining and the bidder shareholders struggling to hold their own raises a number of interesting issues concerning both the acquirer's motive and its ability to translate expected gains from the proposed acquisition into wealth gains for its shareholders. Indeed, arguably, the evidence may be consistent with managerial motives dominating takeover decisions. It appears that there is many a proverbial slip between acquisitions and value creation in the post-acquisition period. Apart from managerial self-interest, which may drive at least some of the acquisitions, there are other aspects of the acquisition process which need to be explored before the actual source of acquisition failure can be reasonably traced.

In large corporations, investment decisions such as acquisitions are subject to a wide variety of intra-organisational conflicts. It may be the acquisition process, with ill-defined objectives and messy political compromises, which leads to poor acquisition decisions. We will explore the impact of the organisational dynamics of the acquisition decision process on acquisition success.

The dynamics of the takeover process

Another aspect of the acquisition process which may determine its success is the market dynamics external to the firm. Takeovers have been referred to as the market for corporate control, with rival management teams competing for the right to manage the corporate assets of the target. In this market, as in others, there are intermediaries whose profitability depends upon the volume of takeovers they handle.

The incentives that some of the intermediaries, such as merchant bankers, have in M & A deals may create conflicts of interest between bidders and their advisers. Such incentives may lead to pressures for 'closing the deal'. In this event, acquirers, unable to resist such pressures, may overpay for the targets, and post-acquisition added value may not match, let alone exceed, this overpayment. It is, therefore, necessary to understand the dynamics of the takeover process. We will describe the role of the inter-mediaries in the bid process and the areas of potential conflicts of interest between bidders and targets on the one hand and inter-mediaries on the other.

Economic consequences of takeovers

So far we have focused on the shareholders and managers as gaining or losing from acquisitions. But mergers and acquisitions have wider constituencies than just these two groups. Indeed, either or both of the groups can gain at the expense of these other constituencies. The latter include employees, consumers and com-munities in which the operations of the acquired and acquirer firms are located.

Takeovers often lead to rationalisation of operations of the firms involved as well as renegotiation of the terms of employment. There have been, for instance, cases in the recent past when acquirers attempted to reduce the value of pension benefits which employees of the acquired company had enjoyed. Rationalisation may also lead to plant closures and consequent redundancies, with often devastating impact on local communities.

Where the acquisition is driven by the desire to achieve market dominance or increased market power, the shareholders and manager groups may gain from the merger, but to the detriment of consumers. Such reduction in competition may also have long-term consequences for the competitiveness and growth of the economy as a whole. For these reasons, takeovers in the UK and many other countries are subject to antitrust screening. The antitrust authorities have statutory powers to block a merger or allow it subject to certain acceptable conditions.

UK bidders are subject to the antitrust regime policed by the Office of Fair Trading (OFT). They also have to observe the rules of the European Union (EU) Merger Regulation. While the UK antitrust rules empower the OFT to take into account wider criteria than just competition, since 1984 there has been a major shift in emphasis towards competition as the primary ground on which mergers are investigated in the UK.

The dual antitrust regime to which EU companies are subject sometimes creates a jurisdictional conflict between member states and the European Commission. As the EU Merger Regulation has been in existence only since September 1990, it is still evolving, with a corpus of case law on individual mergers being built up. The motivation behind the promulgation of the EU Merger Regulation was to create 'a one-stop shopping' for antitrust clearance. We will examine to what extent this aim has been achieved and look forward to the future evolution of the EU regime.

Cross-border acquisitions

There has been a substantial increase in the amount of funds flowing across nations in search of takeover candidates. The UK has been the most important foreign investor in the USA in recent years, with British companies making large acquisitions. With the advent of the Single Market, the European Union now represents the largest single market in the world. European as well as Japanese and American companies have, therefore, sought to increase their market presence by acquisitions in this huge market.

British companies have made acquisitions both on Continental Europe and in the USA. They have also increasingly been the targets of acquirers from overseas. The number of European acquisitions made by UK companies in 1993 was 196, amounting to £3.96 billion. The corresponding figures for acquisitions in the USA were 107 and £13.80 billion.

Cross-border acquisitions pose many of the same problems as domestic ones, as regards identifying appropriate targets with high value creation potential, the scope for overpayment and post-acquisition integration. However, these problems may be of a higher order of magnitude in cross-border mergers because of the acquirer's lack of familiarity with the acquired firm's environment and organisational culture.

There are many instances of UK companies making a hash of their US acquisitions. The commonality of language may have induced in these acquirers a false sense of familiarity, and dulled their awareness of the idiosyncratic nature of the US corporate environment and cultural norms. Acquirers need to sensitise themselves to the cultural and other nuances of targets in foreign countries before they venture abroad.

Corporate divestments

As noted earlier, the 1980s witnessed a high level of corporate divestments. Together, acquisitions and divestments constitute corporate restructuring. The ease with which divestments could be carried out has endowed firms with a great deal of flexibility and capacity to adapt their business and corporate strategies to the changing environment. Firms can reconfigure their businesses less traumatically than in the past, and with greater speed, when they find that a particular business fits ill with their changed strategic vision.

The existence of an intercorporate market in corporate assets does not require that the ownership of the legal entity owning those assets has to change before the portfolio of its businesses can be reshuffled. Thus a predatory acquisition followed by asset stripping is not the only mechanism available for transferring assets to those who can exploit their potential to the full. Provided firms are perceptive enough to see when a particular business in their portfolio has outlived its strategic *raison d'être*, they could use the divestment mechanism to improve the value of their businesses, and thereby avoid falling into the hands of asset strippers.

Strategic alliances as alternatives to acquisitions

In recent years, many companies have sought to advance their strategic goals through strategic alliances in preference to straight acquisitions. This preference has resulted partly from the 'failure' of many acquisitions. But strategic alliances also have certain inherent advantages. Since they are created to achieve specific and fairly narrowly defined strategic objectives, there is a greater clarity of purpose than in 'fuzzy' acquisitions. Further, with these ventures and alliances, the problem of post-acquisition integration does not arise.

There are, however, pitfalls in strategic alliances which are co-operative arrangements among actual or potential rivals. This paradoxical co-operative–competitive game is not easy to manage. Often joint ventures fall apart for organisational reasons because of cultural conflicts or divergent managerial philosophies between the venture partners. We shall set out the relative attractions and shortcomings of strategic alliances.

Objective of the book

The objective of the book is to provide the readers with an overview of the subject of mergers and acquisitions. It seeks not to give conclusive answers to the questions raised by corporate mergers and acquisitions, but to indicate the balance of evidence in favour of one or the other of many answers to these questions. The practical aspects of mergers and acquisitions are as important as the theoretical constructs used to explore the various aspects surrounding them. The practical perspective is enhanced by numerous examples from actual mergers and strategic alliances. It is hoped that after reading this book the reader will be stimulated to explore the subject further, and to this end a list of further reading is provided at the end of each chapter.

Outline of the book

Chapter 2 discusses the possible motivations for firms to undertake mergers and acquisitions. The neoclassical profit maximisation model is contrasted with the managerial utility model. The agency problem, a concomitant of the divorce of management from ownership of large modern corporations, is seen as particularly relevant to the acquisition decision and the post-merger performance of the acquirer.

The acquisition decision is placed in Chapter 3 in the context of the acquirer's business and corporate strategies. Techniques for the strategic evaluation of potential acquisition targets are described. The relationship between acquisition strategy and business strategy is illustrated. Chapter 4 examines the organisational context of the acquisitions process and highlights how, in a large corporation, this process may not produce a unified view of the objective or the benefits of an acquisition. It is argued that the seeds of post-merger problems may actually be sown in the acquisition decision process.

Chapters 5 and 6 explore the regulatory environment in which takeover bids are conducted in the UK. The antitrust regime in the UK and at the European Union level is described, and the shortcomings of this regime are critically examined. The role of the City Panel on Takeovers and Mergers (the Panel) in regulating the conduct of bids for public companies in the UK is discussed and illustrated.

The external dynamics of the market for corporate control are explored in Chapters 7 and 8. The various players in that market, the intermediaries, the arbitrageurs and the financial institutions, and their influence on the level of activity and outcomes of takeover contests, are described. The bid offence strategies and tactics in hostile bids are delineated.

Chapter 9 is concerned with the valuation of targets. Various approaches to target valuation and their limitations are considered. Accounting rules for mergers and acquisitions are discussed in Chapter 10. The choice of payment medium in acquisitions is a very complex decision based on liquidity, tax and accounting rules, and valuation uncertainty considerations. The determinants of the choice of payment method are discussed in Chapter 11.

Chapter 12 examines the different types of defensive strategy that target companies in hostile bids deploy, and provides evidence of their relative effectiveness. In Chapter 13, evidence from numerous studies on the post-acquisition performance of merged firms is presented. This performance is evaluated from the perspective of different stakeholders.

Evidence, based on managerial surveys, on the post-merger performance of acquirers is presented in Chapter 14, which also examines the possible reasons for the wide perception that acquisitions 'don't pay'. The problems of post-merger integration of the acquired with the acquirer are highlighted.

Chapter 15 describes the recent phenomenon of divestments and similar forms of corporate restructuring. The relationship between such restructuring and the 'failure' of earlier acquisitions by divestors is traced. The variety of forms which divestment has taken, and the logic and motivation behind them, are discussed. The wealth impact of divestments on the divestor shareholders is examined with empirical evidence from a number of studies. The structure of MBOs and their performance are discussed.

Chapter 16 describes the recent trend towards increasing cross-border acquisitions. The reasons for this trend are set out, and the problems associated with cross-border acquisitions are examined. The differences in the environments of different countries are highlighted, and the impact of these differences on bid and defence strategies is discussed.

The alternatives to full-scale mergers and acquisitions are described in Chapter 17. Companies, having burnt their fingers with unwise or intractable acquisitions, increasingly look to strategic alliances as part of their business strategies. The various types of strategic alliance, and their advantages and disadvantages compared to acquisitions, are examined.

References and further reading

Bannock, G. (1990) 'The takeover boom: an international and historic perspective', Hume Occasional Paper 15, The David Hume Institute.

2

Acquisition motives

Acquisition motives may be defined in terms of the acquirer's corporate and business strategy objectives. For example, a large food company with well-established brand names or distribution network may acquire a small, less well-known target in order to achieve marketing and distribution synergies. Other acquisitions may be motivated by the desire for increased market power, control of a supplier, consolidation of excess production capacity and so on. However, as noted in Chapter 1, while strategic objectives are the proximate motives for acquisitions, these strategies themselves are formulated to serve the interests of the stakeholders in the acquiring firm.

Strategies are formulated and acquisition decisions are made by the managers of the acquiring firm. Managers may be taking these decisions to further the interest of the owners of the firm, i.e. the shareholders. This is the neoclassical view of the firm, in which the shareholder interest is paramount and managerial interests are subordinated. Where managerial interests differ from those of the shareholders, acquisitions may be undertaken to serve the former.

In large, publicly owned modern corporations, managers wield considerable power and discretion, and are often subject to only feeble oversight by shareholders. This gives managers much scope to pursue their own self-interest at the expense of the shareholders. Acquisitions driven by managerial self-interest may fail and cause wealth losses for shareholders.

In the literature there is a wide perception that acquisitions 'don't pay' for the shareholders of the acquirer (see Chapter 13 on assessment of acquisition performance). A possible reason for this is that they are motivated by managerial self-interest. In this chapter, we describe the alternative shareholder and managerial perspectives, and draw out the implications for the success of the acquisition when either the shareholder or managerial considerations dominate the other. It must be remembered that the conflict between the two perspectives may permeate all decisions made by managers and not just acquisitions.

The causes of failure of acquisitions cannot be unambiguously attributed to managerial selfishness. Even if managers do act in the shareholder interest, acquisitions may fail for a variety of other reasons, such as weak acquisition strategy, bid dynamics and problems of post-acquisition integration. It may be argued that these are themselves an affirmation of managerial misconduct arising from pursuit of managerial self-interest. However, managerial incompetence untainted by malice towards the shareholders is at least a plausible villain in the acquisition drama.

Shareholder wealth maximisation perspective

In this neoclassical perspective, all firm decisions including acquisitions are made with the objective of maximising the wealth of the shareholders of the firm. This means that the incremental cash flows from the decision, when discounted at the appropriate discount rate, should yield zero or positive net present value. Under uncertainty, the discount rate is the risk-adjusted rate with a market-determined risk premium for risk (see Chapter 9 on determination of the discount rate).

With acquisitions, the shareholder wealth maximisation criterion is satisfied when the added value created by the acquisition exceeds the cost of acquisition:

Added value from   = Value of acquirer and the acquired after
acquisition   acquisition − Their aggregate value before

Increase in acquirer = Added value − Cost of acquisition
share value

Cost of acquisition   = Acquisition transaction cost
                         + Acquisition premium

Acquisition transaction cost is the cost incurred when an acquisition is made, in the form of various advisers' fees (see Chapter 7), regulator's fees, stock exchange fees, cost of underwriting and so on. The acquisition premium is the excess of the offer price paid to the target over the target's pre-bid price. It is also called the control premium. Where managers seek to enhance shareholder wealth, they must not only add value, but also ensure that the cost of the acquisition does not exceed that value. Value creation may occur in the target alone, or in both the acquirer and the acquired firm. The calculation of added value for the acquirer's shareholders is illustrated in the following example.

Predator plc makes a cash bid for Sitting Duck plc. Their equity market values ahead of the bid are respectively £100 million and £20 million. Predator expects that, as a result of the operational and strategic improvements made to Sitting Duck, its value will, post-acquisition, increase to £30 million. It pays a premium of £5 million to Sitting Duck shareholders to win control in a hostile bid, which also entails transaction costs, in the form of advisers' fees etc., of £0.5 million.

Added value from acquisition $= £(100 + 30)m - (100 + 20)m$
$= £10m$

Cost of acquisition $= £5m + 0.5m = £5.5m$

Increase in Predator's share value $= £10m - 5.5m = £4.5m$

Assuming that the stock market correctly anticipates the expected benefits from the acquisition and the transaction costs, the market value of Predator will increase by £4.5 million at the time of the takeover.

Managerial perspective

The modern corporate economy is characterised by large corporations with widespread diffusion of ownership which is divorced from management. With the separation of ownership from control, the relation between shareholders and managers may be viewed as one between a principal and his or her agent. In this agency model, managers as agents may not always act in the best interest of the principal. The cost to the shareholders of such behaviour is called the agency cost and represents loss of value to the shareholders.

Managers may act in disregard of their principal's interest in order to promote their own self-interest. In the acquisition context, such self-interest pursuit may result in bad acquisitions and loss of shareholder value. Acquisitions lacking in value creation rationale may be undertaken to satisfy managerial objectives such as an increase in firm size.

Where the acquisition does have value creation potential, it may be overestimated. Managers may overpay for the acquisition or incur high transaction costs by launching hostile bids. Managers may make genuine errors in estimating the value creation potential, since such an estimation is often based on incomplete information about the target at the time of the bid. If managers are unaware of such errors, they may unwittingly pay an excessive bid premium or enter into a hostile bid with attendant high transaction costs.

Disentangling managers' true intentions from their decisions poses problems both before and after a takeover. *Ex ante*, managers can be very persuasive about the merits of an acquisition and the potential for shareholder wealth increase. *Ex post*, managerial intentions may be obscured by alternative explanations for acquisition failure. Thus evidence of acquisition failure may point to either an agency problem or managerial failure unrelated to agency conflict.

Managerial motives in acquisitions

Managers may undertake acquisitions for the following reasons:

1. To pursue growth in the size of their firm, since their remuneration, perquisites, status and power are a function of firm size (the empire-building syndrome).
2. To deploy their currently underused managerial talents and skills (the self-fulfilment motive).
3. To diversify risk and minimise the costs of financial distress and bankruptcy (job security motive).
4. To avoid being taken over (job security motive).

The above motives are not mutually exclusive, but to some extent reinforcing. They are now discussed in turn.

1. Managerial compensation may be related to firm size because of the greater complexity of larger firms. Managers may derive

intangible benefits such as power and social status when they run large firms. Executive compensation may increase as a result of an increase in firm size (e.g. in terms of assets or sales), even when there is no corresponding increase in shareholders' wealth (Jensen, 1986). Managers may pursue growth if their compensation is a function of sales growth.

2. Where a firm is in a mature or declining industry, the survival of the firm may depend on an orderly exit from that industry and entry into one with greater growth opportunities. The present industry operations may not exhaust the managerial energies and talents available to the firm. Without moving into a growth industry, the firm may lose young managers and thereby accelerate its own decline.

3. Risk diversification may be achieved when the acquiring and the acquired firms' cash flows are not highly positively correlated, thereby reducing the overall variability of the combined entity's cash flows. Such diversification is not necessarily value creating for the shareholders. In a well-functioning capital market, shareholders may construct their portfolio to include the shares of both companies and achieve the required diversification, perhaps at a lower cost than the firm. Thus, shareholders' do-it-yourself diversification may be a superior alternative to firm diversification.

Risk diversification may, nevertheless, be of value under certain circumstances. For example, when the acquired firm's shares are not traded, diversification into that firm is only possible for investors via corporate diversification. Second, the reduction in the overall variability of the firm's cash flows reduces the probability of financial distress and bankruptcy. Financial distress is the condition where the firm finds it difficult to meet its obligations and is forced to make suboptimal operating, investment and financing decisions. Firm failure results in receivership or winding up of the firm. Financial distress and firm failure may have a greater impact on managers than on shareholders.

Managers are generally overinvested in their own firms. This overinvestment arises from three sources. They depend on their firms for their income in the form of salaries and bonuses. They may have developed firm-specific human capital which outside their present firm may not be valued as highly. Finally, where they receive compensation in the form of stocks and stock options, they increase their investment in their own firms.

Thus, unlike shareholders, managers hold highly undiversified portfolios which are overwhelmingly invested in their own firms. This suggests that total risk, which includes firm-specific risk such as the risk of failure, is more important to managers than systematic risk: that is, market-movement-related risk appropriate to well-diversified shareholders.

Shareholders may also benefit from a reduction in the risk of financial distress and bankruptcy through corporate diversification. However, the more stable cash flows of the combined firm resulting from a diversifying merger may strengthen the security available to the debt holders of the firm. Thus debt holders, rather than shareholders, may be the beneficiaries of risk reduction.

4. The last of the motives – avoiding being taken over – is perhaps the least plausible or respectable and, for that reason, is often clothed in euphemistic and lofty managerial rhetoric about the value of the company's continued independence. Target managers often go to extraordinary lengths to defeat hostile takeover bids (see Chapter 12). To achieve immunity from the threat of a takeover, managers may undertake acquisitions, assuming, quite falsely at times, that increased firm size confers such immunity.

At least in the 1980s, large firms were not so protected. In the USA, RJR Nabisco, the food and tobacco conglomerate, was taken over in a hostile leveraged buyout for $25 billion. In the UK, the Hoylake consortium bid £13 billion for BAT Industries in 1989. Consolidated Goldfields was taken over in a hostile bid by Hanson in 1989 for £3.1 billion. In the mid-1980s, several UK companies like Imperial Group and Distillers were taken over in bids worth nearly £2 billion. Those were the days of megabids when hostile bidders were not deterred by target size.

Acquisitions to increase firm size, or to move into growth industries and away from the declining ones in which the firm currently operates, are consistent with the defensive motive of avoiding becoming a takeover target.

Free cash flow and the agency problem

Free cash flow is normally measured as the operating cash flow after the firm has met its tax commitments, and after it has financed the currently available investment opportunities. According to Jensen (1986), 'free cash flow is cash flow in excess of that required to fund all projects that have positive net present values when discounted at the relevant cost of capital' (see Chapter 9 on calculation of free cash flow).

Such free cash flow is generally available to profitable firms in mature industries with few growth prospects. Managers of those firms have the option to increase the dividend payout or recapitalise their firms, that is, to buy back equity, and have more debt and less equity in their firms' capital structure. Either course would reduce the size of the free cash flow. Alternatively, managers could use the free cash flow to finance diversifying acquisitions, which might turn out to be negative net present value investments. In the 1960s, many firms in tobacco, food, oil and other mature industries diversified into unrelated businesses with poor subsequent financial performance and value decline for their shareholders. In the 1980s, such firms themselves became targets of hostile takeovers.

How can managers be induced to make use of the free cash flow in an optimal way from the shareholders' perspective? 'For shareholders the problem is how to motivate managers to disgorge the excess cash rather than investing it at below the cost of capital or wasting it on organisational inefficiencies' (Jensen, 1986). This suggests that free cash flow is not in itself a manifestation of the agency conflict between shareholders and managers, but that, when put to 'improper' use by managers, it can accentuate that conflict.

Mechanisms for controlling the agency conflict

A number of control mechanisms exist to minimise the incidence and cost of the agency conflict to shareholders. They are both internal and external to the firm. Internal controls include shareholder–manager alignment devices, a rigorous policing of managerial conduct and managerial compensation contracts. External mechanisms rely on the discipline imposed on managers by the product market in which the firm sells its output, the managerial labour market where managers with a reputation may command premium wages, and the market for corporate control in which management teams compete for the right to manage corporate assets.

Internal agency conflict control mechanisms

Since the source of agency conflict is the divorce of ownership from control, such a conflict may be mitigated by aligning the interests of the managers and shareholders. When managers own shares in their own companies, their interests are at least partly aligned to those of shareholders. Executive share option schemes operated by many companies are intended to accomplish such an alignment. Managers receive their reward in many forms – returns to their shareholding; direct pecuniary remuneration in the form of salaries, bonuses and perquisites; and indirect, psychological rewards of control, power or status.

Making managers part owners of the firm by offering share

options may, however, not influence their behaviour towards alignment if they derive more reward from the other two sources. Further, share ownership by managers may potentially facilitate their entrenchment and protect them from the discipline of other internal controls as well as external controls. It is not clear at what level of managerial shareholding alignment gives way to entrenchment.

Policing of management requires an institutional arrangement such as the presence of outside, non-executive directors. Similarly, performance-linked remuneration to managers requires a mechanism for clearly metering managerial performance and establishing a formula for rewarding that performance. The recent Cadbury Report (1992) has sought to improve corporate governance in UK companies by proposing the inclusion of a sufficient number of non-executive directors and the establishment of remuneration committees.

The effectiveness of policing by non-executive directors and determination of performance-linked managerial remuneration by remuneration committees is yet to be assessed. But these controls may be weak, since executive directors can 'pack' the board and the remuneration committee with their own henchmen. A recent survey of 235 UK companies found that more than half of all non-executive appointments of directors were personally made by the chairperson (KPMG Peat Marwick, 1994). In the same survey, more than half of the non-executive directors felt that they had not been given the full range of financial and non-financial (e.g. strategic) information. Another survey found that non-executive directors were not perceived as very effective by institutional shareholders (BDO Binder Hamlyn, 1994).

With the increasing concentration of shareholdings in the hands of financial institutions, it may be thought that these institutions can play the policing role effectively. While, a priori, their large block holdings enable the institutions to monitor managements effectively, in practice, they have been rather reluctant to play that role. Institutions have pleaded lack of expert knowledge to assume an interventionist role. Institutions may also receive side payments for other business relationships with firms, such as underwriting. Such relationships may create a conflict of interest and dilute monitoring by institutions in their role as shareholders.

In the 1990s, there has been a trend in the USA towards shareholder activism, with managers being subjected to much greater scrutiny and questioning by active shareholder groups. Often institutional investors have taken on such activist roles in response to criticism of their earlier inertia in the face of perceived 'managerial excesses'. In the UK, the Cadbury Report also envisages a more active monitoring role for institutional investors.

External agency conflict control mechanisms

The product, managerial labour and corporate control markets have been proposed as agency conflict control devices. They are not specifically designed for that purpose, but nevertheless can play a correctional role when managerial failure has occurred. It is the fear that these markets will punish managerial failure by allowing displacement of the failed managers that is supposed to act as a deterrent against the pursuit of managerial self-interest. Of course, these markets may discipline failing managers whatever the cause of such failure.

Of particular relevance to acquisitions is the disciplinary role of the market for corporate control. In this market, corporate assets are traded between competing management teams. The management teams which can create more value out of those corporate assets will then outbid other teams less capable of value creation. Hostile bids which are resisted by the incumbent target managements are a necessary part of the disciplinary role of the market for corporate control: indeed, they are its defining characteristic.

The operation of the market for corporate control, therefore, rests on inefficient teams being weeded out by superior management teams. There are two 'flies in the ointment' concerning this view. First, conceptually, the winning management team may make the acquisition from motives inconsistent with shareholder wealth increase. Empirical evidence shows that acquisitions generate, on average, little or even negative wealth changes for acquiring company shareholders (see Chapter 13). Moreover, acquirers in many cases overpay for the targets. Second, it has been argued that hostile takeovers may be an inefficient and expensive method of correcting managerial failure (Kay, 1989).

Empirical evidence on acquisition motives

Whether managers act in shareholders' or in their own interest has been tested in a few studies. One of the implications of managerial self-interest pursuit, that managers will emphasise size or growth, has been tested by Meeks and Whittington (1975). They find, for a UK sample, that sales growth is positively related to directors' pay increases, although such pay increases are also due to higher profitability. The profitability effect in fact dominates in the short term.

Baker *et al.* (1988) report, for the USA, that the average elasticity of compensation with respect to firm size is 0.3: that is, a 10 per cent increase in firm sales raises executive compensation by 3 per cent. This suggests that executive compensation can increase with an increase in firm size, even when shareholder wealth is not enhanced as a result. This, Baker *et al.* argue, could explain some of the vast amount of inefficient expenditures of corporate resources on diversification programmes that have created large conglomerate organisations in the past.

Acquisitions and managerial compensation

Ravenscraft and Scherer (1987), from their case studies of US acquisitions and sell-offs, find that empire building through conglomerate acquisitions may have been an important motive behind the original acquisitions. Other studies have sought to establish a more explicit link between acquisitions and managerial compensation.

Firth (1991) tests whether executive reward increases with acquisitions for a sample of 254 UK takeover offers during 1974–80. He finds that the acquisition process leads to an increase in managerial remuneration, and that this is predicated on the increased size of the acquirer. Making acquisitions in which shareholders gain leads to significant increases in managerial rewards. Even in acquisitions where shareholders lose, executives gain. Firth (1991) concludes that the evidence is 'consistent with takeovers being motivated by managers wanting to maximise their own welfare'.

A more recent study of managers' compensation by Conyon and Clegg (1994) finds, for a sample of 170 UK firms between 1985 and 1990, that directors' pay is positively related to sales growth. Further, expansion through takeovers increases such pay, and the relationship between frequency of takeovers and pay is positive. The above studies may be summarised as suggesting that managers stand to gain from acquisitions in terms of their compensation, even though such acquisitions may not always benefit their shareholders.

Target management behaviour in hostile offers

Target management may resist takeover bids in order to secure their jobs or safeguard their empire. Alternatively, they may resist in order to maximise the premium paid by the bidder. While increasing the premium, target resistance may reduce the probability of a successful bid. Where a bid is abandoned, if the target shareholders lose their earlier gains, one may infer that the resistance was driven by managerial entrenchment motives rather than shareholder welfare considerations. Such value-reducing target management behaviour may, however, by constrained by a watchful board with independent, outside directors.

Cotter *et al.* (1993) find, with a US sample, that board composition influences the target management decision to resist, the outcome of tender offers and the wealth gains to target shareholders. They study US tender offers which are generally hostile and made directly to the target shareholders. In those offers where target boards are numerically dominated by outside directors, target management resistance to a bid is significantly more probable and the offer less likely to succeed.

However, more reputable outside directors and those who have a large share ownership in the target company exercised a more restraining influence on target managers' resistance. These results suggest that board oversight of management can be effective, but that it depends on the characteristics of the board.

Target management attitude to bids is also influenced by the incentive structure for managers. If the takeover is successful, managers may be replaced and so lose future compensation, as well as non-financial rewards such as status. On the other hand, they can enjoy capital gains on their shareholding in their firms and also receive 'golden parachute' payments (see Chapter 12 on golden parachutes). Managers, in deciding whether or not to oppose an offer, have to strike a trade-off between these potential gains and losses.

Cotter and Zenner (1994) present evidence on the relation between changes in managerial wealth and the tender offer process for a US sample. They find that initial target management resistance is greater, the smaller the managerial wealth changes and, in particular, the smaller the capital gains on the managers' shareholding in the target. Moreover, once the offer premium is allowed for, managerial resistance reduces wealth gains to target shareholders, presumably because such resistance reduces the probability of offer success. The probability of a tender offer success is increased when managers' wealth increases. It appears that share ownership may align managers' interest with that of other shareholders.

Overview

In this chapter, we have examined alternative perspectives on what motivates acquisition decisions – the neoclassical model, which assumes that such decisions are made to maximise shareholder wealth, and the managerialist model, which assumes that managers act in their own self-interest. The implications of either perspective for the success of acquisitions have been drawn out. The various prescriptions to bring about convergence of interest between shareholders and managers have been discussed. We have also provided some empirical evidence which supports the managerialist view that managers' acquisition decisions lead to an increase in their wealth. There is also evidence that control mechanisms like board composition and managerial share ownership may be effective in restraining the potentially opportunistic behaviour of managers in the context of acquisitions. In Chapter 3, the place of acquisitions in the broader context of a firm's corporate and business strategies is examined.

References and further reading

Baker, G.P., M.C. Jensen and K.J. Murphy (1988) 'Compensation and incentives: practice and theory', *Journal of Finance*, **43**, 593–616.

BDO Binder Hamlyn (1994) 'Non-executive directors: watchdogs or advisers?', Special Briefing No. 91, London.

The Cadbury Report (1992) *The Financial Aspects of Corporate Governance*, Committee on the Financial Aspects of Corporate Governance, London.

Conyon, M.J. and P. Clegg (1994) 'Pay at the top: a study of the sensitivity of top director remuneration to company specific shocks', *National Institute of Economic Review*, August.

Cotter, J.F., and M. Zenner (1994) 'How managerial wealth affects the tender offer process', *Journal of Financial Economics*, **35**, 1, 63–97.

Cotter, J.F., A. Shivdasani and M. Zenner (1993) 'The effect of board composition and incentives on the tender offer process', working paper, University of North Carolina.

Firth, M. (1991) 'Corporate takeovers, stockholder returns and executive rewards', *Managerial and Decision Economics*, **12**, 421–8.

Jensen, M. (1986) 'Agency costs of free cash flows, corporate finance and takeovers', *American Economic Review*, **76**, 2, 323–9.

Kay, J.A. (1989) 'Introduction', in J.A. Fairburn and J.A. Kay (eds.), *Mergers and Merger Policy*, Oxford University Press.

KPMG Peat Marwick (1994) *Survey of Non-Executive Directors*, London.

Meeks, G., and G. Whittington (1975) 'Directors' pay, growth and profitability', *Journal of Industrial Economics*, **24**, 1, 1–14.

Ravenscraft, D.J., and F.M. Scherer (1987) *Mergers, Sell-offs and Economic Efficiency*, The Brookings Institution, chapter 7.

3

Acquisitions and corporate strategy

An acquisition is a means to an end, the end being the achievement of certain strategic objectives of the acquirer. These strategic objectives may be varied, including growth of the firm, gaining competitive advantage in existing product markets, market or product extension, or risk reduction. Like all other strategic decisions, acquisitions should satisfy the criterion of added value. Where managers make decisions in their own interests, this added value may be appropriated by managers to the detriment of shareholders. Where they act in shareholders' interests, the added value will be reflected in wealth gains for shareholders.

For certain types of strategy such as market or product extension, acquisition may be one of several alternatives for achieving the same objectives. The other alternatives include organic growth, joint ventures and co-operative alliances. Preference for acquisition over the alternatives should be justified by their relative benefits and costs.

Acquisitions need to be placed in the context of the firm's broader corporate and business strategy framework. Different types of acquisition are dictated by the firm's strategic imperatives and choices. These acquisitions are differentiated by the source of value creation in each. The acquisition type also dictates the acquisition logic, the framework for the evaluation of targets, the acquisition target profile and the post-acquisition integration (see Chapter 4 on integration).

In this chapter, we describe an analytical framework for strategic evaluation of acquisitions. Various conceptual models discussed in the corporate strategy literature are drawn upon and applied to the acquisition context. Models for identifying and assessing value creation sources are suggested.

Corporate and business strategies

Corporate strategy is concerned with arranging the business activities of the corporation as a whole, with a view to achieving certain predetermined objectives at the corporate level. These objectives include orderly redirection of the firm's activities, deploying surplus cash from one business to finance profitable growth in another, exploiting interdependence among present or prospective businesses within the corporate portfolio, and risk reduction.

Apart from this portfolio management role, corporate strategy aims to develop a number of distinctive capabilities or core competencies (Hamel and Prahalad, 1994: 220), which the firm can translate into sustainable competitive advantage and, in turn, into added value. These distinctive capabilities include the firm's architecture, reputation and innovation. Architecture comprises the internal relations between the firm and its employees, the external relations between the firm and its suppliers or customers, and networks within a group of collaborating firms (Kay, 1993: 66). A management style appropriate to managing the business units is part of the architecture of the firm.

Business strategy is concerned with improving the competitive position of an individual business, with a view to maximising the contribution that the individual business makes to the corporate objectives. It also aims to exploit the strategic assets that the business has accumulated. Kay (1993, ch. 8) defines strategic assets to include: natural monopolies, barriers to entry in the form of sunk costs, the experience curve effect, reputation, advertising and market knowledge, and exclusivity through licensing.

Corporate and business strategies differ in the level within the firm at which strategy is formulated and implemented, and in the breadth of focus. Corporate strategy has an all-firm encompassing focus and may exploit the dependencies between component businesses, whereas business strategy focuses on a narrow range of markets. The distinctive capabilities that the firm has built at the corporate level, such as reputation or innovatory flair, are available to be exploited together with the strategic assets to enhance the competitive advantage of the component businesses.

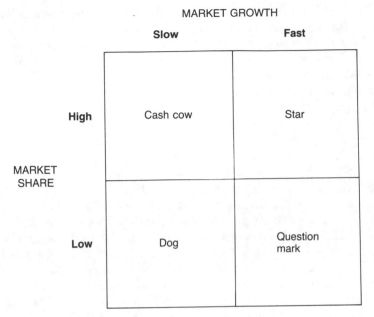

Figure 3.1 Boston Consulting Group business portfolio matrix.

Analytical framework for generic strategies

A simple model of this analysis is the Boston Consulting Group (BCG) matrix, shown in Figure 3.1. This matrix classifies a firm's portfolio of businesses on two dimensions – market growth rate and the firm's relative share of that market. Market growth rate is used as a proxy for the attractiveness of the market. When demand for the products sold in a market rises rapidly, firms have more profitable opportunities, hence the attractiveness of the market. Market share represents the firm's competitive strength in that market. The positive impact of market share on profitability has been demonstrated in a number of studies, the most substantial being the PIMS (Profit Impact of Market Share) study of thousands of firms by the Strategic Planning Institute in the USA.

A 'star' is a product sold in a market with high growth opportunities and where the firm commands a high market share. A 'cash cow' is a mature business with low growth opportunities, but where the firm has a high market share. A 'question mark' is a young business with plenty of growth prospects, but where the firm has a low market share and faces heavy competition. A 'dog' is a business in which the market growth is low and the firm's market share is also low. The four types of business have different profiles in terms of profitability, investment needs and free cash flows. Free cash flow, as defined in Chapter 2, is the cash flow from a firm's operations after it has met its investment needs.

A dog is a low-profit (possibly loss-making) business with low free cash flow and low investment (possibly disinvestment). It represents a product market which is declining for a variety of reasons. A question mark is a high-investment business with potentially high profits and a low (or negative) free cash flow. The high investment is necessary to build up the market and the firm's market share. A cash cow is a profitable, low-investment business with high free cash flow. Since the business is mature and probably oligopolistic, investment in market development, research and development (R & D) or additional production capacity is no longer needed. Thus a cash cow throws off surplus cash. A star is a high-profit, high-investment business with low free cash flow. The high profits are retained to make additional investments in order to maintain the high market shares held by the firm in a fast-growing market.

The product life cycle

It can be seen that the classification in Figure 3.1 derives its rationale from the nature of the product and its life cycle. The product life cycle concept is depicted in Figure 3.2 and traces the evolution of a product and its associated market over time. The four stages of a product's life are: launch, growth, maturity and decline.

The firm which launches a new product has the advantage and burden of a first mover. The market for the product is small, but the profit margin is high. The first mover must expend resources on building up the demand for the product and on additional production capacity. Market development expenditure takes the form of further product development in response to customer preferences, and the development of marketing and distribution channels and advertising. As the market expands, the first mover enjoys high margins on increasing sales volume.

The expanding market with high profits now attracts competing producers. This increased supply leads to a lower profit margin and, consequently, to further expansion of market demand. Firms now begin to compete on a wide front – in terms of price, product differentiation, and non-price dimensions such as product quality

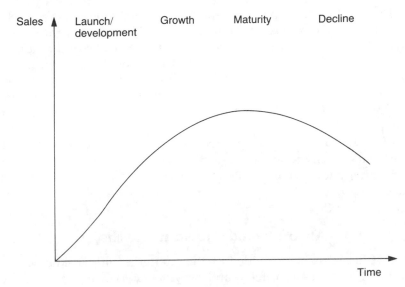

Figure 3.2   The product life cycle.

and after-sales service. This phase is characterised by tough competition, but in a still-growing market.

Thereafter, market growth slows down, which leads to excess
production capacity. Competition gets keener, profit margins are
squeezed and the shake-out starts. In this phase, reduction of excess
capacity is often achieved through defensive mergers. Shake-out
tends to lead to a better matching of production capacity to market
demand and to a smaller number of competitors. We have now
reached the maturity stage of the product's life.

The market has settled down to the slower and more certain
rhythms of oligopolistic competition. Profit margins are low, each
competitor has significant but fairly stable market shares, and
investment requirements are low. In the case of some products
which are necessities, and for which substitutes emerge slowly, if at
all, the maturity phase can be one of relative and prolonged
serenity.

For other products, consumer tastes may have changed or
substitutes may have been invented, bringing about the decline of
the product. At this stage, volumes are falling, profit margins are
low, and investment needs are also low. Indeed, this phase requires
disinvestment, which may become a source of cash inflow. That is
the end of story.

The product life cycle concept helps us to identify the market opportunities for a single product and the position of the firm in that market: for example, whether it is in the growth or decline phase. The BCG matrix expands this analysis to the firm's portfolio of businesses, each of which may be at a different stage of its own life cycle: for instance, a star is a business in the growth phase, a dog is in the decline phase, and so on. Thus the two models are complementary.

While the BCG matrix explicitly considers the interaction between the market environment (growth) and the firm's competitive strength (market share), this is implicit in the product life cycle model.

Ansoff's model of strategic choice

The BCG matrix helps to identify the strengths and weaknesses of a corporate business portfolio, and provides guidance as to which of those businesses should be divested, retained or further strengthened through additional investment. Thus it indicates the direction of a firm's strategic movement in terms of market attractiveness and competitive strength. The Ansoff model maps out the alternative directions in which it can choose to go.

The Ansoff matrix is shown in Figure 3.3. It depicts four possible strategic choices for a firm, depending on the relation between its existing products/markets and those which it wishes to enter. These are as follows:

- Market penetration, with the firm increasing market share in its existing markets.
- Market extension, with the firm selling its existing products in new geographic markets.
- Product extension, in which the firm sells new products related to its existing ones in its present markets.
- Diversification, in which the firm sells new products in new markets.

The particular choice that a firm makes depends on its evaluation of the attractiveness of the market that it wishes to enter or deepen its commitment to, its own competitive strengths, and the potential for value creation when these strengths are matched to the demands of the market. The core competencies or distinctive capabilities of the firm have a decisive influence on its strategic choice. Neither the

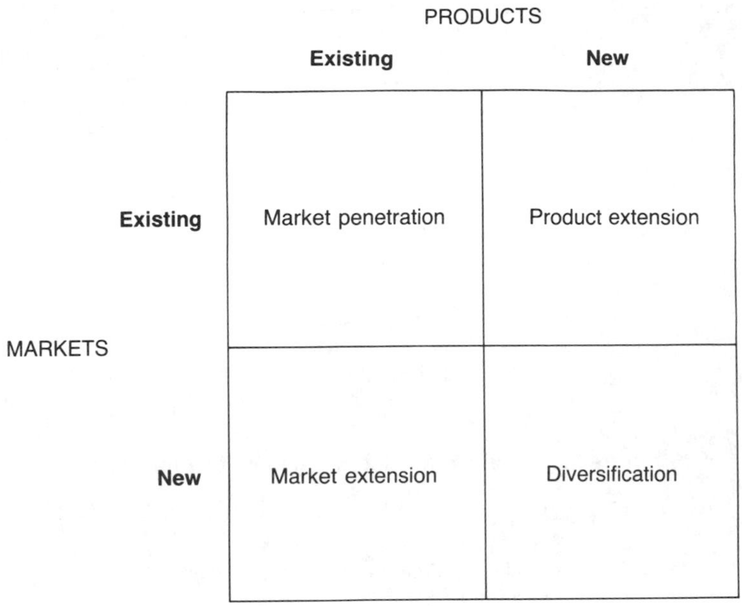

PRODUCTS

	Existing	New
Existing	Market penetration	Product extension
New	Market extension	Diversification

MARKETS

Figure 3.3 Ansoff product–market matrix.

BCG nor the Ansoff model captures the rich complexity of factors which determine the competitive environment of markets, or the factors which constitute a firm's competitive strength.

Porter's five forces model

Porter portrays the competitive structure of a firm's environment in five dimensions, as shown in Figure 3.4. These five dimensions are: existing competition in the firm's industry, the threat of new entrants, the relative bargaining power of suppliers of inputs, the relative bargaining power of the buyers of the firm's output, and the threat of substitutes. These five forces are not of equal strength within the same industry or across industries at any time. Their relative strength may also change over time. Indeed, forces such as the threat of new entrants or the threat of substitutes are essentially of a dynamic nature and are based on expectations, whereas the current rivalry, and the bargaining powers of suppliers and buyers, are more static and reflect current realities.

The strength of each of the five competitive forces is determined by a number of factors, some of which are listed in Table 3.1 by way

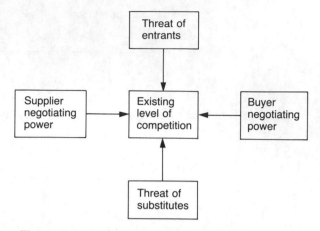

Figure 3.4   Porter's five forces model of competition.

Table 3.1   Determinants of strength of the five competitive forces

Competitive force	Strengthened by
New entrant	Low level of entry barriers (e.g. scale economies, capital requirements).
Product substitution	Low relative price of substitute, buyer propensity to substitute, low (product) switching costs to buyers.
Supplier power	High (supplier) switching costs to buyers, non-availability of substitutes, supplier concentration.
Buyer power	Buyer concentration, low cost of switching to other sellers.
Current rivalry	Low industry growth, high fixed operating costs, low product differentiation.

of example. An assessment of market attractiveness depends in turn upon an assessment of the strength of these factors.

Strategic situation and strategic choice analyses

Strategy formulation is a loosely sequential process which consists of two broad steps: strategic situation and strategic choice analyses. Strategic situation analysis is self-examination of the corporation's existing strategic posture, whereas strategic choice analysis is a forward-looking, scenario-building approach to the firm's future strategic posture.

The Porter model can be used for both strategic situation and strategic choice analyses. A firm can employ it to examine the strategic strength/market attractiveness configuration of its existing portfolio of businesses. Such an examination enables the firm to assess its competitive strengths (S) and weaknesses (W), and to match these against the opportunities (O) and threats (T) posed by the five forces. Such a SWOT analysis may reveal a mismatch between the firm's present capabilities and those that are needed to create, sustain or strengthen a competitive advantage in a market.

The Porter model is also useful in examining the future configuration of strategic strength and attractiveness of markets which the firm wishes to enter. It is this configuration which will determine the strategic choice that the firm makes.

Corporate strategies for market entry

From its strategic situation and strategic choice analyses, a firm selects the particular markets to serve. The market entry mode is then a choice among several alternatives: organic growth, acquisition or strategic alliance. The choice of entry mode depends on a number of factors:

- Level of competition in the host market.
- Start-up risk in greenfield (organic growth) investments.
- Availability of organisational resources for organic growth.
- Ability to appropriate potential added value.
- Advantage of speed of entry.

If level of competition in the host market is already high and there is excess capacity, building new capacity is likely to invite retaliation from the existing players. In this case, acquisition of an existing firm will reduce the risk of retaliation. A start-up venture is often more risky than the acquisition of an ongoing operation, or is not feasible for other reasons (see Case Study 3.1). However, it may avoid the problems of integration with an acquisition (see Chapter 4).

The firm may not possess all the necessary resources and capabilities to compete effectively in the host market. Access to these resources and capabilities may be possible only through acquisition or strategic alliance. The ability of a firm to appropriate the added value from the new market entry depends on the organisational form of that entry. The ability to appropriate is maximised with entry via organic growth, and becomes more difficult with acquisition, strategic alliance and joint venture.

CASE STUDY 3.1 Sainsbury prefers acquisition to greenfield investment in Scotland

When Tesco, the UK food retailer, made a £154m bid for Wm Low, the Scottish food retailer, Sainsbury joined the fray with a counter-bid of £210m. Sainsbury had only four stores in Scotland and wished to increase its market share quickly and relatively cheaply. Its ambitions had been hampered by intense competition for sites and struggles with local authorities over planning permission, thus preventing a greenfield expansion.

Source: *Financial Times*, 29.7.1994.

Acquisition is the quickest means of entry into a new market, and confers a strategic advantage when 'time to market' is important. However, acquisitions may be more expensive due to the control premium that the existing owners of the target firm have to be paid. There is evidence, reviewed in Chapter 13, that this premium is often high. Acquisition may also not be possible if suitable targets are not available. The choice of entry mode is, therefore, based on a careful evaluation of the above alternatives. Strategic alliances are discussed in Chapter 17. In this chapter, we describe the framework for a strategic evaluation of acquisitions.

Acquisition as strategic choice

The strategic choice made by a firm dictates the type of acquisition it undertakes and the target firm's profile. Market penetration strategy suggests acquisition of a target selling the same product: that is, a horizontal merger. With market extension, the target serves as a channel for distributing the firm's existing products, as with a cross-border acquisition. The target in a product extension acquisition is selling complementary products, thus increasing the product range that the combined entity can sell in their present markets. In a diversification strategy, the target is in an unrelated business, as with a conglomerate merger. Case study 3.2 exemplifies an acquisition including elements of horizontal expansion, and product and market extension.

CASE STUDY 3.2   Acquisition reflecting strategic choice

Greene King (GK) made a £104 million bid for fellow brewer Morland in 1992. GK's strategy was to become the largest regional brewer in southern England. While GK operated in the south and west of London, Morland operated in the Thames Valley. Thus the two companies were operating in complementary areas. GK argued that this provided a natural geographical fit between the two companies. The acquisition would provide economies in production, distribution and marketing, and in purchasing of supplies. Since GK and Morland had complementary brands of beer, GK expected to sell its own brands alongside Morland's, thus increasing the product range in Morland's area. GK estimated that combining with Morland would produce £2.5 million of extra trading profit per year, to the benefit of the shareholders of the enlarged group.

Source: Greene King offer documents.

Value creation in different acquisition types

When a firm makes an acquisition, it buys 'off the shelf' a bundle of tangible and intangible resources and capabilities, all wrapped up in a particular organisational form. An acquisition also brings together two such bundles – the acquirer and the acquired.

In acquisitions and mergers, sustainable competitive advantage is created when there is a mismatch between the resources, capabilities and opportunities available to the two firms. Resources include marketing excellence, a distribution network, R & D and surplus operating capacity. Some of these resources are in the form of strategic assets such as market power and entry barriers such as the experience curve or size. As noted earlier, a firm's distinctive capabilities can be a source of sustainable competitive advantage, and these include the firm's architecture, capacity for innovation and reputation. The firm's architecture encompasses its management style and reputation as distinct from the reputation of its products.

Value created in acquisitions may be differentiated by the source of that value. There are three broad generic modes of value creation in acquisitions: the donor–recipient mode; the participative mode; and the collusive mode.

Donor–recipient mode

In this mode, there is a transfer of resources and/or capabilities from the acquirer to the acquired firm. Value is created when such a transfer improves the strategic and financial performance of the acquired. An example of this method of value creation is the takeover of a poorly performing firm by an acquirer with a superior and reputed management, such as Hanson or BTR. In this process the acquirer must guard against the transplant rejection syndrome: that is, the acquired firm being resistant to the transfer.

Participative mode

In this mode, there is a pooling of the resources and capabilities of the two firms. Such pooling is a two-way exchange process, and a great deal of interaction and mutual learning between the firms takes place. This pooling makes more effective use of the two firms' resources and enhances their joint capabilities. Scope and scale economies may be achieved from this pooling.

Collusive mode

This involves the pooling of strategic assets. Kay (1993: 114) defines strategic assets as those characteristics of the market structure which give a firm its competitive advantage. In this mode, the coming together of the two firms in an acquisition creates or strengthens those strategic assets. Examples of the collusive mode include cartels, vertical integration and licensing. The enhancement of strategic assets is the source of sustainable competitive advantage and added value.

Analysis of the value chain

Value chain analysis is generally carried out at the business unit level and seeks to identify the cost structure of a firm's activities. Porter (1985: 36) defines a firm as a 'collection of activities that are performed to design, produce, market, deliver, and support its product'. Each of these activities contributes to the cost structure of

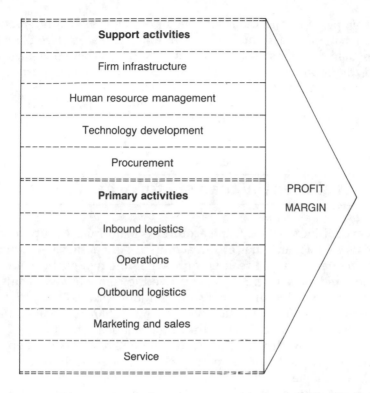

Figure 3.5 Value chain for a manufacturing firm.

the firm. Some of these activities, such as design and customer support, are intended to differentiate the firm's offerings from those of its competitors.

A value chain represents the breakdown of the value of the total output (sales revenue) into its component profit margin and costs, as shown in Figure 3.5. The costs are broadly divided into those expended on primary activities and those expended on support activities. These costs are then broken down into various functional costs. Primary activities are those directed towards the creation of the product, its sale and transfer to the buyer, and service after the sale. Study of a firm's value chain enables a manager to understand the behaviour of costs, and also to identify the possible sources of differentiation.

According to Porter, a firm secures its competitive advantage by differentiating its value chain. Cost-based competitive advantage (i.e. being the lowest-cost producer) is reflected in the value chain:

for example, in scale economies in operations. Similarly, product differentiation as a competitive advantage is also reflected in the value chain – for instance, in technology development. A firm can create or improve its competitive advantage by reconfiguring the value chain. A firm's distinctive capabilities as described by Kay can be traced to Porter's value chain. For example, innovation is clearly related to technology development.

Value chain analysis for acquisitions

In the acquisitions context, the acquirer is concerned with two value chains – its own and that of the acquired. Any anticipated synergy from the merger can be realised only when the two value chains are reconfigured so as to create or improve the competitive advantages for the combined firm. The reconfiguration process may involve changing one or both of the value chains. Changing value chains necessarily involves changing the organisational structures of two firms. The ease with which the latter can be accomplished depends on the political and cultural processes which define those organisations (see Chapter 4).

Different value creation logic drives different types of acquisition. The way the value chain of either or both of the merging firms is reconfigured depends upon this logic. For example, where the logic is economy of scale and the production facilities of both firms are rationalised and integrated, the operating cost component of the value chain will fall. Where economy of scale in purchase of inputs is the logic behind the acquisition, the input logistics component will be altered. Where the acquirer aims to put a larger volume of the acquired company's output through its own distribution network, the distribution cost to the acquired firm will fall (see Case Study 3.2 above).

A conglomerate merger may be motivated by an expected reduction in cost of capital. In this case, the firms' infrastructure costs will decline. In other cases, some of the activities of the acquired firm may be considered redundant, such as R & D and design capability. If these activities are then terminated, the support activities component of the acquired firm's value chain will be slimmed. If the takeover is financial control oriented and efficiency driven, leading to a reduction in head office staff and to other central functions being transferred to the acquirer, the infrastructure component of the acquired firm's value chain will be reduced (see Case Study 3.3).

CASE STUDY 3.3   Tomkins' plans for RHM

Tomkins, a British conglomerate without previous experience in the food industry, acquired RHM, a baking and grocery group, for £935m in 1992. Its options to improve RHM's profit performance included the following:

- Closing RHM's head office.
- Rationalising production.
- Introducing a more devolved management structure.
- Divesting some of RHM's brands.

Source: *Financial Times*, 9.11.1992.

Any changes in the value chain will be reflected in the revenues, costs, profit margin and investment requirements of the acquired or the acquirer. These changes represent the source of incremental cash flows arising from the acquisition. Where there are financial synergies, the cost of capital may also be reduced. The present value of these incremental cash flows at the new cost of capital is the added value due to the acquisition. In order to estimate the incremental cash flows, the acquirer needs to relate the changes in the value chain to the revenue, cost and investment cash flows. The valuation of potential targets on the basis of incremental cash flows is discussed in Chapter 9.

Acquisition criteria and target profile

Following its strategic situation and strategic choice analyses, a firm is in a position to specify the kind of target firms which would help achieve its strategic objectives and create value. Thus the desired target profile can be constructed and the acquisition criteria drawn up. The acquisition criteria should not be a 'wish list', since no potential target is likely to fit such a list. Active acquirers prepare the acquisition criteria as a spin-off from their ongoing strategic planning and review, as shown in Case Study 3.4.

CASE STUDY 3.4   *Acquisition criteria for target selection*

Booker

Booker, the UK food distributor and manufacturer, set three acquisition criteria:

1. Synergy – the merger should yield quantifiable benefits.
2. Strategy – targets should have leading market positions in growing markets.
3. Simplicity – the acquisition should not involve massive reorganisation or restructuring.

Wassall

Wassall, the acquisitive conglomerate, has six main acquisition criteria which a target should satisfy:

1. The target should be among the market leaders in established markets.
2. It should sell everyday, low-technology products.
3. It should have sufficient assets (i.e. purchase price is backed by target assets).
4. It should be potentially cash generative.
5. It is an underperformer relative to its industry standard.
6. It has a history of underinvestment.

The above criteria were applied by Wassall in its recent acquisition of the US firm General Cable for $270m.

Sources: Angear and Dewhurst (1989: ch. 4); *Financial Times*, 6.5.1994.

Overview

In this chapter, acquisitions and mergers have been placed in the broader context of a firm's corporate and business strategies. It is the firm's strategic objectives which dictate whether, and what type of, acquisition will be undertaken. A strategic analysis of acquisitions should also be underpinned by the value creation logic and identify the sources of value creation.

An analytical framework for a strategic analysis of acquisitions has been provided. Using the models derived from this framework, acquirers can develop the acquisition criteria which potential targets must satisfy. This chapter has been concerned with the hard analysis of quantifiable economic and financial aspects of acquisitions. Analysis of soft, non-quantifiable factors is often more important than the hard analysis. These soft factors include the political and cultural dimensions of both the acquirer and the target. We turn our attention to such factors in the next chapter.

References and further reading

Angear, T.R., and J. Dewhurst (1989) *How to Buy a Company*, Director Books.
Hamel, G., and C.K. Prahalad (1994) *Competing for the Future*, Harvard University Press.
Kay, J.A. (1993) *Foundations of Corporate Success*, Oxford University Press.
Porter, M. (1985) *Competitive Advantage*, Free Press.
Rappaport, A. (1986) *Creating Shareholder Value*, Free Press.

4

Organisational dynamics and human aspects of acquisitions

The previous chapter described the framework for a strategic analysis of acquisitions and mergers. This framework is useful in evaluating the choice of acquisitions and mergers as a means of achieving the firm's strategic objectives, and it leads to the selection criteria for screening potential candidates for acquisitions and mergers. In this chapter, alternative perspectives on the acquisition decision process within firms are presented.

An understanding of the acquisition decision process is important, since it has a bearing on the quality of the acquisition decision and its value creation logic. Success of post-acquisition integration is determined at least partly by the thoroughness, clarity and fore-thought with which the value creation logic is blueprinted at the acquisition decision stage. Under certain circumstances, the deficiency of the decision process can diminish the chance of a successful acquisition.

Value creation in acquisitions remains a potential until the target is successfully integrated with the acquirer. The post-acquisition integration process starts in the cold morning after the heady euphoria of a successful deal has died down. Value creation depends upon the quality of this integration. In this chapter, we describe the alternative approaches to post-acquisition integration.

We provide an organisational perspective on the post-acquisition integration process. Different types of integration approach are described, and the contingency of their choice on the underlying strategic rationale of the acquisition is emphasised. An important aspect of integration is the cultural integration of the acquiring and the acquired firms. The concept of acquisition culture risk is explained, and its implications for the integration process are drawn out. The human side of mergers and acquisitions is described, and the need for acquirers to handle this aspect carefully is highlighted.

A model of the acquisition process

An acquisition or merger involves three stages: preparation, negotiation and integration. The various steps involved in each of these stages are shown in Figure 4.1. Stage 2 is the technical and transactional stage involving the target company, the acquirer's advisers and financiers. This stage is thus very much external to the acquirer's organisation and is discussed in later chapters. Here we focus on the organisational aspects of stages 1 and 3.

Acquisition decision making

Haspeslagh and Jemison (1991) contrast two perspectives of acquisition decision making – the rationalist and the organisational process based. Figure 4.2 delineates the conventional rationalist view of acquisition decision making. This view is based on hard economic, strategic and financial evaluation of the acquisition proposal, and

---

STAGE 1

- Development of acquisition strategy, value creation logic and acquisition criteria.
- Target search, screening and identification.
- Strategic evaluation of target and acquisition justification.

STAGE 2

- Development of bidding strategy.
- Financial evaluation and pricing of target.
- Negotiating, financing and closing the deal.

STAGE 3

- Evaluation of organisational and cultural fit.
- Development of integration approach.
- Matching strategy, organisation and culture between acquirer and acquired.
- Results.

Figure 4.1 Three stages of an acquisition.

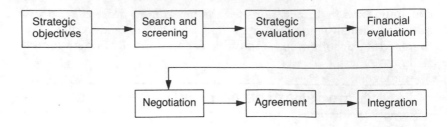

Figure 4.2 Rationalist view of acquisitions.

estimates the potential value creation based on such an evaluation. The acquisition justification is articulated in terms of the strategic goals, how the acquisition will serve these goals, and the sources of value gains. An important aspect of the rationalist procedure is the emphasis on quantification of expected costs and benefits of the acquisition.

In the rationalist view, the acquiring firm is a black box, and the acquisition decision emerging out of the black box is a unified view held by the firm. Any discord among various players within the firm, such as top managers, operating managers and different functional managers, has been neatly ironed out. The resulting decision will then command the wholehearted commitment and loyalty of those players. Thus acquisitions are the result of coldly rational decision processes, with the acquiring firm regarded as an undivided, homogeneous decision unit.

The organisational process perspective

The process perspective differs from the rationalist model in that it considers the organisational context as relevant at both the pre-acquisition decision-making and the post-acquisition integration stages. The process perspective adds the soft dimension to the rationalist, strategy-oriented approach, and takes a peep into the black box.

In the process perspective, stage 1 of the acquisition process starts with an idea and progresses through acquisition justification. The acquisition decision-making process is a complex one, giving rise to a number of problems. This process therefore has to be carefully managed, and the firm must have the necessary organisational structure for such management. The acquisition decision process in a large firm is characterised by four potentially debilitating factors.

The four factors are not mutually exclusive and indeed are inter-related:

- Fragmented perspective on the acquisition held by different managers.
- Escalating momentum in decision making, which may dilute the quality of the decision.
- Ambiguous expectations of different managers about the benefits of the acquisition.
- Diversity of motives among managers in lending support to the acquisition.

Impact of the process characteristics

The fragmented perspective arises from the fact that evaluating an acquisition is a complex, multidisciplinary exercise. Specialists from different functional areas, such as finance, R & D, marketing, personnel, environmental audit and antitrust law, are involved in making such an evaluation. Each of these specialists analyses the separate aspects of the acquisition with an essentially narrow focus. Sometimes, where the acquirer lacks specialists in certain areas, outside consultants such as environmental specialists may be co-opted into the evaluation team.

Communication among these different specialist groups may be limited. Integration of the narrow specialist perspectives becomes difficult as the complexity of the acquisition and the number of specialists increase. As a result, the top management in charge of the acquisition may focus on easily and quickly communicated issues and on quantified factors. Where outside specialists such as investment bankers are brought in, the problem of fragmented perspectives is accentuated.

The danger of such a narrow perspective is that the more subtle and soft issues which are relevant to the success of post-acquisition integration may be given scant attention. For example, the acquisition may be conceived by the top management without the active involvement of the operational-level managers, although the latter may have much greater familiarity with the proposed acquisition.

Further, an acquired firm is normally a bundle of different capabilities and opportunities. Not all the managers involved in deciding upon the acquisition may be fully aware of them or their impact on the acquirer's competitive strength. Thus they develop a partial view of the potentialities of the acquisition (see Case Study 4.1).

CASE STUDY 4.1   BTR learns after the acquisition of Hawker Siddeley

BTR is an experienced and successful acquisitive British conglomerate. It acquired Hawker Siddeley (HS), an engineering company, in a £1.55bn hostile bid in 1991. Though the bid was made after an intensive study of HS lasting several months, BTR nevertheless found that it did not know everything about HS. It dropped its proposal to create a global electrical engineering business, suggesting that HS knew more about its businesses than BTR. BTR also slowed its pre-bid integration plan until it learnt more about HS.

Source: *Financial Times*, 11.3.1992.

Acquisitions often generate a momentum of their own, even in friendly mergers. Hostile takeovers, in addition, can generate a hothouse atmosphere. Managers often find the acquisition process full of excitement and are propelled by the thrill of the chase. Moreover, acquisitions may create the need for external advisers such as merchant banks. These external advisers may have an incentive in closing the deal, especially if their fees are not fixed in advance, but are success related. Such an incentive structure will add to the pressure on acquiring firm managers (see Chapter 7). These pressures tend to reduce the attention that the acquisition receives (see Case Study 4.2).

There are also other kinds of pressure on managers making acquisition decisions. They may have staked a great deal of their prestige on the acquisition, and will be reluctant to pull out for fear of being stigmatised by this 'failure'. On the other hand, success in an acquisition may increase their career prospects and compensation levels by increasing the size of businesses under their control (see Chapter 2).

Managers may also fear that, if the acquisition decision making is prolonged, word may get out and the firm's competitors may make a pre-emptive bid, thus increasing the chances of an auction for the target and raising the eventual bid premium. Moreover, disclosure of the acquisition move may trigger resistance from stakeholders such as employees, where the acquisition is motivated by efficiency and rationalisation considerations and may lead to job losses.

CASE STUDY 4.2   *Advisers pile pressure on bidders*

In a survey of the acquisition experience of 40 UK acquirers conducted during the mid-1980s, some inexperienced acquirers relied heavily on their merchant bank advisers. Many acquirers were unhappy with their bankers' excessive orientation towards deals and fee earning. British acquirers making US acquisitions intensely disliked banks 'hassling' them or 'scoring points against each other in amicable deals'. Some acquirers were also critical of their banks' lack of understanding of their businesses which caused acrimony and delay. According to one acquirer, 'when advisers get into a win/lose situation, it is potentially disastrous to successful negotiations'.

Source: Hunt *et al.* (1987: 25).

The acquisition proposition has to be 'sold' internally to different managers. In selling the idea, managers who are championing, and who perhaps stand to gain most from, the acquisition may play up the attractions to those managers whose consent is needed, while playing down the potential problems associated with the acquisition. This information asymmetry can lead to different managers developing different expectations of the value of the acquisition.

This expectational ambiguity may be used tactically by the acquisition sponsor to sell the idea and win support from other managers. After the deal, resolution of such ambiguity is left to operating managers, who may not have been involved in the negotiations. While ambiguity is useful in developing political coalitions and evolving a consensus in favour of the acquisition, it hinders a smooth post-acquisition integration process.

The essentially political process of selling the acquisition proposal generates multiple objectives from different players in that process. In the post-acquisition phase, these objectives lead to conflicting claims on priorities and resource allocation, thereby diminishing the effectiveness of the integration process. For example, the same acquisition may aim to create value through capacity rationalisation, product development, merging of distribution networks or vertical integration. Where different managers are responsible for bringing about these changes, they may have to agree on how fast and in what sequence these must be achieved.

The acquirer's normal resource allocation planning styles have a significant impact on the quality of acquisition decision making. Companies with a robust allocation style can handle acquisition decisions much more effectively. Characteristics of a robust style of resource allocation include a long-term strategic orientation, firm commitment of the top management, an analytical rather than a political approach, and consensus rather than dominance by individual managers.

Managing acquisition decision making

In some companies the acquisition decision process may be separately established from the normal corporate planning function. The need for a separate acquisition function depends on the expected level of acquisition activity, the complexity and variety of the anticipated acquisitions, and the prior acquisition experience of managers sponsoring or implementing acquisitions.

The acquisition function, if separate, is likely to be located at the corporate level. At the business unit level, individual acquisitions have to be handled by the business unit managers, but subject to approval and monitoring by the corporate-level senior managers.

The acquisition team

In some major companies, such as ICI, the corporate-level acquisition function is carried out by an acquisition team (the A team) headed by an acquisition manager. The acquisition function performs several roles. Essentially it acts not as a supreme authority on acquisition decisions, but as a conduit and catalyst for promoting acquisitions as a means of achieving the firm's broad corporate and business strategy objectives.

The A team needs to be proactive and search for acquisition opportunities. It serves as a focal point and as a clearing house for ideas emanating from within and outside the firm. Over time it becomes a repository of learning, experience and distilled wisdom in acquisition-related matters and skills in identifying acquisition opportunities, evaluating them and negotiating deals. Finally, the A team serves as an internal consultant to acquisition task forces concerned with specific acquisitions.

The acquisition team must be composed of managers with the required experience and authority, so that the team commands the respect of the operational managers and the board to whom it will make its recommendation. The team must also be accessible to managers in its role as a diffuser of acquisition learning and knowledge.

The task force

For specific acquisitions, a task force may be constituted, made up of business unit managers and corporate-level managers. The involvement of the corporate acquisition function in the task force is helpful in overcoming many of the problems associated with acquisition decision making. It can eliminate fragmentation of perspectives by taking a broad overall view of the proposed acquisition. It can regulate the momentum of the acquisition process and reduce ambiguity by requiring a clear articulation of different managerial expectations and objectives. The role of an acquisition team or task force is illustrated in the case of BTR's acquisition of Hawker Siddeley in 1991 (Case Study 4.3).

CASE STUDY 4.3 BTR's A team in Hawker Siddeley takeover

Prior to its £1.55bn bid for the British engineering group Hawker Siddeley (HS), the British conglomerate BTR had formed its A team of 30 senior managers. They had been studying HS intensively for months. In the weeks before BTR's victory, the A team managers had been allocated to follow HS's seven business divisions and after the bid were paired with their counterparts in those divisions. The role of each manager so allocated was as 'minder, godfather, counsellor but not the boss'. Further, it was his function to acquaint the HS managers with BTR.

Source: *Financial Times*, 11.3.1992.

The accumulation of acquisition-related expertise and skills within the corporate acquisition function is itself a distinctive capability which can confer a competitive advantage in the market for corporate control. By increasing the credibility of the acquisitions that the firm makes, its acquisition function can ensure that overpayment to targets is avoided and the chances of a successful integration are improved. This is one of the strengths of companies like Electrolux of Sweden, and Hanson and Tomkins of the UK, as substantial and frequent acquirers.

The post-acquisition integration process

This stage of the acquisition process is the all-important determinant of the success of the acquisition in creating value. As indicated in Chapter 3, value creation often depends on the transfer of strategic capabilities between the acquirer and the acquired firms. There are four broad sources of added value, of which three involve some capability transfer between the acquiring and the acquired firms. These three require operational resources pooling or functional skills transfer or general management skills transfer. The fourth is size related and derives from the increased size of the combined entity relative to the pre-combination firms. These capabilities/benefits are outlined in Table 4.1.

The extent of integration depends upon the degree of strategic interdependence between the two firms as a precondition for capability transfer and value creation. The timing of integration also depends on the type of capability being shared or transferred. Rationalisation of operating capacity is often done much faster than the transfer of functional or management skills.

Strategic interaction versus autonomy

The strategic value creation logic behind the acquisition dictates the extent to which the capabilities of the two firms need to be merged within a single organisational structure or maintained within the

Table 4.1   Types of strategic capability/size benefits in value-creating acquisitions

Category of capability/benefit	Specific capabilities/benefits transferable
Operating resource sharing	Sales force, manufacturing facilities, trade marks, brand names, distribution channels, office space, etc.
Functional skills	Design, product development, production techniques, material handling, quality control, packaging, marketing, promotion, training and organisational routines.
General management	Strategic direction, leadership, vision, resource allocation, financial planning and control, human resource management, relations with suppliers, management style to motivate staff.
Size benefits	Market power, purchasing power, access to financial resources, risk diversification, cost of capital reduction.

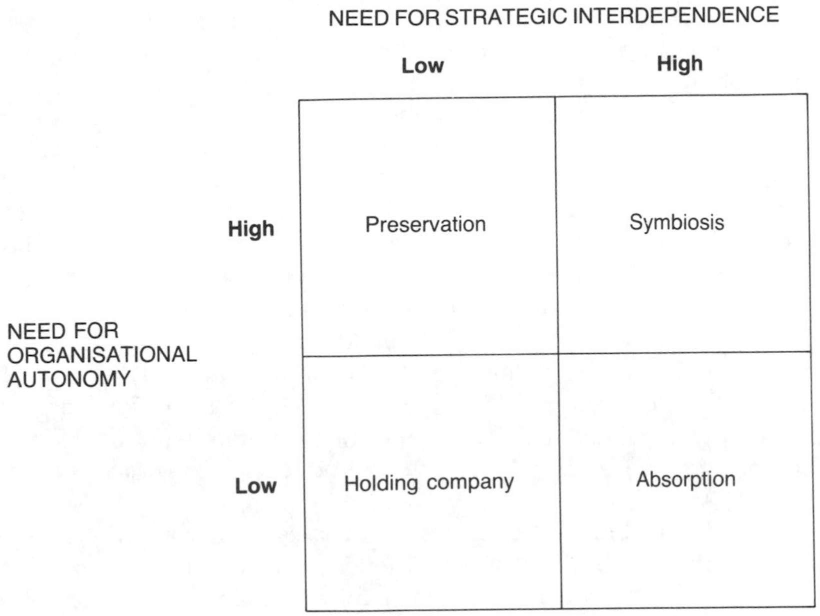

NEED FOR STRATEGIC INTERDEPENDENCE

	Low	High
High	Preservation	Symbiosis
Low	Holding company	Absorption

NEED FOR
ORGANISATIONAL
AUTONOMY

Figure 4.3   Strategic interdependence versus autonomy in integration.

boundaries of the firms. There is a trade-off between the need for strategic interdependence and the need for autonomy for the acquired firm (Haspeslagh and Jemison, 1991). This trade-off is represented by Figure 4.3. At the two extremes are complete preservation and complete absorption. Most acquisitions require a mixture of interdependence and autonomy. This taxonomy leads to four types of post-acquisition integration: portfolio management, preservation, symbiosis and absorption.

Under absorption, integration implies a full consolidation of the operations, organisation and culture of both firms over time. In a preservation acquisition, there is a great need for autonomy. The acquired firm's capabilities must be nurtured by the acquirer with judicious and limited intervention, such as financial control, while allowing the acquired firm to develop and exploit its capabilities to the full. In a symbiotic acquisition, the two firms initially coexist but gradually become interdependent. Symbiosis-based acquisitions need simultaneous protection and permeability of the boundary between the two firms.

Acquiring company managers select an appropriate integration approach that will lead to exploitation of the capabilities of the two firms for securing sustainable competitive advantage. In an absorption approach, operational resources need to be pooled to eliminate duplication. An acquisition aimed at reducing production capacity in a declining industry dictates an absorption approach. In a preservation approach, only general management skills may be transferred. A conglomerate-type acquisition is characterised by this approach.

In a symbiotic integration, no sharing of operational resources takes place, but there may be a gradual transfer of functional skills. A telecommunications firm acquiring a computer firm in order to create multimedia products needs to preserve each firm within its boundary, but also to allow interaction across the boundary. For example, after its acquisition of the computer firm NCR in 1991, AT&T, the telecommunications giant, allowed NCR to take charge of all computer-related activity, but also co-operated on developing 'computing telecommunications products' (*Financial Times*, 27.1.1993).

Strategic capabilities transfer encompasses numerous interactions between the two firms at different levels, and requires management of the interface between the two organisations and the personnel of the two firms. The interactive process is also a process of learning and consequential adaptation of the original acquisition blueprint to the realities of the two firms.

Identifying the capabilities to be transferred is not enough. A proper atmosphere conducive to this transfer needs to be created. Where the capabilities to be transferred are not properly identified due to deficiencies of the pre-acquisition decision making outlined above, or the necessary atmosphere is not created or the interface is mismanaged, value destruction rather than value creation may result from the integration process.

Political and cultural perspectives of integration

Schweiger *et al.* (1994) propose a model of integration in which the value chains (see Chapter 3) of the acquirer and the acquired need to be reconfigured in order to achieve the value creation objectives of the acquirer. Such a reconfiguration has three dimensions: the technical, political and cultural. The technical reconfiguration is similar to the capabilities transfer model discussed above, with an impact on the different components of a value chain.

However, the value chain represents more than a technical configuration. It is also 'a configuration of social interaction and political relationships' (Schweiger *et al.*, 1994: 31). These represent the informal processes and systems which influence people's ability and motivation to perform. A manager's position, power and influence may not be fully captured by his or her formal and official title. In carrying out integration, the acquirer should have regard to these political relationships if acquired employees are not to feel slighted or unfairly treated.

The culture of an organisation is embodied in its collective value systems, beliefs, norms, ideologies, myths and rituals. They can motivate people and can become valuable sources of efficiency and effectiveness. Four different organisational culture types have been suggested, as shown in Table 4.2 (Cartwright and Cooper, 1992: ch. 5). The four culture types have as their patron gods Zeus (power), Apollo (role), Athena (task) and Dionysus (person) in Handy's (1993: ch. 7) delightful pantheon of management.

Cartwright and Cooper (1993) suggest that the following factors are likely to be important in determining merger outcomes:

- The degree of cultural fit which exists between the combining organisations, given the objectives: that is, whether the mode of acculturation is one of cultural integration, displacement or maintenance of cultural autonomy.

- The impact of the event on the individual: that is, the degree and scale of stress generated by the merger process and its duration.

Poor culture fit or incompatibility is likely to result in considerable fragmentation, uncertainty and cultural ambiguity, which may be

Table 4.2 Types of organisational culture

Type	Main characteristics
Power	Essentially autocratic and suppressive of challenge; emphasis on individual rather than group decision making.
Role	Bureaucratic and hierarchical; emphasis on formal rules and procedures; values fast, efficient and standardised customer service.
Task/achievement	Emphasis on team commitment; task determines organisation of work; flexibility and worker autonomy; needs creative environment.
Person/support	Emphasis on equality; seeks to nurture personal development of individual members.

Table 4.3 Good and bad corporate marriages based on cultural compatibility

Culture of acquirer	Culture of potential partner in marriage type		
	'Good'	'Problematic'	'Disastrous'
Power	–	Power	Role, task, person/support
Role	Power, role	Task	Person/support
Task	Power, role, task	Person/support	–
Person/support	All types	–	–

experienced as stressful by organisational members. Such stressful experience may lead to their loss of morale, loss of commitment, confusion and hopelessness, and may have a dysfunctional impact on organisational performance. Cartwright and Cooper (1992: ch. 6) argue that mergers between certain culture types can be disastrous. They identify which cross-cultural mergers are likely to make good corporate marriages (see Table 4.3).

David and Singh (1994) consider acquisition culture risk, which is a measure of cultural incompatibility or distance between the acquirer and the acquired firms, and which is capable of impeding the efficient integration of the two. In assessing the advisability of an acquisition, the acquirer must, in addition to strategic issues, consider cultural risk. There is in general a cultural distance between the two firms. They often differ in organisational culture and may also differ in professional (e.g. scientist versus accountant) and national culture. Acquisition culture risk, however, depends on the following contingencies:

- Whether operational integration occurs. Different types of synergy imply different degrees of risk. Operational integration increases the risk.
- The division being integrated. Within a firm there are subcultures: for example, a task-oriented research and development division compared to a role-oriented service division.
- The mode of integration adopted by the acquirer.

Companies differ in their tolerance of cultural diversity. For example, Electrolux, the Swedish multinational, has made numerous acquisitions in different countries. Its integration approach has been to accept and even preserve the cultural identity of the acquired companies. It tends to retain target firm executives, unambiguously giving them operational control, negotiating performance goals and relying on them to co-operate and integrate themselves voluntarily with the rest of the group. The importance that some acquirers attach to 'the people dimension' is illustrated in Case Study 4.4.

CASE STUDY 4.4   Beecham's integration approach

Beecham made several European acquisitions in the mid-1980s. Its integration policy acknowledged the importance of the human dimension thus:

The key is to acknowledge that people are the most important asset, to take into account the feelings, problems and attitudes of those you are dealing with. Before making any changes the business should be examined to see what makes it tick and to discover the strengths and weaknesses of the people. The findings should be compared with previous assumptions and data-gathering before settling on a strategy. To implement changes straight away is a waste of opportunity.

Source: British Institute of Management (1986).

Problems in integration

Since pre-bid acquisition justification is generally based on limited information about the true financial, strategic and organisational strengths and weaknesses of the target, it seldom corresponds fully to post-acquisition reality. This means that pre-bid expectations usually have to be modified in response to this reality, and the integration process should be flexible enough to accommodate this response.

Integration problems may arise from three possible sources: determinism, value destruction and leadership vacuum (Haspeslagh and Jemison, 1991: ch. 7). Determinism is a characteristic of managers who believe that the acquisition blueprint can be implemented without change and without regard for ground realities. They tend to forget that the blueprint was based on incomplete information and is often a wish list to accommodate the political compulsions of decision making in the acquirer. They do not consider that the implementation process is one where mutual learning between the acquirer and the acquired takes place, and that the process is essentially adaptive in the light of this learning.

Determinism leads to a rigid and unrealistic programme of integration, and builds up hostility from managers on both sides when they do not share the blueprint's assumptions about the capabilities to be transferred or the time scale for the transfer. Such a hostility engenders a non-cooperative attitude among managers, vitiating the atmosphere for a healthy transfer.

Where the integration experience of managers and other personnel in the two organisations is contrary to their expectations, they may feel that they stand to lose from the acquisition. Thus at a personal level the acquisition is value destroying. Value in this context includes both pecuniary and non-pecuniary, psychological compensations that managers have earned in the past. Value destruction may take the form of reduced remuneration in the post-acquisition firm, or of loss of power or of symbols of corporate status. For example, the target firm managers may be given positions which fail to acknowledge their seniority in the pre-acquisition target or their expertise.

A very heavy-handed integration approach may bruise the sensibilities of the target managers and hinder the development of a trusting and co-operative atmosphere conducive to creative interaction between managers of the two firms and necessary for valuable capability transfer. Where there is perceived value destruction of this kind, again smooth integration is not possible.

Finally, the management of the interface requires tough and enlightened leadership from the top managers of the acquirer. Where the integration task is delegated to the operational managers of the two firms without visible involvement or commitment of the top management, the integration process can degenerate into mutual wrangling and recrimination. Top management must be on hand to iron out the inevitable frictions that arise between groups of managers in the integration process (see Case Study 4.5).

CASE STUDY 4.5   *Importance of managing the interface*

The survey by Hunt *et al.* (1987) shows that UK acquirers attach considerable importance to regulating the interface between the acquirer and acquired management teams. In their view, where there was lax management of the interfaces, without a single, overall authority, the consequences were inevitable displays of politics, interfunctional conflict, uncertainty and 'both sides playing footsie under the table'.

The personnel director of one of the acquirers said, 'we had two management teams resenting each other during the first year. There were far too many of our people "sniffing around" the other [i.e. the seller's] side to see who they could integrate into the company'.

Stages in the integration process

Integration proceeds in two stages. At the preparatory stage, the acquirer must take stock of the acquired firm. In some cases, before any functional or general management skills can be transferred, the operations of the target may have to be strengthened by infusing fresh capital, say, for working capital purposes.

The interface between the two firms has to be managed carefully, and an interface management team may be set up. This team, made up of a senior manager of the acquirer, the head of the acquired firm and some support staff, must identify what capabilities can and need to be transferred and in which direction. It must keep out unwanted interactions between the firms, which dilute the effectiveness of the transfer process. It may have to regulate the pace of interaction to enhance its quality.

Often the morale of managers in the acquired firm may be low, without a sense of direction or purpose. The interface managers have the important function of restoring the confidence of these managers by instilling a new and vigorous sense of the purpose which underlies the acquisition. They also need to restore an external, market focus so that the competitors are put on notice that the acquired firm is back in business.

The second stage of the integration process involves the actual capability transfer. The mode of transfer and the length of the transfer process depend upon the type of integration – preservation, symbiosis or absorption. Each integration mode is characterised by specific tasks which lie at the heart of the process.

Overview

This chapter has emphasised that the acquisition process is much more than the strategic and financial evaluation of the target company and negotiating a good deal. Making a successful acquisition requires that all three stages of the acquisition process –

preparation, negotiation and post-acquisition integration – must be understood as interrelated processes with their own dynamics. We have examined the organisational processes that drive acquisition decision making and acquisition integration. The acquisition decision process is characterised by a number of different problems which may detract from the quality of decisions reached. Similarly, the post-acquisition integration process also gives rise to problems arising from cultural incompatibility between the acquiring and acquired firms. The importance of human aspects of acquisition and the dangers of ignoring them have been highlighted.

References and further reading

British Institute of Management (1986) 'The management of acquisitions and mergers', Discussion Paper 8.

Cartwright, S., and C.L. Cooper (1992) *Mergers and Acquisitions: The human factor*, Butterworth–Heinemann.

Cartwright, S., and C.L. Cooper (1993) 'The psychological impact of merger and acquisition on the individual: a study of building society mergers', *Human Relations*, **46**, 3.

David, K., and H. Singh (1994) 'Sources of acquisition culture risk', in G. Von Krogh, A. Sinatra and H. Singh (eds.), *The Management of Corporate Acquisitions*, Macmillan.

Handy, C. (1993) *Understanding Organisations*, Penguin.

Haspeslagh, P., and D. Jemison (1991) *Managing Acquisitions*, Free Press.

Hunt, J., S. Lees, J.J. Grumbar and P.D. Vivian (1987) *Acquisitions: The human factor*, London Business School.

Jemison, D., and S. Sitkin (1986) 'Corporate acquisitions: a process perspective', *Academy of Management Review*, **11**, 1, 145–63.

Schweiger, D., E.N. Csiszar and N.K. Napier (1994) 'A strategic approach to implementing mergers and acquisitions', in G. Von Krogh, A. Sinatra and H. Singh (eds.), *The Management of Corporate Acquisitions*, Macmillan.

5

Antitrust regulation

In the UK, mergers have been the subject of antitrust regulation since 1965, during which period the UK government's policy has gone through distinct phases. While the main thrust of the antitrust regulation has been the maintenance of effective competition, many other issues of public interest have been, from time to time, considered relevant in determining whether a merger should be allowed. In this chapter, we describe the functioning and record of the UK antitrust regulatory framework. We also highlight the problems associated with the regulatory process.

Mergers of enterprises operating within the European Union (EU) are, since 1990, subject to EU-level merger regulation. This regulation was promulgated with the aim of achieving the 'one-stop shop' clearance of mergers. The result is that there is now a hierarchy of merger regulation in the EU, with very large mergers having a European Union-wide impact being examined by the European Commission (EC), while smaller mergers with their impact predominantly within a single member state are investigated by that state's own antitrust regulator.

In this chapter, we describe the institutional arrangements behind the EU merger regulation, the criteria and the procedures for merger investigation by the European Commission, and the division of jurisdiction between the European Commission and the member states. The limitations of the one-stop shop approach to merger regulation are discussed.

Where a UK firm makes a bid for a target in a non-EU country, such as the USA, the bid will be subject to the antitrust regime of the target country. In some countries antitrust regulations are still inchoate, whereas in others they are extremely rigorous. Bidders must be aware of the different regimes which will impact on their bids.

Intervention of the antitrust regulator, either at the UK or at the EU level, may cause a bid for a UK public company to be abandoned at least for the duration of the antitrust inquiry. We discuss the consequences of an antitrust investigation for the bid process.

The UK antitrust regime

Regulation of mergers is part of the UK government's competition policy, aimed at maintaining effective competition in various product markets within the UK or a substantial part of it. Although restrictive trade practices have been subject to government scrutiny since 1948, mergers became the explicit focus of government competition policy only in 1965, with the enactment of the Monopolies and Mergers Act. This Act adopted an administrative means of merger control in the form of a Monopolies and Mergers Commission (MMC) to investigate a merger when called upon to do so. The UK merger control regime is neutral in its attitude to mergers. There is no presumption that mergers are *per se* undesirable.

Currently, merger investigation in the UK is a two-stage process. The first stage is a preliminary screening by the Office of Fair Trading (OFT), created under the Fair Trading Act 1973 (FTA). This stage may lead to a recommendation to the President of the Board of Trade (previously called the Secretary of State for Trade and Industry) for a more detailed investigation by the MMC (the second stage). The MMC undertakes such an investigation and presents its report to the President, who then accepts or rejects its recommendation.

Office of Fair Trading and its operation

The OFT, created under the Fair Trading Act, is an independent competition watchdog and monitors all merger proposals or actual mergers in the UK. From its initial screening of a merger or a proposal, the OFT has to determine whether it is 'a merger situation qualifying for investigation' by the MMC. A merger situation covers transactions aimed at majority or minority control of one enterprise by another. Such a situation exists when all of the following conditions apply:

1. Two or more enterprises cease to be distinct.
2. At least one of them is a UK or UK-controlled company.
3. The merger, if already completed, has taken place in the last six months before the reference.
4. (a) The combined market share of the merging firms will exceed 25 per cent (the market share test); *or*
    (b) the gross book value of the assets of the acquired enterprise exceeds £70 million (the size test).

Although a qualifying merger situation may be identified by the OFT, not every such situation is recommended for an MMC reference. There are no simple and predictable rules for the recommendation. The OFT judges each case on its merits and has to weigh whether sufficient reasons for a reference exist. It takes into account the impact of the proposed merger on the following factors:

1. Competition in the UK.
2. Efficiency of the merging firms.
3. Employment and regional distribution of industry.
4. International competitiveness of UK firms.
5. National strategic interest.
6. The viability of the merging firms as a result of the method of financing.
7. The scope for turning around the acquired firm.

In considering the above factors, the OFT has regard for the policy of the government of the day. Over the years, there have been several shifts of emphasis between competition and non-competition factors. In the period 1965–73, the government encouraged consolidation of UK firms in order to enhance their international competitiveness. The aim was to build up the 'national champions'. This led to a policy of 'benign indifference' towards mergers, which reduced competition in the UK.

In the period 1974–83, this policy was somewhat reversed, and many mergers, including conglomerate ones, were vigorously scrutinised and some of them disallowed. In 1984 Norman Tebbit, the Secretary of State, introduced guidelines emphasising the primacy of competition grounds for referral to the MMC. Immediately thereafter at least two references were made because of their highly leveraged financing arrangements: the Elders bid for Allied-Lyons in 1985 and the Gulf Resources and Chemicals Corporation bid for

Imperial Continental Gas in 1986 (see Chapter 11 on leveraged bids). The former was cleared by the MMC, while the latter was abandoned on reference. More recently, there seems to have been a dilution of the pure competition approach (see Case Study 5.1).

There is no statutory obligation for the merging firms to notify the OFT of their merger. There is also no time limit for the OFT to make its recommendation. In practice, however, the OFT endeavours to complete its assessment quickly, having regard to the timetable for a public company bid under the City Code on Takeovers and Mergers. Under this Code, a bid lapses on its being referred to the MMC (see Chapter 6).

In general, the President of the Board of Trade accepts the OFT's recommendation. However, there have been a few, relatively rare, instances of the OFT recommendation being rejected, as in the case of the Airtours bid for Owners Abroad (see Case Study 5.1). This ruling attracted much criticism from the smaller firms in the travel industry as promoting industry concentration.

CASE STUDY 5.1   Mr Heseltine defies advice from the OFT

In early 1993, Airtours (AT) made a £225 million hostile bid for rival holiday company Owners Abroad (OA). The two companies were Britain's second and third largest holiday companies, and the takeover would have created a single company with between 25 and 30 per cent of the market. The OFT judged that this takeover raised serious competition issues and recommended reference to the MMC for investigation. However, Mr Michael Heseltine, the President of the Board of Trade, overruled the OFT and allowed the bid to proceed.

Source: *Guardian*, 25.2.1993.

Monopolies and Mergers Commission

The MMC is an independent advisory body headed by a full-time chairman, and includes a number of part-time commissioners made up of business people, lawyers, economists, accountants and other specialists. The first task of the MMC upon a referral is to establish whether the merger situation qualifies for investigation. It must then determine whether the merger as a whole or in parts operates against the public interest, using the following criteria:

1. Maintenance of effective competition in the UK.
2. Promotion of consumer interests.
3. Promotion of cost reduction, new techniques and products, and new competitors.
4. Balanced UK distribution of industry/employment.
5. Promotion of UK companies' international competitiveness.

The MMC's deliberations are investigative and not adversarial. There are no definitive rules of evidence, procedure or fairness. Informality and flexibility characterise MMC's proceedings.

The MMC may reach one of three conclusions:

- The merger does not operate against the public interest and can, therefore, be allowed to proceed or stand.
- The merger operates against the public interest and should, therefore, be prevented.
- The merger can be allowed subject to the adverse effects on competition being remedied.

The President of the Board of Trade is bound by the MMC's conclusion that the merger does not operate against the public interest. On the other hand, he or she can override the MMC's adverse finding of the merger being against the public interest and allow a merger to proceed. Overturning the MMC's adverse conclusion is again a rare event, an example being the bid for Anderson Strathclyde by Charter Consolidated in 1982. Case Study 5.2 provides an example of a conditional clearance of a merger.

CASE STUDY 5.2   *Allied-Lyons and Carlsberg merger*

Allied-Lyons (AL) and Carlsberg (C) proposed in 1992 to merge C's one UK brewery and AL's five beer plants to form Carlsberg-Tetley, which would have sales of £1 billion and an 18 per cent share of the beer market, creating the third largest force in the UK industry. The MMC, after investigating the proposal, concluded that it would have significant but not large adverse effects on competition affecting small brewers and independent wholesalers, and recommended a conditional clearance.

AL and C provided undertakings that the terms of supply to C's existing customers would not be worsened, and that the supply agreement with AL's pubs would be reduced from seven to five years.

AL also agreed to free 400 of its tied public houses so that they could source their lager from suppliers of their own choice. With these undertakings, the merger proposal was cleared.

Source: *Financial Times*, 28.11.1992.

Fast-track OFT and MMC investigations

The UK government introduced a fast-track procedure under the Companies Act 1989. This provides for voluntary pre-notification of a publicly announced merger bid to the OFT, and a time-bound screening process by the OFT. Under the fast-track procedure, the OFT must make its reference recommendations within 20 working days (the consideration period). However, where relevant information has not been provided, a maximum of 45 working days is allowed.

The OFT can also be approached by potential acquirers for confidential guidance before making a formal and public bid. This enables the merging parties to assess the likelihood of a referral and modify their merger proposal if necessary. The confidential guideline is, however, not a guarantee against subsequent reference, since a recommendation for reference can be made only after the merger has been announced and there has been an opportunity for the OFT to seek views from third parties.

Another device for speeding up merger clearance is the system whereby the President of the Board of Trade accepts binding and enforceable divestment undertakings from the merging companies in lieu of making a reference. The undertakings must be appropriate to remedy the effects adverse to public interest specified in the OFT advice. Where the offeror can give acceptable undertakings, a reference to the MMC can be avoided and disruption of the bid timetable minimised.

The appropriate undertakings may be negotiated by the OFT (see Case Study 5.3). Upon acceptance of these, the OFT monitors compliance with the undertakings and enforces them. The divestments covered by the undertaking must be carried out before a deadline which is publicly announced. Such a public disclosure will add to the pressure on the bidder, and may cause it to divest on disadvantageous terms.

FTA contains automatic prohibitions on the parties to a proposed merger acquiring interests in each other's shares after a reference has been made to the MMC. The bidder is not normally allowed to

CASE STUDY 5.3   Williams Holdings gives undertakings to escape MMC reference

Williams Holdings (WH) made a £703 million bid for Racal (R) in 1991. On the OFT's recommendation, the Secretary of State decided to refer the bid to the MMC unless WH provided suitable undertakings to remedy the adverse effects of the takeover. Both WH and R were suppliers to the market in locks. The combined group would dominate the market with more than 50 per cent market share. The OFT concluded that the merger might operate against the public interest by reducing competition in that market. WH then undertook to dispose of R's locks and safes businesses in the UK within 15 months. Although the bid was cleared on this undertaking, it failed for other reasons.

Source: *Financial Times*, 21.11.1991.

increase its shareholding or exercise voting rights above 15 per cent in the target.

Criticisms of UK antitrust regime

The shifting emphasis on competition and non-competition grounds for MMC references has introduced much uncertainty and unpredictability into the regime. Even when a merger qualifies for MMC investigation, a reference is not a foregone conclusion. Between 1965 and 1986, out of a total of 3540 qualifying mergers, only 107 (3 per cent) were referred. Of these, 33 (31 per cent) were abandoned by the bidders. Thus only a tiny proportion of qualifying mergers is actually investigated (Fairburn, 1993).

The criteria used by the MMC in framing the competition issues, and in defining the appropriate product and geographical markets to determine market share, are not clearly and consistently spelt out. Once the relevant market is defined, the MMC then assesses competition within it by computing market shares of the merging firms and the competitors. There is ambiguity both about the relevance of market shares as a measure of competition and about the threshold level of market shares at which the merger will be deemed against the public interest. In the past, the unacceptable thresholds have ranged from 28 to 71 per cent (Fairburn, 1993).

Market shares may not be a good indicator of the state of competition. Other factors such as buyer power, supplier power and potential competition need to be, and often are, considered.

However, whether these criteria are consistently applied is difficult to assess from the MMC's reports. The discretion of the President of the Board of Trade to reject the OFT's recommendation for a reference pre-empts the role of the MMC. This undermines the rigour of the antitrust regime. There is some suspicion that the referral process is not wholly free of political expediency.

Antitrust regulation in the European Union

The Treaty of Rome incorporates a strong emphasis on the maintenance of competition within the Community (the terms Community and Union are used interchangeably in this chapter and elsewhere in this book). The EU rules are designed to prevent distortion of competition in the Common Market through cartels and abuses of dominant market positions. Article 85 of the Treaty aims at preventing arrangements among enterprises which have the effect of distorting competition. Article 86 is designed to preclude firms from abusing their dominant position so as to restrict competition and interstate trade.

Both Articles 85 and 86 have been held by the European Court to have application in the merger area, but their scope is not well defined, since they were not originally designed for regulation of mergers. To remedy this shortcoming, a new regime of merger regulation was installed in September 1990. Articles 85 and 86, however, still have force in certain types of business combination, such as joint ventures (see Chapter 17).

European Union competition rules

Article 85 is the *anti-cartel* rule, which prohibits (1) agreements between undertakings and (2) decisions by associations of undertakings or concerted practices, which prevent, restrict or distort competition within the market and affect trade between member states.

Under Article 85, not all agreements/arrangements are prohibited. The European Commission, which administers the rules, recognises that certain agreements/arrangements may improve production or distribution of goods, or promote technical or economic progress. Such arrangements, if they allow consumers a fair share of the benefits, may then be exempted by the Commission under Article 85(3). Article 85 also provides for pre-notification of agreements so as to allow the Commission to determine whether they are consistent with the Common Market of the EU.

Any agreement prohibited under Article 85 is automatically void with retrospective effect. Further, the exemptions under Article 85(3) may be for a limited period, after which they come up for review.

Article 86 is the *anti-dominance* rule, prohibiting the abuse of dominant market positions within the Common Market in so far as it affects trade between member states. Dominant position *per se* is not prohibited. Unlike Article 85, however, there is no provision for pre-notification or exemption on grounds of compensating benefits. Examples of abuse of dominant position are refusing to supply to a dependent undertaking, and predatory pricing. Remedies under both articles are available through the medium of the national courts.

EU merger policy evolution

'Concentration' is the somewhat ambiguous word used in EU competition law parlance to cover merger, acquisition and takeover, whether they involve acquisition of controlling or minority interest in shares or assets. Some joint ventures may also be considered concentrations. Until the promulgation of the new merger control regulation in 1990, the Commission had applied Articles 85 and 86 to prevent or modify mergers. There was no system specifically designed to screen and regulate mergers, and no single authority to implement that system. This deficiency goes back to the Treaty of Rome.

Two landmark cases decided by the European Court somewhat remedied the situation – *Continental Can* (1973) and *Philip Morris* (1987). The decisions extended the application of Article 86 and Article 85 respectively to mergers. Prior to the Philip Morris case, it was thought that Article 85 did not apply to agreements to buy shares, such as in acquisitions and mergers. Similarly, the Continental Can case decision laid down the principle that, if a company which already held a dominant position in the Common Market sought to take over a competitor, it would amount to abuse of its dominant position, thereby attracting Article 86.

Application of Article 86

In the Continental Can (CC) case, CC, the giant American manufacturer of metal packages and packing materials, first acquired a West German subsidiary, which gave it a dominant position in that country. Subsequently, CC, through another subsidiary, agreed to purchase a controlling interest in its Dutch licensee, the largest manufacturer of metal containers in Benelux. The Commission charged CC with violation of Article 86, and this was upheld by the European Court, which ruled that acquisitions which strengthened a dominant position could amount to an abuse if they 'subsequently fettered competition'.

In subsequent cases, the definition of abuse has been less stringent. For example, any behaviour could be contrary to Article 86 if it had 'an appreciable effect on competition'. The Commission has used Article 86 to intervene in a number of proposed mergers, either to prevent them altogether or to modify them. An example of such intervention was in the British Airways offer for British Caledonian in 1988. The Commission imposed additional undertakings from British Airways over and above those demanded by the UK MMC, in order to maintain competition on routes in and out of the UK.

Despite these attempts to extend Article 86 to cover mergers, it was an inadequate rule:

- It did not apply where dominant position was created, only where it already existed.

- The Commission could not authorise mergers on the basis of clear and explicit criteria.

- There was no power to prevent mergers, only to unscramble them after their consummation.

Application of Article 85

Although originally designed to apply in the context of cartel agreements, this article was extended by the European Court to acquisition of share ownership in *Philip Morris* (1987). Philip Morris agreed to acquire a 24.9 per cent shareholding in one of its competitors, Rothmans International, from the latter's holding company, Rembrandt. The proposal had already been cleared with conditions imposed by the European Commission, but it was challenged by rival cigarette manufacturers BAT and Reynolds.

The Court held that the arrangement did not infringe Article 85, but it laid down the general principle that there was no basic difference between an agreement to purchase shares in a competitor and other types of agreement leading to cartels. Article 85 might be infringed if an acquisition was likely to result in a change in the competitive behaviour of the companies involved.

Despite the Philip Morris ruling, extending Article 85 to mergers, the article was not altogether suitable for a number of reasons. It did not provide a well-ordered system of procedure and timetable for vetting mergers. The procedures under the article were also time consuming. Moreover, the exemptions were subject to review, whereas mergers once carried out are generally irreversible. To overcome these defects and those of Article 86 noted earlier, the Merger Regulation (the Regulation) was put into effect on 21 September 1990.

The Merger Regulation

The new regime lays down size and other criteria for concentrations (including mergers) which will be subject to screening by the Merger Task Force of the Commission. It sets up a procedure for notification and also a timetable for the Commission's deliberations. It seeks to minimise the overlap between EU and national antitrust regulations and procedures. A concentration can arise in any of the following circumstances:

1. Two or more previously independent undertakings merge.
2. One undertaking acquires, through purchase of shares or otherwise, direct or indirect control of another.
3. Persons who already control at least one undertaking acquire direct or indirect control of another.

Direct or indirect control, derived from rights, contracts or other means, confers the possibility of exercising decisive influence on an undertaking. This means that even a minority stake can be deemed to lead to *de facto* control if the minority holder exercises decisive influence. Once a person has acquired decisive influence over an undertaking, a concentration generally occurs. However, arrangements which confer decisive influence for a temporary period only are unlikely to be considered as bringing about concentration. What constitutes decisive influence is reviewed by the Commission on a case-by-case basis, but it may occur at shareholding levels as low as 20 per cent.

The Merger Regulation exempts certain types of shareholding, such as investment by security firms, and certain types of control, such as administrators in receivership, from the definition of concentration.

Concentration with a Community dimension (CCD)

A 'concentration' will fall under the EC's jurisdiction only if it has a 'Community dimension'. Thus, for a transaction to fall under the Merger Regulation, it must be a concentration and must have a Community dimension. A CCD is defined in terms of three turnover size thresholds – global, Community-wide and country. These are designed to catch large concentrations that are not limited to a single member state, but have Community-wide impact.

Under the Merger Regulation, a CCD is present when:

- the combined worldwide turnover of all the companies involved totals ECU 5 billion or more; *and*
- the aggregate EU turnover of each of at least two of the companies is ECU 250 million or more; *unless*
- each of the companies concerned achieves more than two-thirds of its total EU turnover within one and the same member state.

An example is shown in Table 5.1. Although each company achieves about 72 per cent of its turnover in its home country, they are from different countries. So the merger is a CCD. If we alter the scenario and assume that German AG is also a British company, then the two-thirds rule is infringed and the merger will fall under UK jurisdiction.

The Commission has exclusive jurisdiction over CCDs except in certain circumstances permitted under the Regulation (see below). This avoids the need for companies involved in CCDs to satisfy antitrust authorities in different countries. As we have seen, this elimination of multiple jurisdictions is known as the 'one-stop shopping' principle. The thresholds have been arrived at as a compromise between advocates of Community-wide merger regulation, who see merit in one-stop shopping, and the reluctance of some member states to cede too much power to Brussels.

Mergers with a Community dimension must be notified by the

Table 5.1 UK plc bids for German AG

Company	Turnover (ECU millions)		
	World	EU	Home country
UK plc	4000	2500	1800 (72%)
German AG	3000	1500	1100 (73%)

participating companies to the European Commission within a week of announcement, and should be suspended for three weeks. Within one month of notification, the Commission must decide whether the concentration is compatible with the Common Market (the first phase). If not, it will proceed with its investigation, which should be concluded within four months (the second phase). If the Commission initiates proceedings, a bid covered by the City Code immediately lapses (see Chapter 6). A bidder can approach the Merger Task Force of the Commission for confidential advice prior to making an offer, and obtain a non-binding preliminary opinion.

If a merger threatens competition in the EU, the Commission may prohibit it altogether or allow it to proceed subject to undertakings by merging companies to eliminate the anticompetitive aspects of the merger (see Case Study 5.4).

Conflict of jurisdictions

There are at least two types of jurisdictional conflict which can conceivably arise in the operation of the Merger Regulation. The first is the conflict between the European Commission and the member states. The second is the conflict between the EU and non-EU countries, such as the USA or Japan.

CASE STUDY 5.4   European Commission clears merger subject to undertakings

In 1992 the Commission cleared the acquisition by British Airways (BA) of a 49.9 per cent stake in TAT European Airways (EA), operating in the French domestic market. The acquisition also gave BA the option to buy out EA's French parent. BA had no share of the French domestic market, whereas EA had only 3.8 per cent. BA and EA overlapped on the Paris/London and Lyons/London routes, and they had a combined market share of over 50 per cent on these routes. On the Gatwick and Lyons route, there was no effective competition for them. The Commission accepted BA's undertaking to make slots available to competitors at Heathrow and Gatwick airports in the UK, and cleared the acquisition. Here the Commission defined the relevant market as being the services between the UK and French airports affected by the acquisition.

Source: *Financial Times*, 31.5.1994.

Although the aim of the Regulation is to avoid multiple antitrust investigations of the same concentrations, in practice both the Commission and the antitrust authority of a member state can claim jurisdiction in a particular case. Articles 9 and 21 of the Regulation allow member states to claim jurisdiction under certain circumstances.

Under Article 9, the Commission may refer a merger to the national authority upon a claim by that authority that the merger threatens to create or strengthen a dominant position impeding effective competition in 'a distinct market' within the member's territory, *provided the Commission finds the claim justified*. An example of this transfer of jurisdiction is given in Case Study 5.5. This clawback provision is known as the 'German clause', so called because the Germans, not willing to trust the Commission's competition credentials too much, insisted on it.

CASE STUDY 5.5   European Commission transfers jurisdiction to the UK

Steetley and Tarmac, both UK companies, agreed in 1992 to merge their brick, clay roof tile and concrete products, with large market shares in the UK. For the first time after the introduction of the Merger Regulation, the UK government asked to investigate the merger, since it raised serious competition issues in the UK. Although the merger was a CCD, the EC agreed to relinquish jurisdiction in favour of the UK authorities.

Source: *Financial Times*, 25.1.1992.

Under Article 21, member states may intervene and claim jurisdiction to protect 'other legitimate interests' not already subject to Community rules. Such interests include public security, media plurality and prudential rules affecting, for example, banks. Where the concentration is not a CCD, Articles 85 and 86 cannot be invoked by the Commission. However, it can be investigated by the national antitrust authorities.

Where a company becomes the target of multiple bids, both the EU and a member state may exercise jurisdiction over the different bids, with the result that they may be investigated with different and potentially inconsistent criteria. This situation is illustrated by the bids by the Hongkong and Shanghai Banking Corporation and the UK's Lloyds Bank for the UK target, Midland Bank, in 1992 (see Case Study 5.6).

CASE STUDY 5.6   Takeover bids for Midland Bank lead to split jurisdiction

The Hongkong and Shanghai Banking Corporation (HSBC) made a bid for Midland Bank (MB) in March 1992. MB was one of the four high street retail banks in the UK. HSBC had no retail banking operation in the UK. HSBC notified the European Commission of the bid under the Regulation. Lloyds Bank (LB), another UK high street bank, launched a rival bid in April 1992. LB's bid was conditional on both bids being treated identically under the same regulatory regime.

Of the two bids, the HSBC bid was clearly a CCD, and the European Commission assumed jurisdiction and cleared the bid after two weeks. The LB bid was not a CCD, and the OFT recommended its referral to the MMC. LB then withdrew its offer.

Had the Secretary of State in the UK claimed jurisdiction under Article 9, both bids could have been investigated by the OFT. But he did not do so. Since the Bank of England had cleared the HSBC bid, no claim for UK jurisdiction under Article 21 was tenable.

Source: Love (1994).

Conflicts may also arise when a merger between companies which originate from outside the EU is attempted. Because of their turnover levels breaching the Regulation thresholds, the companies may be subject to the European Commission investigations. Thus such a merger may be prohibited despite being cleared by the antitrust authority of the country of origin of the companies. For example, in 1991 the Commission made a preliminary investigation of the merger between AT&T, the telecommunications giant, and NCR, the big computer company, both of which are American. This merger was cleared, but it did raise the problem of the extraterritorial reach of the EC Regulation.

Assessment of the Merger Regulation

While concentrative joint ventures which are similar to mergers fall under the Merger Regulation, co-operative joint ventures which resemble cartel arrangements attract Article 85 of the Treaty. The distinction between the two types is very difficult to make. This problem is discussed further in Chapter 17 on strategic alliances. Further, definitions of 'controlling interest', 'corporate group', for the purpose of calculating the turnover thresholds, and 'markets', where the proposed concentrations are likely to impede effective competition, are still not very clear.

The Regulation has a provision for vetting concentrations on grounds which may include contribution to 'technical and economic progress' and 'social cohesion'. Thus there is room for 'public interest' considerations, as in the UK, to influence the outcome of merger investigations. This may in the future introduce further ambiguity into the Regulation.

From the inception of the Regulation to January 1994, the EC considered 197 merger cases, of which only one (Aerospatiale and Alenia's joint bid for de Havilland of Canada in 1991) was prohibited. In eight cases the mergers were cleared subject to certain conditions, and another eight were cleared without conditions after a second-phase investigation. This low prohibition rate has created the impression that the EU-level regulation is rather lenient. To its credit, however, the European Commission has met the deadline in every case, and has won some confidence among companies.

Stock market reaction to MMC references

Franks and Harris (1993) investigate the shareholder wealth impact of the OFT references to the MMC, using monthly returns data for a sample of about 80 UK takeover bids. The returns to bidder and target shareholders at different times around a reference to the MMC are shown in Table 5.2. MMC referrals lead to wealth losses for target shareholders. They lose further when the MMC report is adverse.

The average gain for target shareholders when the bids for their companies are cleared by the MMC is 38 per cent over the period from twelve months before to one month after the report. This suggests that, where bids are not rejected by the MMC, the gains to the merger may arise from sources other than increased market power. In the case of rejected mergers, the target shareholders gain only 9 per cent over the same interval. Thus most of the gains on bid announcement which are subsequently lost might have arisen from increased market power of the merging firms. For the bidders, the return over the period from twelve months before to one month after the MMC report is not significant. Both referrals and MMC reports have a broadly neutral impact for bidder shareholders.

Table 5.2   Value changes on MMC referral and report (%)

	In referral month		In report month	
	Target	Bidder	Target	Bidder
All referrals	−8	−1	−3	1
Accepted	−9	−1	2	2
Rejected	−8	0	−9	1
Laid aside (abandoned)	−9	−2	(no report)	

Note: The returns are average risk adjusted using the market model (see Chapter 13 on this methodology). All target returns except for 'accepted' in report month are significant at the 5 per cent level. None of the bidder returns is significant.
Source: Franks and Harris (1993).

Forbes (1994) investigates the abnormal returns to bidder shareholders around three dates – bid announcement, MMC referral and MMC decision dates – using a sample of 53 UK bids and daily returns. The impact of referral on returns is not significant, whereas bidders whose bids are cleared by the MMC enjoy a significant 0.3 per cent over three days and 0.81 per cent over 21 days surrounding the MMC decision. Bidder shareholders whose bids are stopped by the MMC experience non-significant gains over the same periods. Thus Forbes' results are broadly in line with those of Franks and Harris (1993).

Antitrust regulation in the USA

Among other countries, the USA has the longest tradition of antitrust regulation, starting with the Sherman Act of 1890. This Act declared contracts and combinations which restricted interstate trade or trade with other countries illegal, and any attempt at monopolising this trade a criminal offence. The Sherman Act was not particularly suitable for the prevention of prospective mergers and monopolies, especially in the form of acquisition of stock to gain control of companies.

The Clayton Act 1914 was passed to overcome the shortcomings of the Sherman Act, and was subject to later amendments to make it a more effective mechanism for dealing with mergers. Section 7 of the Clayton Act prohibits full or partial acquisition by a commercial corporation of the stock or assets of another engaged in commerce in the country, if the effect of such an acquisition may be substantially to lessen competition or tend to create a monopoly. The prohibition applies to horizontal, related and conglomerate acquisitions.

The various statutory rules are enforced by the federal Department of Justice (DOJ) and the Federal Trade Commission (FTC). Prospective mergers have to be notified to these agencies. Both agencies then investigate and, if necessary, initiate proceedings in federal courts. The FTC also has various appeal procedures involving the administrative law courts and the independent FTC commissioners.

In addition to the above federal regulation, individual states have their own antitrust laws applying to mergers that would not affect interstate trade. The state Attorney General can bring a suit in the state courts. Affected parties can bring or join proceedings under both federal and state laws. This contrasts with the EU and the UK position, where affected parties cannot bring a legal action to force the European Commission or the OFT to investigate a merger. Antitrust enforcement in the USA has in the past fluctuated from great vigour to deep indifference, depending upon the political current of the times.

Merger control in the USA

Merger transactions in which the parties have significant assets or sales are regulated by the Hart-Scott-Rodino Act (HSR). HSR requires such parties to notify the DOJ and the FTC of the transactions, and observe a prescribed waiting period before completing them. Like the EU's Merger Regulation, HSR stipulates a threshold test of applicability based on the size of the parties, but HSR has an additional test based on the transaction size, similar to the UK's for a qualifying merger. Like the Merger Regulation, HSR is also a two-phase process, with an initial filing and a 'second request' for more elaborate information.

The USA has in the past attempted to investigate mergers or cartels among two or more non-US corporations which have significant operations in the USA. This claim for extraterritorial jurisdiction has been resisted by regulatory authorities in other countries, such as France, Canada and the UK, which even prohibited their own national companies from supplying documents to the US antitrust authorities. More recently, the guidelines issued by the DOJ and the FTC say that the USA may act against a foreign cartel if the cartel members make substantial sales to the USA (*Financial Times*, 19.10.1994).

Antitrust regulation in Continental Europe

Antitrust regimes in Continental European countries differ in terms of their approach, institutional structure and the zeal with which antitrust regulation is enforced (Carrington and Pessôa de Araújo, 1994). Germany is well known for its vigorous antitrust policing, and has an administrative approach to antitrust regulation through the Federal Cartel Office. Its decisions are subject to appeal to the Federal Department of Economy. Prior approval of the Cartel Office is required if the merging parties exceed certain turnover thresholds. Pre-notification of large mergers is mandatory. The Cartel Office clearance is through a time-bound process of up to four months. In the case of smaller mergers, post-merger notification to the Cartel Office is required. The Cartel Office can prohibit a merger or order it to be dissolved if already completed.

In France, the approach is again administrative. The Competition Council investigates mergers satisfying both total turnover and market share tests. Neither pre- nor post-merger notification is mandatory, but there is a voluntary pre-notification procedure. The final decision rests with the Minister of the Economy, who can prohibit a merger or clear it subject to certain conditions, such as divestiture or undertakings about future competitive conduct.

The Netherlands has a more relaxed antitrust regime. There are no clear guidelines except in the case of banking and insurance company mergers. In Sweden, which has just joined the European Union, antitrust rules are modelled on the EU laws. The Competition Authority investigates mergers above a certain threshold of worldwide turnover of merging companies. Pre-notification is required and the clearance procedure is time bound. The Competition Authority must within 30 days of notification start proceedings in Stockholm's City Court, which decides whether the merger can go ahead. Its decision can be appealed to the Market Court. The City Court can prohibit a merger, or require the acquirer to divest the whole or part of the acquired business.

Overview

This chapter has provided an introduction to the rules and regulations governing mergers and acquisitions in the UK and the European Union from the antitrust perspective. It has described the hierarchy of these regulations divided between the EU and the national authorities. The principle of one-stop shopping upon which this division of jurisdiction is based, and its practical manifestation in the definition of concentration with a Community dimension, have been discussed. The limitations of one-stop shopping arising from jurisdictional frictions, procedural uncertainties and definitional ambiguities have been highlighted. Progress of the EU's Merger Regulation has been reviewed. A brief description of the antitrust and merger control regime in the USA and in some Continental European countries has been provided to illustrate the diversity of approaches to antitrust regulation.

References and further reading

Bell, R. (1994) 'Regulatory aspects of acquisitions in the EU', in *Company Acquisitions Handbook*, Tolley Publishing Co.

Carrington, N., and B. Pessôa de Araújo (1994) *Acquiring Companies and Businesses in Europe*, Chancery Law Publishing.

Fairburn, J. (1993) 'Evolution of merger policy in Britain', in M. Bishop and J. Kay (eds.) *European Mergers and Merger Policy*, Oxford University Press.

Forbes, W. (1994) 'The shareholder wealth effects of Monopolies and Mergers Commission decisions', *Journal of Business Finance and Accounting*, **21**, 6, 763–90.

Franks, J., and R. Harris (1993) 'Shareholder wealth effects of UK takeovers: implications for merger policy', in M. Bishop and J. Kay (eds.), *European Mergers and Merger Policy*, Oxford University Press.

Love, J. (1994) 'The operation of the EC mergers policy: the Midland Bank takeover', *Journal of General Management*, **20**, 1, 29–43.

Peacock, A., and G. Bannock (1991) *Corporate Takeovers and the Public Interest*, chs. 6, 7 and 8, The David Hume Institute, Edinburgh.

Woolcock, S. (1989) *European Mergers: National or Community controls?*, Royal Institute of International House, London.

6

Regulating takeover bids

In the previous chapter, we discussed the statutory regime governing the antitrust and public interest aspects of mergers. This chapter describes the framework within which takeover bids are conducted. The UK framework, in the form of the City Panel on Takeovers and Mergers and its rule book, the City Code on Takeovers and Mergers, is mainly concerned with bids for public companies. Bids for private companies are regulated by the provisions of the UK Companies Act 1989. After describing the UK regime for takeovers, we briefly compare it to its counterpart in the USA and in European countries. The European Community draft directive on takeovers, which seeks to provide a Community-wide framework for bids, together with its shortcomings, are discussed.

Importance of regulating the bid process

In a takeover bid involving an offer by the bidder to purchase shares from the target company shareholders, there is much scope in principle for manipulative tactics from both the bidder and the target management. Some of these tactics are as follows:

- Selective release of information during a bid.
- Special deals with the larger target shareholders denied to the smaller ones.
- Creating a false market in either bidder or target shares.

- Insider dealing.
- Frustrating action by the target management which denies the target shareholders the opportunity to accept a fair offer.

Thus the target company shareholders, especially the multitude of small shareholders, may be the victims of 'sharp practice' unless the process is properly policed. Further, the bid process, if prolonged inordinately, will render the target management unable to manage the firm. Such an incapacitation is to the detriment of managers, staff, shareholders, suppliers and customers of the target firm. Thus a definitive time-bound process is desirable.

Takeover regulation in the UK

A takeover is a means of achieving a controlling interest in the target company. A public offer extended to all the target shareholders is only one way in which the controlling interest can be passed on from the existing to new shareholders. Other transactions which could also result in control transfers include: private contract; issue of new shares by the target; redemption of target shares; share capital reconstruction and schemes of arrangement.

Since shares in private companies are not widely held, the need for regulation of takeover bids is much less for them than for public and listed companies. In the UK, takeovers where the target company is a public company are regulated by the City Panel on Takeovers and Mergers (the Panel) under the City Code on Takeovers and Mergers (the Code) (also called the Blue Book because of the colour of its binder).

A scheme of arrangement is carried out under Section 425 of the UK Companies Act 1985 (CA 1985). It is a scheme between the target company and its shareholders, and requires the co-operation of the target. A takeover proposal may be the subject of a scheme. Such a scheme, when agreed by three-quarters in value of shareholders, needs to be sanctioned by the court. Once sanctioned, the scheme is binding on all shareholders, thus obviating the problem of minority shareholders after acquisition. Because of the involvement of the court, a scheme is tedious, time consuming and expensive. For this reason, mergers by schemes of arrangement are much less frequent than public offers under the Code. For example, in their study of UK mergers during 1955–85, Franks and Harris (1989) find only 121 schemes of arrangement compared to 1693 public offers.

The Takeover Panel

The Panel was promoted by the Bank of England in response to rising concern about some of the market 'rigging' and manipulative activities of bidders and target managements. It came into being in 1968. It was created as a self-regulatory, non-statutory authority, a character which it retains to this day. Its aim is to provide a speedy response to takeover situations, and ensure a fair and orderly transfer of ownership of companies in the stock market. Its philosophy is to promote best practice rather than minimally acceptable conduct among those involved in takeovers. This philosophy permeates the 10 General Principles and 38 Rules of the Code.

The membership of the Panel includes nominees of the Bank of England, and representatives of investment institutions, banks, self-regulatory organisations (SROs), the accountancy profession and industry. The chairperson and two deputy chairpersons are all Bank of England nominees. The Panel Executive is headed by the Director General, normally on secondment from a merchant bank, and is staffed by a mixture of permanent Panel employees and those seconded from the City firms and the Bank of England.

The day-to-day work of the Panel is carried out by the Panel Executive, whose decisions and interpretations of the Code can be challenged before a full Panel. There is also a right of appeal from the Panel to the Appeal Committee, which is headed by someone with experience of high judicial office.

Although the Panel does not derive its authority from the law, its role has been recognised and its jurisdiction over takeovers supported by the court and other self-regulatory organisations such as the Stock Exchange. In the landmark Datafin case in 1986, which involved two rival bids for McCorquodale, Datafin challenged the Panel ruling. The Court of Appeal held that the proceedings of the Panel were subject to judicial review. This review does not amount to an appeal. The focus of the review is to ensure that the Panel has observed its own rules and procedures fairly. The effect of this ruling is to prevent any tactical litigation in challenge of the Panel's rulings while a bid is in progress. This position of the court has been affirmed in further cases in 1988 and 1992.

The Panel's authority is also recognised by the UK government and regulatory bodies under the Financial Services Act (FSA) 1986. The Panel can receive information from the Department of Trade and Industry (DTI) which the latter obtains in the course of an investigation, and can use this information to form its own rulings. An example of this co-operation was the Guinness case in 1988 (see Case Study 6.1).

CASE STUDY 6.1   DTI passes information to the Panel

Guinness, in its 1985 competitive bid for Distillers, had entered into share purchase arrangements without disclosing them, and paid a higher price under this arrangement than was made available to other target shareholders. This contravened the Code's highest price and equality of treatment rules. The Panel ordered Guinness in 1989 to compensate the other shareholders for £85 million. Guinness' challenge in the Court against this ruling was not successful. The Panel's ruling was based on information it had received from the DTI inspectors investigating the Guinness affair.

Source: Panel Report for the year to 31.3.1989.

The rules of the Securities and Investments Board (SIB), the apex regulator of financial services in the UK under FSA, and other self-regulating organisations (SROs) such as the Securities and Futures Authority, provide that the firms authorised to carry on investment business should not act for clients or with professionals who are not prepared to comply with the Code ('the cold shoulder rule'). Further, practitioners in breach of the Code may be deemed by their respective SROs as not 'fit and proper' to carry on investment business. Such a judgement may lead to loss of authorisation to carry on investment business.

The City Code

The Code operates principally to oversee conduct of bids and to ensure fair and equal treatment of all shareholders in relation to takeovers. The Code is not concerned with the financial or commercial advantages or disadvantages of a takeover. Nor is it concerned with competition and other public policy issues, which are the province of government. The Code represents the collective opinion of professionals involved in takeovers as to good business standards and how fairness to shareholders can be achieved.

Further, the Code seeks to achieve a fair balance between the interests of the offeror (the bidder) and of the offeree (the target) company and its shareholders. The Code has jurisdiction over bids for UK resident public companies (both listed and unlisted) and certain statutory, chartered and private companies. These private companies must have been, in the previous ten years, listed at any time on the Stock Exchange or involved in the sale of their equity share capital, or must have had dealings in their shares advertised. (For a more detailed description of the jurisdiction, see the Code.)

The Code is based on 10 General Principles and 38 Rules. These Rules are clarified by Notes which accompany them. The Panel promulgates new Rules or provides new interpretation of existing Rules in response to developments in the takeover market. Speed and flexibility of such response are the hallmarks of the self-regulatory system which the Panel embodies. The General Principles of the Code can be summarised as follows:

- Equality of treatment and opportunity for all shareholders in the same class in takeover bids.

- No selective or preferential release of information to some shareholders not made available to all shareholders.

- Adequate information in a timely manner, and advice to enable shareholders to assess the merits of the offer.

- Offeror should make an offer only after the most careful consideration of its ability to implement the offer.

- No action which might frustrate an offer is taken by a target company during the offer period without shareholders being allowed to approve it.

- The maintenance of fair and orderly markets in the shares of the companies concerned throughout the period of the offer.

- Information provided by offerors, offerees and their advisers to shareholders must be prepared with the highest standards of care and accuracy.

- Rights of control must be exercised in good faith and oppression by a minority is unacceptable.

- Directors must act and offer advice solely in the interests of their shareholders, employees and creditors and not in their own personal interests.

- Where control of a company is acquired or consolidated by a person, he or she must normally make a general offer to all other shareholders.

The Rules flesh out these principles, to give direction to concerned parties and their advisers in specific situations. The Rules impose obligations as well as enjoin certain courses of action. Where a particular situation is not covered by a Rule, the Panel will apply the relevant General Principle to arrive at its ruling. At all times in the interpretation of the Rules, the Panel seeks compliance with their spirit, and not merely their letter. A brief summary of some of the more important Rules now follows. This summary carries the health warning that one must use it as a signpost to the Rules and not as a substitute.

- *Mandatory bid:* When a person or a group acquires shares carrying 30 per cent or more of the voting rights of a company, they must normally make a cash offer (or a share offer with a cash alternative) to all other shareholders at the highest price paid in the previous twelve months. Similarly, if the holder of 30 per cent or more of the voting rights adds more than 1 per cent to that holding in a year, a mandatory bid is generally required. (For exceptions to this rule, see the Code.)
- *Mandatory cash offer:* When shares carrying 10 per cent or more of the voting rights have been acquired by an offeror in the offer period and in the previous twelve months, the offer must include a cash alternative at the highest price paid by the offeror.
- *Uniform price offer:* If the offeror buys shares in a target company at a price above the offer value, the offer must be increased to that price.
- *Independent advice for target shareholders:* The target management must obtain competent and independent advice on the offer, and communicate it to its shareholders with its own views.
- *Equality of information:* All shareholders must be given the same information.
- *Equality of rival bidders:* Prospective rival bidders should have access to the same information from the target company.
- *Equality of treatment:* Favourable deals for selected shareholders are banned.
- *Integrity of information:* Profit forecasts and asset valuations must be made to high standards and reported on by professional advisers, who must declare their responsibility.
- *No distortion of information:* Misleading or unsubstantiated statements made must be publicly corrected immediately.

- *No frustrating action:* The target company cannot undertake any frustrating action during the offer unless shareholders approve.

- *Disclosure of share dealings:* There are stringent disclosure requirements for share dealings during an offer.

- *Timetable for a bid:* In general, offers must close 60 days after the posting of the offer document. Parties must observe other deadlines in the offer period (see Table 6.2).

- *Impact of antitrust actions:* A bid lapses if it is referred for Monopolies and Mergers Commission or European Commission investigation. Bids must be made subject to this condition.

- *Twelve-month moratorium:* No renewal of a failed bid is allowed for twelve months unless a rival bid for the target emerges. This prohibition does not apply to bids cleared by the MMC or EC.

The Code's mandatory bid rule (Rule 9) embodies a concept of effective control defined in terms of the threshold of 30 per cent of voting rights. When effective control of their company changes hands, the shareholders must be given the opportunity to decide whether they want to continue to hold their shares in the same company. The Code also covers voluntary bids made when the effective control threshold has not been breached. Table 6.1 compares the conditions attached to mandatory and voluntary bids under the Code.

In a voluntary offer, the offeror may set a high minimum acceptance such as 90 per cent for the offer to become unconditional, but can reserve the right to waive this condition and to declare the offer unconditional at even 51 per cent acceptance level. Moreover, a minimum acceptance level of 90 per cent is often advantageous as it could allow the successful offeror to buy out the minority compulsorily under Section 429 of CA 1985. A 90 per cent acceptance level would also enable the acquirer to qualify for merger accounting or merger relief (see Chapter 10 for details).

Acquisition of 75 per cent voting rights is also useful from tax, financing and control perspectives. The target can form part of a 75 per cent tax group with significant tax advantages to the acquirer (Stedman, 1993: 643–9). Any special resolution to convert the target into a private company is passed more easily when the acquirer already owns 75 per cent of voting rights. Such a conversion may be a prelude to the target providing financial assistance to the offeror. This assistance may be used to finance the acquisition itself (Stedman, 1993: 596–9). If the acquisition is being financed by debt, with the target's assets providing security for the borrowing, the

Table 6.1 Conditions for mandatory and voluntary bids

Mandatory bid	Voluntary bid
Required if bidder has acquired 30 per cent of target's voting shares or, if already owning 30 per cent or more, has increased the holding by 1 per cent or more in one year (Rule 9).	Made when bidder has not breached mandatory bid threshold.
Offer extended to all target shareholders.	Offer extended to all target shareholders.
Offer must be cash or with cash alternative at the highest price paid in the previous twelve months.	Offer need not be cash unless bidder breaches the mandatory cash offer rule (see the summary of Rules).
Offer must become unconditional when acceptances lead to bidder holding more than 50 per cent of voting rights in target.	Bid may be conditional on a higher minimum of acceptances.
Offers for voting non-equity shares must be made.	Not required, but offer cannot be declared unconditional unless acceptances for at least 50 per cent of total voting rights are received.
	Offer conditions must be objective and not subject to offeror directors' judgement.

offeror's lenders may want a 90 per cent acceptance. This increases the offeror's control over those assets, for example through the ability to buy out the minorities. The increased control enhances the security to lenders. Further, if more than 25 per cent of the target shares are still in public hands, they may, under the London Stock Exchange rules, still be listed, with a consequent loss of control to the acquirer.

Setting a high minimum acceptance level means the offer may perhaps have to be kept open longer, with the outcome of the bid more uncertain. However, a voluntary offer is much more flexible and conditions under the Code are less stringent. A mandatory offer is generally to be avoided if possible.

The bid timetable

It is the objective of the Code that the bid process should be brought to a definitive conclusion within a predictable time frame, in general of no more than three months. The reasoning behind this stance is that any protracted siege of the target will detract from the target management's task of managing the company, and may create uncertainty for managers, employees, customers and suppliers, and lead to loss of value for shareholders. The Code, therefore, lays down milestones on the timetable for a hostile bid. This timetable is shown in Table 6.2.

Where an offer becomes unconditional as to acceptances, it must also become unconditional in all respects not later than 21 days thereafter. The Code also allows another 21 days for the payment of

Table 6.2 Bid timetable under the Code

Announcement day	The bidder announces the offer with all terms and conditions.
Posting day (Day 0)	Offer document must be posted within 28 days of offer announcement.
Day 14	Last day for target recommendation to its shareholders and for response to offer document.
Day 21	First offer closing day. Offer may be extended. Offeror may buy target shares in the market above 30 per cent under voluntary offer rules.
Day 35	End of grace period for acceptance when offer went unconditional on Day 21.
Day 39	Last day for target to release new information, e.g. profit forecast.
Day 42	After this day target shareholders can withdraw their acceptances if offer was not declared unconditional on Day 21.
Day 46	Last day for bidder to revise and post offer terms, e.g. raise offer price, or release new information, e.g. dividend forecast.
Day 60	Final closing date, i.e. last day of offer period. Bid either fails or is declared unconditional as to acceptances.
Day 81	Last day for clearing all other conditions attached to bid.
Day 102	Last day for delivery of consideration.

consideration from the day the offer becomes wholly unconditional. The timetable can be extended at the discretion of the Panel. For example, if there is any delay in the OFT decision to refer the bid to the MMC, the Panel can 'stop the clock', thus allowing the bid to proceed after the OFT has cleared the bid. Where a competing offeror for the target emerges, its bid timetable is available to the first offeror.

The Code recognises that bidders and target companies may camouflage their intentions and actions before and during an offer. It therefore employs the concepts of 'concert party' and 'associate' in defining the obligations and responsibilities of parties to a takeover. 'Persons acting in concert comprise those who, pursuant to an agreement or understanding (whether formal or informal) actively cooperate, through the acquisition by any of them of shares in a company, to obtain or consolidate control of that company' (The Code Definitions). The obligations under the Code are extended to the concert parties. For example, in determining whether a mandatory bid has become necessary, the share purchases by the offeror's concert parties will be taken into account.

The term 'associate' is intended to cover all persons (whether or not acting in concert) who directly or indirectly own or deal in the shares of the offeror or the offeree company in an offer, and who have an interest or potential interest in the outcome of the offer (see the Code for a more comprehensive definition). Associates may include subsidiaries, professional advisers like merchant banks, directors and their close relatives, and company pension funds. Ownership or control of 5 per cent of shares may lead to a rebuttable presumption that the holder is an associate. Associates have the obligation to disclose their dealings in the offeror or target company securities and any arrangements concerning those securities such as an indemnity.

Partial offers

The Code allows offers for less than 100 per cent of the voting rights of the target. A partial offer is made to all target shareholders on a pro rata basis and requires the Panel's consent. Up to 30 per cent, consent will normally be given. The Panel will not normally give its consent for a partial offer aimed at over 30 per cent where the offeror or its concert parties have, in the previous twelve months, acquired significant amounts of the target shares. Partial offers are not common in the UK, since, under the Code, an offer for more than 30 per cent can succeed only if shareholders holding more than

50 per cent of the target voting rights (excluding the offeror and its concert parties) vote in favour of the offer.

A detailed discussion of the application of the Code rules is beyond the scope of this book. A flavour of the pragmatic way in which the Panel interprets these Rules and the General Principles is provided from a selection of cases decided by the Panel in Case Study 6.2.

CASE STUDY 6.2   *Panel decisions in a selection of bids*

Accuracy of information
In its defence against the hostile bid from Airtours in January 1993, Owners Abroad (OA) argued that its current trading performance and prospects were strong. The bid failed. In July 1993, OA announced its half-yearly results with a profit warning for the full year, and attributed this to a number of adverse factors since Easter 1993. The Panel investigated whether information provided in OA's defence document had been prepared with the highest care, and whether any material information had been withheld. The Panel concluded there was no breach of the Code (Panel Statement 1993/3).

Extension of timetable
Tootal Group was the target of an offer by Coats Viyella in 1991. OFT was considering a reference to the MMC, but no decision had been made by Day 39, the last day for the target to release any new information. The Panel ruled that Day 39 would be deemed two days after the announcement of the OFT decision (Panel Statement 1991/3).

Breach of equality of information
In April 1992 Dowty Group was the target of a hostile bid from TI Group. During the bid, the public relations adviser to Dowty released a profit forecast which could not be made public, since it could not be made to the standard required by the Code. The Panel judged the behaviour of the PR adviser a serious breach of the Code, and criticised Lazards, the merchant bank adviser to Dowty (Panel Statement 1992/20).

Prohibition of renewal of a failed bid
Robert Maxwell was a concert party to the Demerger bid for Extel in 1986. When the bid lapsed, the concert party arrangement ended. Nevertheless the Panel decided that the twelve-month moratorium on renewal of a lapsed bid would apply to the concert party as well as the bidder (Panel Statement 1986/32).

Quality of profit forecast
During the hostile bid by Dixons Group for Woolworth Holdings in 1986, Woolworth produced a profit forecast. The Panel ruled that this was not

up to the Code standards, and that the Panel had not been consulted as required by the Code. The Panel required the deficiencies in the statement to be made good, and accordingly extended Day 39. The Panel also expressed surprise at the advice given to Woolworth by Rothschilds, its financial adviser (Panel Statement 1986/25).

Highest price to all

Guinness won the bid for Distillers in 1986. It had an undisclosed concert party arrangement with Pipetec of Switzerland, which bought Distillers shares on behalf of Guinness during the bid, but at a higher price (731 pence) than was on public offer (630.3 pence cash alternative). The concert party was only discovered during the DTI fraud investigation into Guinness. It breached the Code that the highest price should be extended to all target shareholders. The Panel ordered Guinness in July 1989 to pay some £85 million compensation to Distillers' shareholders, including interest (Panel Statement 1989/13).

The Substantial Acquisition Rules

In the past, potential bidders built up substantial stakes in the target company before publicly announcing their intention to bid (an acquisition known as a 'dawn raid'). This put the target company shareholders at a disadvantage, since they were denied equality of treatment and the opportunity to judge a bid in the light of full disclosure of relevant information. The Substantial Acquisition Rules (SARs) are designed to make acquisitions between 15 and 30 per cent of the voting rights more transparent and also to slow down such acquisitions.

The SARs are independent of the Code, but are administered by the Panel. They apply only to the range of 15 to 30 per cent where the Code becomes relevant. The SARs also require accelerated disclosure of share acquisitions. Except under certain conditions (for example, purchase from a single seller), acquisitions of 10 per cent or more of the target shares in a period of seven days is not allowed if this would bring the total holding to above 15 per cent. Once the 15 per cent threshold is reached, any 1 per cent or higher increase in the shareholding must be disclosed not later than the following business day. Such purchases must be notified to the target company and the London Stock Exchange by noon the following day.

One of the SARs deals with a tender offer which is restricted to stake building up to a maximum of 30 per cent. This is an alternative to market purchases or privately negotiated purchases. A tender offer is made to all target shareholders and must be for cash. All target shareholders must be treated equally. Tender offers must be advertised, but no argument or persuasion is allowed. Target shareholders may interpret a tender offer as a prelude to a full bid and therefore refrain from tendering. Because of this 'wait and see' posture, and the rule prohibiting any 'top up' whereby the offeror can compensate tendering shareholders in the event of a subsequent full bid, tender offers in the UK are not very popular.

Statutory rules

As noted earlier, schemes of arrangement are carried out under the CA 1985 provisions (sections 425–7). CA 1985 also requires an acquirer to notify the target of purchases resulting in a holding of 3 per cent or more of the voting shares within two days. Any 1 per cent change above that threshold needs to be similarly notified (sections 198–220). The use of target company's resources to provide financial assistance to pay for the acquisition is generally prohibited (sections 151–5). Proposed compensation payments to directors in connection with a takeover for loss of office or retirement must be disclosed in the offer document (section 314).

When the share stake build up is carried out through nominees, CA 1985 gives companies the right to require disclosure of the true owners of the shares (section 212). A company may also assume power, in its articles, to disenfranchise those shares or appeal to the court to do so. An offeror who has 90 per cent of its offer accepted can then compulsorily purchase the remaining 10 per cent of the shares that are the subject of the offer (section 429). This provision helps the acquirer to get rid of any unwanted minority. CA 1985 also lays down the minimum level of acquisition (90 per cent) for the acquirer to claim merger relief (section 131) and also qualify for merger accounting (see Chapter 10 below).

The Financial Services Act (FSA) 1986 requires offer documents which are investment advertisements to be approved by authorised persons (section 57). In a securities exchange, listing particulars must be published and be free of defective particulars. FSA prohibits misleading statements and practices (section 47).

The Company Securities (Insider Dealing) (ID) Act 1985 prohibits a person who has received price-sensitive information about an offer or contemplated offer from a person connected with a company from dealing in shares in the target company. It is a criminal offence not only to deal, but also to counsel or procure others to deal. Under the Criminal Justice Act 1993 it is a criminal offence for an individual who has information as an insider, such as a director, to deal in securities whose price would be significantly affected if the insider information were made public. It is also an offence to encourage insider dealing and to disclose inside information to others with a view to their profiting from it.

The London Stock Exchange rules

The regulations of the London Stock Exchange (LSE) (more formally known as the International Stock Exchange of the United Kingdom and the Republic of Ireland) concern the following:

- The announcement of takeover bids.
- The need for shareholder approval for large transactions.
- The content of offer documents and notification to the LSE.
- The content of listing particulars when securities are issued in consideration.

LSE's Listing Rules divide acquisitions, disposals, takeovers and mergers into size classes. Size is expressed as a percentage of the target's net assets or profits, or the consideration paid or gross capital in relation to the offeror's net assets, market capitalisation or gross assets (for the detailed criteria for size classification, see the Yellow Book containing the Listing Rules). The LSE imposes one or more of the following obligations on the offeror in class transactions: notify the Company Announcements Office (CAO) at the LSE, send a circular to the offeror shareholders with details of the offer, and obtain their approval for the transaction at a general meeting. As the class size of a transaction increases, the obligations become more onerous.

A reverse takeover is one where the size ratio exceeds 100 per cent. This means that in an acquisition the target is larger than the listed offeror, and thus control of the offeror may pass to the target shareholders. When a reverse takeover is announced, the offeror's listing is suspended pending approval by the offeror shareholders at an extraordinary general meeting. If the takeover is approved, the company will have to apply for listing as a new applicant. In that event, the company would normally produce listing particulars conditional on shareholder approval so that listing can be granted immediately following the approval.

The various size classes and their respective obligations under the LSE Listing Rules are shown in Table 6.3. The Listing Rules stipulate deadlines for the dispatch of notification and circulars, and for shareholder approval. Where shareholder approval is required, as

Table 6.3 Transaction class and obligations

Class size	Notify CAO	Send circular	Obtain shareholder approval
3 (less than 5%)	No (except if paid for by securities to be listed)	No	No
2 (less than 15%)	Yes	No	No
1 (less than 25%)	Yes	Yes	No
Super Class 1 (more than 25%)	Yes	Yes	Yes
Reverse takeover	Yes	Yes	Yes

Note: When the CAO is notified, the information becomes public.

for a Super Class 1 or reverse takeover bid, the offeror must take care not to invite the obligation to make a mandatory bid since it cannot be made conditional upon such approval (Rule 9.3 of the Code). Listing particulars are required if offeror share capital is increased by 10 per cent or more as a result of an equity financed offer.

If a listed company enters into an indemnity arrangement accepting liability for costs/losses exceeding 25 per cent of the average net profits of the company over the previous three years, such an arrangement becomes a Super Class 1 transaction. This rule was triggered by the Guinness bid for Distillers in 1985, as described in Case Study 6.3.

CASE STUDY 6.3   Indemnity against losses

In December 1985, Imperial Group was the target of a friendly bid from United Biscuits (UB) and a hostile bid from Hanson Trust. In February 1986, Morgan Grenfell bought Imperial shares on behalf of UB at a price of 320 pence per share against Hanson's cash alternative offer of 293 pence. Thus Morgan stood to lose in the event of a Hanson win, but it was indemnified against this loss by UB.

Guinness made a friendly bid for Distillers Company, which was also the target of a hostile bid from Argyll Group in December 1985. To encourage Guinness to make the bid, Distillers indemnified it against any costs incurred by Guinness.

Source: Dimson and Marsh (1988: 174) and press reports.

Limitations of UK takeover regulation

The current framework, with the Panel as its cornerstone, has been criticised on several grounds:

- The membership of the Panel is biased towards those with a direct financial interest in creating more takeover activity.

- Its consultative procedures in effecting changes to the Code are minimal.

- In establishing principles, in making its rules, in interpreting them and in waiving them, it operates virtually free of public scrutiny.

- Legal representation before the Executive is not allowed, although in any appeal to the full Panel it is (Professor Jeffrey Jowell, *Financial Times*, 9, 15 and 24 May 1991).

Future evolution of UK regulation

With increasing cross-border mergers in the European Union and the spread of Anglo-Saxon-style takeover bids to the Continent, there is a need to evolve a proper takeover regulatory regime. A draft directive concerning 'takeover and other general bids' from the European Commission (the thirteenth Company Law Directive) has been under consideration for several years now. The proposed takeover regime has been inspired by the Code in the UK, and provides for a Supervisory Authority charged with ensuring observance of a number of principles, including fair and equal treatment of all shareholders.

The other principles embodied in the directive include a threshold for a full mandatory bid, requirement to bid for all shares, specification of minimum offer document content, a bid timetable and the offeree company report. Under the directive, takeover regulation will become statutory rather than voluntary.

The takeover directive has been criticised on the grounds that it will give rise to a more bureaucratic, legalistic and costly system. It will also reduce the flexibility and speed of response which are characteristic of the UK Panel. There will also be greater scope for tactical litigation. As it currently stands, the Supervisory Authority will not be able to give general dispensations/derogations.

Takeover regulation in the USA

In the USA, tender offers are regulated under the Williams Act (WA) 1968 by the Securities and Exchange Commission. WA imposes obligations on both offerors and targets, and prevents secret accumulation of large stakes by requiring acquisitions of 5 per cent or more of voting shares to be disclosed within ten days. WA defines when a tender offer commences, and sets out the information to be disclosed, including the source of funds for and the purpose of the offer. Tender offers must be open for twenty business days, and revised offers kept open for another ten business days.

The 'best price' and 'all holders' rule requires that the bidder buys the tendered shares at the best price during the offer, and that the tender be open to all shareholders. During the offer, shares cannot be bought by the offeror except in pursuance of the offer itself. WA makes any fraudulent act, including insider trading in connection with the offer, illegal.

WA imposes obligations on targets in their response to tender offers. It requires the target to inform its shareholders of its position on the tender offer within ten business days. Target management must disclose any conflict of interest and also refrain from materially misleading statements.

Since in the USA companies are incorporated under state laws, the structure of an acquisition is a matter partly of state law and partly of Federal law. Some state laws have recently made tender offers more difficult by allowing certain defensive devices by target companies, such as shark repellents and poison pills (see Chapter 12).

Regulation of takeover bids on the Continent

There are very few Continental European countries which operate a UK-style takeover Code, although many countries have in recent years introduced rules and guidelines incorporating some of the principles of the Code. In this section, the regulations in some European countries are outlined. The reader must bear in mind that the following description is not exhaustive (see Carrington and Pessôa de Araújo, 1994, for further details).

In the Netherlands, the Dutch Social and Economic Council has issued the Fusie Code to be observed during bids for public companies. This code requires full bids to be made to all target shareholders at a fixed price, but there is no mandatory bid requirement. Discriminatory price offers are thus not allowed. Bids must be publicly announced. Adequate information must be provided to target shareholders. Target management must state its position on the merits of the bid, and must not seek to frustrate it without good reason. All target shareholders must be treated equally. The offer should not be false or misleading. The Fusie Code is not law, but violations of the Code may lead to public censure. Disclosure of shareholdings must be made when they reach the thresholds of 5, 10, 25, 50 and 66.66 per cent. There is no provision for compulsory purchase of minority shareholders.

In France, the takeover regulation derives from the law and is monitored and enforced by three bodies – Conseil des Bourses de Valeurs (CBV), Société des Bourses Françaises (SBF) and Commission des Opérations de Bourse (COB). The regulation requires a mandatory bid with a threshold of one-third of the target shares or voting rights, and it must be extended to all the remaining shareholders. Similarly, between the above threshold and 50 per cent of shareholding, if the annual purchase of target shares exceeds 2 per cent, again a mandatory bid is required. The CBV can veto a low price bid. A bid timetable lasting from the day of the offer to 28 stock market days thereafter is followed. Full disclosure of information to shareholders must be made. Disclosure of shareholdings when they reach 5, 10, 20, 33.33, 50 and 66.66 per cent is required. There is no provision for compulsory acquisition of minority shareholders after a successful bid.

In Germany, public company bids, especially hostile ones, have been very rare, but there are guidelines for the conduct of public offers. The principle of non-discrimination towards target shareholders is enshrined in the guidelines, which require mandatory bids in very limited circumstances, such as for the protection of minority shareholders. Shareholding thresholds for disclosure have in the past been 25 and 50 per cent, but have recently been modified to 5, 10, 25, 50 and 75 per cent. There is no provision for compulsory purchase of minorities.

In Sweden, the Stockholm Stock Exchange (SSE) has published a number of recommendations for conduct of public company takeovers. Equality of treatment of target shareholders is laid down. The target management must inform its shareholders of a bid and can express its own opinion. Sufficient information concerning the offer must be provided to enable shareholders to evaluate the offer. The Swedish Companies Act regulates the content of offer documents. Compulsory acquisition of minorities is allowed. No threshold for a mandatory bid is laid down.

It is clear from the above brief review of the regulatory systems in different countries that there is a wide diversity among them. Such a diversity may create barriers to cross-border acquisitions, or at least raise the cost of such acquisitions (see Chapter 16 for further discussion of barriers to cross-border acquisitions). There is, however, a trend among Continental countries towards a UK-style regulatory regime. The EU's proposed takeover directive reflects such a trend, although in many important respects it differs from the UK Code.

Takeover regulation and takeover activity

The Code, in conjunction with the SARs and the Companies Act 1989, requires extensive disclosures of share acquisitions by actual or potential bidders. Do such disclosure requirements raise bid premia and reduce the profitability of acquisitions, and hence reduce the incentive for potential bidders to undertake acquisitions?

The Code also requires a mandatory bid to ensure that target shareholders are given the opportunity to decide whether they wish to remain shareholders when effective control of the target has passed on to the bidder. Further, both mandatory and voluntary bid offers have to be extended to all target shareholders. Do these rules overprotect target shareholders, enhance their leverage against bidders and lead to high bid premia? Do they deter profitable and value-creating takeovers? If value-creating acquisitions are deterred, the result may be a welfare loss to the economy as a whole. We attempt below to answer the above questions.

Grossman and Hart (1980) put forward the 'free-rider' model of the relationship between the ownership structure of a target firm and the incentive for bidders to make bids. In this model, which assumes the US system of strong minority shareholder rights, the target is owned by a multitude of small shareholders (an atomistic shareholder structure). Each shareholder, believing her own decision has a trivially small effect on the probability of success of a particular bid, will have an incentive to decline the bid offer if she expects other shareholders to accept. In this way, the shareholder expects to participate in the post-acquisition performance improvement of the target effected by the acquirer.

Each shareholder thus expects to free-ride on the accepting decisions of her fellow-shareholders. Further, the shareholder free-rides on the acquirer, since she benefits from the efforts of the acquirer in researching the enhanced profit potential of the target and in realising that potential after the acquisition. If all target shareholders expect to free-ride, the bid will fail and there will be no ride at all for anyone. This free-riding behaviour will, therefore, deter any value-increasing bid. That is, there is no incentive for any potential bidder to incur the costs of researching value-creating takeover opportunities and the bid-related costs (see Chapter 8) if he has to pass all the added value to a bunch of free-riders.

Grossman and Hart argue that the Williams Act disclosure requirements in the USA aggravate the free-riding problem, since they prevent the potential bidder from accumulating a substantial stake (the toehold) ahead of a public bid. A toehold allows the bidder to retain some of the value improvements it brings about after acquisition. This compensates it for the cost of making the acquisition. Grossman and Hart suggest a remedy for the free-riding problem – diminished rights for minority shareholders of the target after being acquired by the bidder. Such diminution of rights allows the bidder to retain some of the benefits of acquisition.

In the UK, the free-rider problem may be much less serious. According to Yarrow (1985), protection of minorities in the UK against oppression by the majority shareholder is much weaker. Moreover, the Companies Act 1985 allows an acquirer which has purchased 90 per cent of the target shares to acquire compulsorily the minority. Thus the incentive for free-riding appears to be small. Indeed it may be the small shareholder who perhaps needs protection from being locked into a minority position. The Code rules on equality of treatment and information disclosure, as well as the prohibition of partial bids except in very restricted circumstances, restore some balance in favour of the small shareholders. Yarrow (1985), therefore, argues that the UK regulatory regime does not provide any disincentive to profitable takeover bids.

The assumption of atomistic shareholding underlying the Grossman and Hart model is also weakened by the presence of substantial block shareholdings by institutional shareholders. Moreover, the presence of arbitrageurs (see Chapter 7), who exploit the difference between the market and offer prices of the target shares, leads to accumulation of large block shareholding. Insider trading, though prohibited by law, also allows such large block accumulation. Thus these deviations from the Grossman and Hart assumption may mitigate the impact of free-riding and allow for a greater level of takeover activity (Roell, 1987). We have seen in Chapter 1 evidence of high takeover activity from time to time. This suggests that the free-rider problem may have been considerably mitigated by the countervailing factors described by Roell.

Overview

This chapter has described the statutory and non-statutory framework for the regulation of takeovers in the UK. Alternative takeover and merger procedures have been examined. The role of the City Panel on Takeovers and Mergers and its Code in policing bids for public companies has been set out in some detail. The advantages and disadvantages of this uniquely non-statutory and self-regulatory system in the UK have been described. Takeovers in the UK are also significantly influenced by statutory rules.

The current attempts at developing a common takeover regime for the European Union have been highlighted, along with a critique of its weaknesses. Takeover regulation in the USA and in some Continental countries has been outlined to enable the reader to appreciate the variety of approaches to such regulation. The trend among Continental countries towards a more UK-style regulation has been noted. We have also discussed the impact of takeover regulation on the level of takeover activity, and whether such regulation deters value-creating takeover bids.

Further reading

Begg, P.F.C. (1991) *Corporate Acquisitions and Mergers* (3rd edn), Graham and Trotman.

Carrington, N., and B. Pessôa de Araújo (1994) *Acquiring Companies and Businesses in Europe*, Chancery Law Publishing.

Dimson, E. and P. Marsh (1988) *Cases in Corporate Finance*, John Wiley.

Franks, J., and R. Harris (1989) 'Shareholder wealth effects of corporate takeovers: the UK experience 1955–85', *Journal of Financial Economics*, **23**, 225–49.

Grossman, S., and O. Hart (1980) 'Takeover bids, the free rider problem and the theory of the corporation', *Bell Journal of Economics*, **11**, 1, 42–64.

Karnath, L. (1993) 'France is different', *Mergers and Acquisitions International*, January, 18–22.

Popper, M. (1993) 'The Anglo-Saxon invasion', *Mergers and Acquisitions International*, February, 14–18.

Roell, A. (1987) 'Regulation of takeovers', London School of Economics Discussion Paper 003.

Stedman, G. (1993) *Takeovers*, Longman.

Yarrow, G.K. (1985) 'Shareholder protection, compulsory acquisition and the efficiency of the takeover process', *Journal of Industrial Economics*, **34**, 1, 3–16.

7

Advisers in takeovers

Although takeovers have increased substantially in recent years, for most companies these happen very infrequently. Thus, except in the case of large firms which are also frequent acquirers, firms are unlikely to have the inhouse expertise necessary for carrying out an acquisition, and will have to seek the help of outside advisers. Further, since takeovers are subject to antitrust and other regulatory rules, advisers who are familiar with those rules and can guide the firm in their proper observance are indispensable. Since an acquisition involves transfer of ownership of shares or assets, the contracts to accomplish that transfer should be drawn up very carefully by expert lawyers.

Valuation of the target is an important aspect of an acquisition, requiring a great deal of skill and judgement as to the future prospects for both the acquirer and the acquired firms. This exercise calls for an understanding of the strategic aspects of the acquisition and of valuation models. This again may demand contributions from outside experts.

This chapter describes the different advisers who may become involved in a takeover. The paramount role of the merchant (investment) banks in the UK is detailed. Their responsibilities and relationship to acquirers and targets are described. The role of other advisers, such as corporate lawyers, accountants, strategy consultants, investor relations and public relations consultants and environment consultants, who may also participate in an acquisition or a defence in a contested bid, is also discussed.

Role of advisers in acquisitions

A takeover may involve the use of one or more of the following advisers:

- Merchant banks.
- Lawyers.
- Accountants.
- Stockbrokers.
- Investor relations/public relations consultants.
- Strategy consultants.
- Environment consultants.

In addition, business brokers or specialist acquisitions consultants may often be used by companies to locate potential acquisition targets.

The need for any of the above advisers in a takeover deal depends upon the extent of inhouse expertise available to the company, the stock exchange requirements and the level of complexity of the deal. For example, the acquisition of a private company or the division of another firm may not require the services of a stockbroker or an investor relations adviser. Some acquisitions may not give rise to any environmental concern. Small deals may often be concluded with the help of the firm's accountants and without the involvement of a merchant banker.

The needs of a bidder for external advice are of a different character from those of a company defending itself against a hostile bid. Some of the advisers, such as merchant banks, specialise in advising hostile bidders or targets. Advisers also differ in the range of services they offer.

The advisory services in acquisitions and corporate restructuring have become increasingly competitive, with advisers offering an overlapping range of services: for example, accountants offer corporate finance advice and their strategy consulting arms offer strategic evaluation advice. Lawyers have also encroached upon the role traditionally played by merchant banks. Nevertheless, in the UK, at least in bids for public companies, the role of the merchant bank is still paramount.

Merchant banks

Merchant banks in the UK and their counterparts, the investment banks, in the USA differ in the range of capabilities they can bring to bear upon a takeover deal. Some of them are financial services conglomerates. Examples of such multiservice merchant banks in the UK are Schroders, Barclays de Zoete Wedd and S.G. Warburg. In the USA they include Goldman Sachs, Morgan Stanley and Salomon Brothers.

The services that merchant banks offer include corporate finance services, stockbroking, fund management and securities trading. Corporate finance services include valuation of companies and businesses as well as arranging packages to finance a deal. A merchant bank can act for either the bidder or the target, although some have developed expertise for one or the other role: for example, Goldman Sachs has a great reputation in defending targets in hostile bids. Merchant banks normally act in an advisory capacity. However, often in the UK, they have acted as principals – for instance, in underwriting a cash offer or in financing a deal.

Services offered by a merchant bank in its capacity as an adviser for a bidder are as follows:

- Finding acquisition opportunities, e.g. locating an acquisition target.
- Evaluating the target from the bidder's strategic and other perspectives; valuing the target; providing 'fair value' opinion.
- Devising appropriate financing structure for the deal, covering offer price, method of payment and sources of finance.
- Advising the client on negotiating tactics and strategies for friendly/hostile bids.
- Collecting information about potential rival bidders.
- Profiling the target shareholders to 'sell' the bid effectively; helping the bidder with presentations and 'road shows'.
- Gathering feedback from the stock market about the attitudes of financial institutions to the bid and its terms.
- Identifying potential 'show stoppers', such as antitrust investigation by MMC, and helping prepare the bidder's case in such investigation.

- Helping prepare offer document, profit forecast, circulars to shareholders and press releases, and ensuring their accuracy.

Services offered to targets are as follows:

- Monitoring target share price to track potential bidders and provide early warning to target of a possible bid.
- Crafting effective bid resistance strategies, e.g. dividend increase.
- Valuing the target and its component businesses to negotiate a higher offer price; providing fair value opinion on the offer.
- Helping the target and its accountants prepare profit forecasts.
- Finding white knights or white squires to block hostile bid.
- Arranging buyers for any divestment or management buyout of target assets as part of its defensive strategy.
- Getting feedback from the financial institutions concerning the offer and the likelihood of its being accepted.

The various bid and defence strategies are discussed extensively in Chapters 8 and 12. In devising these strategies, the merchant bank will rely on the other advisers in the team. For example, in preparing the case in an antitrust investigation, the role of lawyers is crucial. In preparing profit forecasts, the accountants assume the dominant role. In defending the bidder's strategic rationale or in picking holes in that for the defence, the role of the strategy consultant is important.

Where the bank does not have sufficient expertise in any area, another adviser will be brought in, such as an accountant for valuing the target. Where several advisers are involved, it becomes important that one of them co-ordinates the team of advisers. This co-ordinator most often in the UK is a merchant banker, although in smaller deals an accountant or a lawyer may fill that role.

Merchant banks provide 'fair value' opinions which bidders and targets often invoke in support of their decisions, and in recommending these decisions to their respective shareholders. It will be recalled from Chapter 6 that under the London Stock Exchange rules, Super Class 1 transactions have to be approved by the bidder's shareholders. In seeking the shareholder approvals, bidders cite the fair value opinion of their merchant bankers, as shown in Case Study 7.1. Sometimes a bank can be criticised for advising the target management to accept a low-value bid, as shown in Case Study 7.2.

CASE STUDY 7.1   Fair value opinion from merchant banks

In June 1992, Yorkshire Television made a recommended £29.8m bid for Tyne Tees Television. Baring Brothers was the merchant bank adviser to Yorkshire, and Kleinwort Benson acted for Tyne Tees.

In the circular to its shareholders, Yorkshire said: 'Your board, which has been advised by Barings, considers the proposed acquisition . . . in the best interests of Yorkshire and its shareholders.'

Tyne Tees recommended the offer to its shareholders, saying: 'Your board, which has been so advised by Kleinwort Benson, considers the terms of the Offer are fair and reasonable.'

Source: Companies' circulars and recommendations.

CASE STUDY 7.2   Baring Brothers draws flak for low-value opinion

In July 1994, Tesco made an opening bid of £154 million for William Low, the Scottish grocery stores group. This offer was recommended as 'fair and reasonable' and supported by Baring Brothers. Tesco's bid provoked a rival bid from Sainsbury, and Tesco was forced to raise its offer to a winning £247.4 million, a 60 per cent increase. Both Wm Low and Barings defended their initial recommendation as the only way to get an auction going and realise the full value of the company. Nevertheless, the Lex column of the *Financial Times* (dated 4.8.1994) commented that 'if advisers want to maintain their credibility, they should think carefully about letting their names be used too casually'.

Merchant bankers play the 'ears and eyes' of the bidders and targets in gauging the mood of the market during bids. Because of the large block holdings of institutional shareholders, it is especially important that a persuasive case for the bid or for the target independence is made to these investors. In many cases, the outcome of a bid hinges on the decisions of institutional shareholders. The importance of presentations to institutions is indicated in Case Study 7.3.

Assessing market sentiment about the bid or the defence is necessary to modify the tactics and offer terms, as illustrated in the IMI bid for Birmingham Mint (Case Study 7.3). Some merchant banks have longer antennae than others in reading these sentiments. Merchant banks with security trading or stockbroking arms

CASE STUDY 7.3   *IMI woos institutions to beat Birmingham Mint*

In October 1990, IMI made a hostile £14 million bid for Birmingham Mint (BM). The initial offer was 85 pence per ordinary share. BM made presentations to its institutional shareholders well before the first closing date, giving more time for IMI to make its own presentations arranged by Samuel Montagu, the merchant bank advising IMI. The feedback from the institutions to IMI was that an increased offer of 95 pence would be successful. IMI purchased 15.8 per cent of BM shares at 95 pence from a fund manager, and subsequently raised the offer to 110 pence. To clinch victory it bought another 4 per cent of BM shares from a financial institution. The bid succeeded.

Source: *Acquisitions Monthly*, April 1991.

are probably better equipped in this regard, since this helps the banks stay close to the ground. Alternatively, the stockbrokers who are normally part of the advisory team to a bidder can collect market intelligence.

In the USA, many investment banks (known as arbitrageurs or 'arbs') operate risk arbitrage departments, which shift from bidder into target shares or vice versa, in order to exploit the differentials between market and offer prices (Williamson, 1988). This kind of securities trading again enables the investment bank to sharpen its market intelligence capabilities. Although risk arbitrage is not as common in the UK as in the USA, it is not unknown, as shown in Case Study 7.4. In this case, Salomon was not acting for the bidder or target.

US investment banks which arrived on the UK M & A scene in the early 1980s also brought many of the defence techniques shaped in

CASE STUDY 7.4   *Salomon 'arbs' its way to profit*

Tesco's cash offer for William Low was accompanied by a share exchange alternative. Salomon International, the investment bank, busily bought 10 per cent of Low shares and sold Tesco shares in order to arbitrage between the two stocks. Salomon was thought to be aiming to benefit from the all-share alternative.

Source: *Financial Times*, 5.8.1994.

the US market. Among them was finding white knights and buyers for divestments and buyouts. Goldman Sachs was able to arrange a buyout of the US tyre interests of Dunlop, facing a hostile bid from BTR in 1985. As a result, BTR was forced to raise the offer from the initial £33 million to a final and successful offer of £101 million.

Merchant banks and the Code

The Code (Introduction to General Principles, 1993) accords a special place to merchant bank financial advisers, and places special responsibility on them in the conduct of bids for public companies. Financial advisers must do the following:

- Comply with the Code.
- Ensure that an offeror and the offeree company and their respective directors are aware of their responsibilities under the Code and comply with them.
- Ensure that the Panel is consulted whenever necessary.
- Co-operate fully with any enquiries made by the Panel.
- Avoid conflicts of interest.

In playing 'minder' to their clients, merchant banks should, therefore, observe the Code with scrupulous care. There have been several instances where they have overzealously transgressed the Code and earned reprimands from the Panel, as evidenced in Case Study 6.2. Conflicts of interest may arise especially where the bank is a financial conglomerate with a market-making or fund management arm.

Such connected market-makers are exempt from a detailed disclosure of their dealings, required of others acting in concert, so that their normal course of business is not impeded. But the Panel seeks to ensure, through Rule 38, that covert purchases of target shares are not made through the exempt market-maker, and it regards violation of that rule seriously, as shown in Case Study 7.5.

CASE STUDY 7.5   Dealings with exempt market-maker invite Panel rebuke

In January 1988, Peachey Property made a cash bid for Estates Property. Its broker, Philips & Drew, bought on behalf of Peachey 0.8 per cent of Estates' shares from Warburg Securities, the exempt market-making subsidiary of S.G. Warburg Group. S.G. Warburg & Co. Ltd, a fellow subsidiary, acted as financial adviser to Peachey. The Panel ruled that the purchase contravened Rule 38, and ordered the shares to be sold to investment institutions unconnected to Peachey. Both Philips & Drew and Warburg Securities were criticised by the Panel for the inadvertent breaches of the rule.

Source: Panel Statement 1988/5.

Merchant banks' financial support role

Merchant banks often provide support to their M & A clients in the following ways:

- Buying shares in either the bidder or target.
- Underwriting a share exchange offer so as to provide a cash alternative to target shareholders.
- Arranging finance for a cash bid.
- Financing the acquisition as a principal.

Share support operations are allowed under the Code, subject to disclosure rules and the rules governing the maximum price, uniform price and mandatory cash offer described in Chapter 6. In buying the target shares on behalf of the bidder, timing is very important, as highlighted by Case Study 7.6. Merchant banks underwriting a share offer to provide a cash alternative have the deal sub-underwritten by financial institutions, although they may retain some of the exposure themselves. The underwriting may be a

CASE STUDY 7.6   Merchant bank buys target shares to support bidder

Enterprise Oil made a complex securities offer worth £1.6 billion for Lasmo, a rival oil explorer, in April 1994. Just before the final closing date on 1 July 1994, S.G. Warburg, one of the two merchant bank advisers to Enterprise, bought a 10 per cent stake from institutional investors for £170 million at a higher price than the market price. Despite this last-minute support, the bid failed and Enterprise was left with a loss on this purchase of £30 million. Moreover, the shares were bought from institutional investors who would have accepted the securities offer anyway. Thus the share support strategy seems to have been misjudged.

Source: *Financial Times*, 25.7.1994.

conventional rights issue type or contingent upon the success of the bid. The differences between these two forms of underwriting are discussed in Chapter 11.

Arranging acquisition financing requires a good deal of placing power from the merchant bank. The success of this effort will depend upon the reputation of the bank in its corporate finance role in general, and its track record of supporting good acquisitions. While even small merchant banks can successfully place the bidder's securities to raise funds, a bank which chooses to finance a part or whole of the deal itself needs a 'deep pocket'. This is where being part of a larger banking group may be of great competitive advantage. The provision of finance by a merchant bank as a principal is exemplified in Case Study 7.7.

CASE STUDY 7.7 Samuel Montagu finances WPP's bid for J. Walter Thompson (JWT)

On 26 June 1987 WPP, a UK firm with net assets of just £2 million, won a contested $566 million all-cash bid for JWT, the venerable US advertising agency. The cash was provided by an underwritten rights issue. But Samuel Montagu initially underwrote the issue along with Credit Suisse before having it sub-underwritten subsequently. Further, it invested $14 million in a new offshore company set up by WPP to avoid problems with obtaining shareholder approval under the London Stock Exchange rules.

Source: *Acquisitions Monthly*, September 1987.

Lawyers

Among the other advisers, lawyers are almost always involved in acquisitions of both private and public companies. They play an important part in a due diligence audit undertaken as part of an acquisition, although other specialists such as chartered surveyors and risk insurers may be co-opted in carrying out these tasks. The important elements of a due diligence audit are as follows:

- The investigating accountant's report, examining the trading results and prospects, the balance sheet, accounting policies, financial systems and controls of the target.

- Strategic evaluation of the target, e.g. assessing strategic strengths and weaknesses of the target and its strategic fit with the bidder.
- Property investigation, e.g. establishing legal title and valuation.
- Assessment of the target company's liabilities both current and contingent, e.g. liabilities for unpaid tax or pension fund deficits, redundancy payments, pending litigation, and obligations imposed by environmental protection laws or practices.
- Assessment of risks and insurance cover arranged by the target, e.g. insurance of physical assets, and insurance of liabilities such as product liability or directors' and officers' liability.
- Warranties and indemnities.

Warranties and indemnities as well as the contract of sale are the lawyers' territory. A warranty is a contractual representation by the vendor which, if it is untrue, entitles the purchaser to claim for damages. For example, a warranty may be to the effect that the vendor company's title to its properties is good, or that the company's latest accounts are true and accurate. An indemnity is similar to a warranty, but provides that the vendor will compensate the buyer in the event of any loss under specified circumstances. For example, an indemnity may cover potential but undisclosed tax liabilities.

The importance of a due diligence audit of the target in a takeover is most dramatically brought out by the disastrous acquisition of International Signal and Control (ISC), an American defence company, by Ferranti in 1987 (see Case Study 7.8). In the case of public company targets, the scope for due diligence audit is very limited.

CASE STUDY 7.8   Ferranti buys a phantom target

Ferranti, the British defence electronics company, was keen to get a foothold in the large American defence contracts business. It acquired ISC, an unlisted company in the UK, in a friendly bid for £215 million. ISC's accounts before the bid had all been audited. After the acquisition, Ferranti discovered that ISC books included £200 million worth of non-existent sales contracts and subcontracts. Ferranti had to write off the entire investment in ISC. The chairman of ISC, James Guerin, was later gaoled for fraud. Ferranti, which at the time of the ISC acquisition was valued at £1 billion, was put into receivership in 1993.

Sources: *Financial Weekly*, 19.12.1989; *Financial Times*, 2.12.1993.

Lawyers in the UK have a lower profile in public company takeovers than their American counterparts. In the 1980s, the latter enjoyed as much visibility as the investment bank superstars. For example, Martin Lipton of the US law firm Wachtell, Lipton, Rosen and Katz is the progenitor of the famous poison pill defence (see Chapter 12). Most of the significant innovations in the hostile takeover business have come from lawyers (Williamson, 1988: 245).

In the UK, lawyers Freshfields invented the 'vitamin pill' for Consolidated Goldfields (Consgold) in its defence against Minorco, described in Case Study 7.9. Consgold did beat off the predator, although it employed other more effective defence ploys. Consgold was in the same year taken over by Hanson.

Lawyers play an important role in preparing the case to be presented to the Office of Fair Trading, the Monopolies and Mergers Commission and the European Commission in connection with any antitrust investigation. Although the Code specifically emphasises that its appeal proceedings must be conducted in a non-judicial manner, lawyers do get involved in preparing the arguments presented to the Panel (J. Grieves and A. Salz, *Acquisitions Monthly*, November 1989).

CASE STUDY 7.9 *Consgold bolsters its defence with a vitamin pill*

When faced with a £3.2 billion hostile bid from Minorco in 1989, Consgold pledged to pay its shareholders a cash dividend of £6 gross per share if the company did not meet a target earnings per share figure of 400 pence cumulative over the following three years. The £6 was to be tied to the issue of special preference shares carrying rights to vote the promised dividend. If the target EPS were met, the special shares would become worthless.

Source: *Financial Weekly*, 6.4.1989.

Accountants

Accountants carry out the due diligence investigation, which may often be wide ranging and cover pre-purchase review, purchase investigation and acquisition audit (M. Allen and R. Hodgkinson, *Acquisitions Monthly*, June 1989). A pre-purchase review provides limited information about the target, its industry and the reasons for sale, but it is not a substitute for a strategic evaluation. The principal aim of the purchase investigation is to identify significant matters relevant to the valuation of the target, or the warranties and indemnities to be obtained. Such matters cover the target's accounting policies and financial projections, and the key commercial assumptions behind those projections.

The acquisition audit, available only in the case of a private company target, examines the quality of the company's accounts and contains the investigating accountant's assessment of that quality. Based on this, the buyer can seek an appropriate warranty from the seller.

Accountants are also involved in preparing profit forecasts, which are then used by the bidder or target to strengthen their argument for or against the bid. As noted in Chapter 6, such forecasts must be prepared to the highest standards of care and accuracy. The financial adviser takes responsibility for observing these standards.

Other advisers

Stockbrokers play an important role as a channel of communication, through their circulars, of bid-related information between the parties to a bid and the investors. They also become involved in market purchases of shares during a bid. Further, where bid financing involves the issue of new securities, they act as sponsors to the issue. Finally, they may also underwrite a share exchange offer to provide the cash alternative.

Strategy consultants may be called in to evaluate the attractiveness of the target company from the bidder's strategic criteria, and to assess the value creation logic of the bid. More recently, due to burgeoning environment protection laws in different countries, acquirers are concerned about the potential costs of complying with those laws, and the liabilities arising from the past failure of the target to comply. The latter influences the purchase price or alternatively forms the basis of indemnities from the target. The high cost of failing to perform an environmental audit is highlighted in Case Study 7.10.

Public and investor relations

Both public relations (PR) and investor relations (IR) consultants play a crucial role in contested takeovers. IR is about convincing the shareholders and potential investors of the merits of the bid or of

CASE STUDY 7.10   *Beazer pays for environmental clean-up*

The British construction company Beazer acquired Koppers, the American building aggregates group, for $1.72 billion in 1988. When it subsequently divested the chemical manufacturing interests of Koppers, the pollution clean-up bill was estimated at £296 million, which Beazer assumed since the management buying out the business declined to accept it. This was a liability which arose before Beazer's acquisition of Koppers and probably reflected the inadequate environment audit done by Beazer.

Sources: A. Laurie-Walker, *Acquisitions Monthly*, December 1989; *Financial Times*, 3.6.1988.

---

defence. PR has a much wider remit, since the targets for a PR exercise are not only shareholders but also the press, employees, politicians and regulatory bodies. The two terms are often used interchangeably. A large number of UK companies employ PR consultants in their corporate advisory team as part of their long-term bid defence plans.

During a contested bid, putting over the bid and defence arguments powerfully and effectively is quite important. PR consultants are used in the preparation of offer and defence documents and in the wording of letters to shareholders, so that the arguments are presented clearly and persuasively. Use of advertising in the print media as well as television and radio is also done with the advice of PR consultants.

Specialist PR consultants often field questions during a bid on very difficult and sensitive questions. For example, an optimistic profit forecast from a target company with a lacklustre performance in the past will naturally arouse much scepticism, if not derision. It is then for the PR person to make a convincing case for the forecast. PR consultants also 'tutor' company executives who are not used to the limelight to face the media with poise and conviction.

A PR person also advises on bid tactics and on effective counter-attacks against the other side. PR consultants have increasingly become part of a bid or defence advisory team, but their activities need to be regulated so that they are always in compliance with the Code. There have been instances where the PR adviser was somewhat overzealous and earned the merchant bank leading the defence a rebuke from the Panel (see Case Study 6.2).

Responsibilities of advisers

While the Code imposes the responsibility of care on the advisers involved in takeover bids for public companies, the extent of any liability for loss or damages to those who rely on the information and opinion provided by the advisers is a matter for the courts to decide. There have been a few instances where contravening the Code or negligence in the provision of information during a bid has been very costly to merchant banks and other advisers, as described in Case Study 7.11.

Conflict of interest in advisory relationship

When engaging advisers for the conduct of a bid, both bidders and targets must be aware of potential conflicts of interest that advisers face. Where advisers are paid a fixed fee regardless of the outcome of the bid, such conflicts of interest are less serious than when their fee is contingent on a successful outcome. In general, advisers other than merchant banks are paid in relation to their input, such as number of hours worked.

Merchant banks' fee structure may have a contingency element, being higher for a successful bid or a successful defence. Further, their fee may also be related to the bid value. In the former case, the banks have an incentive to close the deal whatever its merits, say, for the bidder, and in the latter case they have the incentive to advise or encourage the bidder to pay an excessive bid premium. In survey evidence of UK acquirers (Hunt *et al.*, 1987), some acquirers felt they had been hustled into closing the deals (see Chapter 4 for further discussion of this aspect of the company–merchant bank relationship).

So what are the checks against such incentives for opportunism on the part of merchant banks? The most important is that the banks have to safeguard their reputation capital. After all, a bank which persistently displays opportunism will soon run out of opportunities. Second, the fee structure should not be overly biased in favour of contingency. A well-prepared and experienced acquirer or target management will avoid such an incentive structure.

Recent trends in advisers' roles

Traditionally, accountants were involved in doing due diligence work of a financial and accounting nature, and also in offering

CASE STUDY 7.11   Merchant banks' risk exposure

Hill Samuel breaks the Code and pays the price

T & N made a £257 million bid for AE, which was advised by merchant bank Hill Samuel. T & N lost the bid by a margin of 1 per cent after some hectic dealings in AE shares just before the bid closed. Hill Samuel and Cazenove the stockbrokers were censured by the Panel for not disclosing indemnity agreements with third parties to buy AE shares to prevent T & N winning. The Panel then waived the 12-month moratorium and allowed T & N to bid again immediately. T & N won with a higher bid of £278 million and sued Hill Samuel to recover the difference of £21 million. In January 1990, Hill Samuel settled with T & N out of court.

Slip of the tongue costs Samuel Montagu dear

In August 1987, British & Commonwealth was negotiating the £280 million sale of one of its businesses to Quadrex, for which Samuel Montagu acted. When asked whether Quadrex had its finances in place for the purchase, Mr Ian McIntosh for Samuel Montagu replied, 'they are good for the money' without any qualification. Subsequently, Quadrex was unable to raise the funds, and B & C went into administration in 1990. The administrators sued Samuel Montagu which was ordered by the court to pay £172 million.

Hill Samuel liable for inaccurate defence document

In December 1985, Morgan Crucible (MC) made a bid for First Castle (FC) for which Hill Samuel acted. During the bid, FC and Hill Samuel issued defence documents and circulars, one of them making a profit forecast 38 per cent higher than in the previous year. Both the auditors, Judkins & Co., and Hill Samuel confirmed that the profit forecast had been properly compiled. MC won the bid on a revised offer. In 1987, MC sued Hill Samuel, the auditors and the directors of FC, alleging that the profit forecast was erroneous and negligently prepared. It was held by the Court of Appeal that directors, auditors and financial advisers of a target in a contested bid owed a duty to take reasonable care in making financial statements on which the bidders could foreseeably rely.

Sources: *Financial Times* (4.1.1990); *Guardian* (19.10.1993); *Financial Times* (30.10.1990) respectively.

---

advice on accounting and tax-related matters in an acquisition. They would also provide profit forecasts and valuation of targets.

Corporate finance work involving underwriting, financing, rights issues or providing capital was an area occupied by merchant banks. This enabled them to assume the lead advisory role, especially in public company bids. However, in recent years the big accounting firms have staked a claim to such an advisory role. For example, KPMG, one of the top six accounting firms, with 91 transactions worth £1.3 billion in 1993, was more active as an M & A lead adviser than some major UK merchant banks like Samuel Montagu (*Acquisitions Monthly*, February 1994). In cross-border deals, the big accounting firms probably have a competitive edge over merchant banks because of their international network of offices and associates.

The role of lawyers has in recent years become more important due to the increasingly complex nature of acquisitions, the regulatory rules and a willingness on the part of companies to litigate. Moreover, the European Commission move embodied in the takeover directive discussed in Chapter 6 would make takeover regulation more legalistic exercise, giving more scope for lawyers to take the lead role as in the USA.

Empirical evidence on the impact of advisers

One important question that companies engaging in takeovers and mergers would ask is what difference the choice of an adviser makes to the outcome or cost of a bid. There is very little empirical evidence on this question in the UK. For the USA, Bowers and Miller (1990) examine two propositions concerning the benefits of choosing a high-quality investment banker:

1. Where either of the companies chooses a first-tier investment banker, is the total wealth created from the acquisition greater than when neither chooses such a banker?

2. Does the choice of a banker with a high reputation either on its own or relative to the banker chosen by the other company add value to the shareholders of the company making that choice?

For a sample of 114 acquisitions, Bowers and Miller divide the investment banks into first-tier and second-tier advisers. They measure the abnormal returns on announcement of the takeovers, using daily returns and the market model (see Chapter 13 on this methodology). They find that the total returns to the two companies' shareholders are indeed higher when at least one of them has chosen a first-tier bank. However, they find no evidence that first-tier bankers bring superior bargaining expertise to acquisition negotiations. The shareholders of either company do not gain from the choice of a first-tier banker, even when its wits are pitted against a second-tier banker in the opposite camp.

Survey evidence on advisers

In a survey of 200 companies which had made 251 acquisitions between 1987 and 1989, the following points emerged (Indal Business Research, 1989):

- Accountants and lawyers were appointed in almost all deals.

- Merchant banks were appointed in 53 per cent of the acquisitions, and in 33 per cent of the cases they were the lead adviser. In other cases, the solicitors took the lead. Merchant banks figured in 80 per cent of the large deals above £20 million.

- Merchant banks received fees of between 1 and 1.5 per cent of the value of the deal. They were the highest paid of all advisers. Accountants and lawyers were paid predominantly by the days worked.

- Satisfaction with the level of fees paid was highest for lawyers but much less so for merchant banks. Some companies felt that merchant banks were overpaid.

A second survey (Hunt *et al.*, 1987) reported that some acquirers were unhappy with the excessive preoccupation of their investment banks with fees and closing the deal. Furthermore, the findings regarding the level of satisfaction with lawyers and merchant banks were similar to those of the previous survey. It looks as though all the world loves a lawyer, whereas a merchant banker is a less endearing species.

Overview

In this chapter, the roles played by different advisers in acquisitions have been described, and the central role of merchant banks in UK public company bids highlighted. The responsibilities of advisers, especially of the merchant banker, under the Code are extremely stringent. The risk faced by merchant banks when they fail to meet these responsibilities has been illustrated. The problem of a conflict of interest between bidding and defending companies and their advisers has been discussed, and the factors which may minimise this conflict indicated. Empirical evidence on the impact of advisers on shareholder wealth, and survey evidence on the use of and satisfaction with advisers, have been presented.

References and further reading

Bowers, H., and R. Miller (1990) 'Choice of investment banker and shareholders' wealth of firms involved in acquisitions', *Financial Management*, Winter, 34–44.

Hunt, J., S. Lees, J.J. Grumbar and P.D. Vivian (1987) *Acquisitions: The human factor*, London Business School.

Indal Business Research (1989) *UK Mergers and Acquisitions Survey 1989*, London.

Williamson, J.P. (1988) *The Investment Banking Handbook*, John Wiley.

8

Bid strategies and tactics

A bid strategy is a plan to acquire another company in order to achieve the predetermined business and corporate strategy objectives of the acquirer. In Chapter 3, the place of acquisitions in the overall strategic planning of a firm was discussed. A thorough strategic analysis of acquisitions is a precondition for an effective and successful acquisition programme. Flowing from this general framework of an acquisition programme are individual takeover bids. The objective of a bid strategy is to acquire a suitable target, satisfying the acquisition criteria dictated by the objectives of the firm's acquisition programme. In this chapter, we describe a process by which companies may develop their bid strategies.

Having identified a suitable target, the bidder must adopt the appropriate tactics during the progress of the bid. Bid tactics are a game plan to consummate a bid for a specific target, and should be played according to the regulatory regime policing the conduct of bids. In the UK, bids for public companies are subject to the Code described in Chapter 6. The impact of the Code and the statutory rules on the terms and timing of bids is discussed in this chapter. Bid strategies and tactics need to be adapted to the potential or actual responses of the target company. The defensive strategies and tactics available to a target company are discussed in Chapter 12.

Bid strategies

A takeover bid may be made on an opportunistic impulse because a seemingly attractive target company is being offered as a takeover candidate. Often companies with a poor performance record, limited growth opportunities or management succession problems when the founder-manager retires look for potential acquirers. Sometimes a company may be bounced into a bid because of an acquisition move made by a rival, as illustrated by Sainsbury's bid for William Low (see Case Study 8.1).

CASE STUDY 8.1   Sainsbury catches up with rival Tesco

In July 1994, Sainsbury, the UK supermarket store group, made a £210 million bid for William Low, the Scottish supermarket chain, in response to the recommended bid for the same company by Tesco, Sainsbury's rival. Both bidders had been attempting to increase their market share in Scotland, but without much success. Sainsbury had talked about a possible bid for Low a year earlier, but had been rebuffed. On seeing its rival make the first move, Sainsbury moved quickly to mount its competing bid.

Source: *Financial Times*, 15.7.1994.

Unplanned takeover bids may turn out, serendipitously, to be winners. However, there is an element of risk in such acquisitions that the underlying value creation logic is glossed over, or the target is overvalued and a high bid premium paid, or the post-acquisition integration problems are not foreseen. It is, therefore, important to undertake acquisitions only after much deliberation and as part of the firm's strategic planning.

Acquisition criteria

The strategic situation and strategic choice analyses described in Chapter 3 lead to the establishment of acquisition objectives intended to promote the firm's strategic goals. Case Study 8.2 shows how Trafalgar House's acquisition objectives guided its acquisition bid strategy. Having defined the acquisition objectives, the firm then has to draw up the acquisition criteria which potential takeover targets must satisfy. Subsequent search for potential targets will be guided by these criteria. They can also be used to short-list those targets which need to be researched in detail before a bid for any of them can be launched. Case Study 8.3 lists the acquisition criteria

CASE STUDY 8.2   Trafalgar House plc's acquisition objectives

Trafalgar House (TH) was, in the early 1980s, a diversified UK firm operating in engineering, construction, shipping, hotels and property. It developed a strategy to concentrate on the 'brainpower' end of the engineering business: that is, designing and managing complex process plant projects worldwide. It also aimed to gain access to several key areas of process technology. To fulfil these strategic objectives it developed an acquisition strategy to take over John Brown and Davy Corporation, two leading UK engineering contractors. John Brown was acquired in 1986 and Davy in 1991.

Source: *Financial Times*, 5.7.1991.

CASE STUDY 8.3   BTR plc's acquisition criteria

The targets should satisfy the following criteria:

- Predominantly definable niche businesses.
- Companies which are not making the best return on assets.
- Potential high-margin businesses.
- Unlikely to be in sectors like heavy engineering, mainstream retailing and mass production businesses.
- Small enough to fit into the BTR structure.

If they are US targets, the object is to gain market position and American management experience in well-established niche businesses.

Source: British Institute of Management (1986).

employed by BTR, an acquisitive UK conglomerate firm, in screening potential targets.

The homework

Researching potential targets, identifying acquisition opportunities and planning the bid may be done by the company's own staff, provided they have the necessary expertise. As noted in Chapter 4, in large firms the internal acquisition team (the A team) may be part of the ongoing strategic planning exercise. As was emphasised, the composition of the A team depends on the nature of the proposed acquisition, the business area which will be affected in terms of the acquisition rationale and post-acquisition integration, the complexity of the proposal and the amount of inhouse expertise available.

Where the internal A team lacks the necessary expertise, or feels that the size and complexity of the proposed acquisition demand further contribution from outside experts, external advisers need to be co-opted on to the A team. Such advisers include strategy consultants, accountants, lawyers, surveyors and actuaries. Merchant bankers and stockbrokers will also become part of the external advisory team. If a contested or hostile bid is foreseen, the services of public relations consultants and political lobbyists may become necessary. The role of these advisers in takeover bids was discussed in Chapter 7. The functions of the A team in the bid context are as follows:

- Bid opportunity identification.
- Target evaluation.
- Crafting bid tactics.
- Planning and making the approach to selected targets.
- Assessing the target response.
- Determining the bid premium range.
- Defining the lines of attack if the bid becomes hostile.
- Day-to-day conduct of the bid.
- Communication with the media, important shareholders and regulatory authorities.

In carrying out its multiple functions under the demanding conditions of an impending or ongoing bid, the A team must have clearly demarcated lines of authority and responsibility, so that there is no schism between different members of the A team and between the A team and the external advisers. The members must be aware of the statutory rules against insider dealings. The City Code imposes on the directors the overall responsibility for the conduct of a bid (see Chapter 6). Thus the board must authorise and be kept informed of the actions taken by the A team and its advisers.

In order to ensure that the A team and its external advisers are not working at cross-purposes, the A team must be clearly briefed as to the objectives, strategies and tactics, the regulatory rules and lines of responsibility.

Bid opportunity identification

One of the first tasks of the A team is to locate potential targets and prepare a shortlist of those satisfying the firm's acquisition criteria. The search for potential targets may be narrow or wide in terms of industry and geography. In the case of horizontal or vertical integration, the industry spectrum of the search will be narrow, but, depending upon the global strategy of the firm, it may span several countries. In the case of conglomerate acquisitions, one may scan both diverse industries and numerous countries.

Opportunity identification is often facilitated by intermediaries. Business brokers, accounting firms, stockbrokers and merchant bankers may be able to suggest potential targets. These intermediaries may provide additional services, such as preliminary soundings of the targets. The A team also needs to undertake its own detailed research of the target industries and target companies.

In the case of target industries the same as or related to the bidder's, its line managers will be aware of the relative performance of those industries and their competitors. This internal database may be supplemented by research based on external sources of information. Publicly available information, such as company annual reports, industry surveys, trade journals, stockbrokers' circulars in the case of stock market listed targets, and credit ratings of targets from rating agencies such as Dun & Bradstreet, may be used to assess the relative attractiveness of industries and companies.

Having identified a strategically attractive target industry and a shortlist of potential targets in that industry, one has to draw up the profile of the targets in terms of their strengths and weaknesses. This profile should cover, *inter alia*, the following aspects:

- Quality of management in terms of strategic thinking, effective implementation of strategic plans and delivering performance.
- Industry status of the target company, the level of competition in the industry and the company's competitive strengths.
- Future technological and competitive evolution of the industry, and the target's ability to cope with this change.
- The target's financial and stock market performance.

Such an evaluation of the strengths and weaknesses helps the A team formulate the appropriate strategy for negotiating with the target management or for launching a hostile bid, if necessary. Valuation of the targets under the bidder's management may then be undertaken as described in Chapter 9. Such a valuation, including a sensitivity analysis under varying assumptions of future scenarios about target performance, provides the bidder with a price range over which to negotiate with the target or vary the terms of a public offer.

Often the firm may not be the first to spot an attractive opportunity. The target may have been 'in play' explicitly as the object of other bids. Or, it may have been stalked by a potential predator which has built up a toehold in the target. Moreover, the likelihood of a rival bid either by a white knight or by a competitor provoked by the firm's bid, and the value of the target to the competitor, must be factored into the firm's bidding strategy. The importance of this point is illustrated in the Tesco bid for William Low described in Case Study 8.4.

When a target is in play, the potential bidder faces an opportunity as well as a threat. Such a target is very vulnerable and may be persuaded by a friendly overture to recommend a bid. On the other hand, a competitive bid with two or more rival bidders may develop, pushing the bid premium inexorably high.

The identified targets must be matched against the acquisition criteria. Although these criteria may be satisfied, the bid can yet run into trouble. The firm must look for any potential 'show stoppers'

CASE STUDY 8.4   Tesco's bid for William Low – Sainsbury jumps into the ring

On 14 July 1994, Tesco announced its recommended bid for Wm Low, the Scottish supermarkets group, with a cash offer of 225 pence, valuing Wm Low at £154 million. Wm Low had a market share of 6.6 per cent compared to Tesco's 7.1 per cent in Scotland. J. Sainsbury, Tesco's great rival in England and Wales, had a market share of only 4.9 per cent and had unsuccessfully attempted a year earlier to arrange a friendly bid for Wm Low. Both Tesco and Sainsbury had been seeking to increase their market share in Scotland, but had been frustrated by lack of planning permission or by prime locations being pre-empted by their rivals. Thus when Tesco announced its bid, Sainsbury could not sit back and let its rival steal a march. It launched a counterbid of 305 pence, which valued Wm Low at £210 million. There ensued a bidding war between the two bidders. Thus for Tesco, securing the target's recommendation was no guarantee of success.

Source: *Financial Times*, 29.7.1994.

which can thwart the bid. Of these impediments, the most important is the antitrust regime. In the UK, the bidder can obtain confidential guidance before announcing a bid from the Office of Fair Trading (OFT), as to the chances of the bid being referred to the Monopolies and Mergers Commission (MMC). After announcing its bid, a bidder may use the OFT's fast-track procedure to obtain an OFT decision within 35 to 45 days. Similar confidential guidance and fast-track clearance procedures are available under the European Union Merger Regulation (see Chapter 5).

If a bid is referred by the OFT or the European Commission for full investigation, under the City Code the bid lapses. It may be relaunched if the MMC or the Commission clears the bid, but this may take up to about four months. Thus valuable time may be lost by the bidder, giving an opportunity to rival bidders or time for the target management to bolster their defences. A careful vetting of the bid proposal for any antitrust implications is therefore necessary. Other show stoppers could be litigation initiated by the target as a defence strategy (see Chapter 12). The potential for such an action must be considered as part of the bid strategy.

Pre-bid stake building in target

After a specific target has been identified, the potential bidder may start to build up a significant stake in it (the toehold). Any pre-bid purchase has to be carried out subject to the rules of the City Code and the Substantial Acquisition Rules (SARs) (see Chapter 6). In particular, acquisitions which result in a holding of 15 per cent or more are regulated by the SARs. If the holding reaches the 30 per cent level, a mandatory bid has to be made. The disclosure rules for share purchases of 3 per cent or more under the Companies Act 1989 must also be taken into account. Pre-bid stake building has both advantages and disadvantages, as shown in Table 8.1.

Because of the stringent disclosure rules, toehold build-up cannot be done on a quiet prowl. Neither can it be done on the sly using nominees, since the target can notify the nominees to reveal the beneficial owners or disenfranchise the shares (see Chapter 6).

Toehold, bid premium and bid outcome

Toehold has been suggested by Grossman and Hart (1980) as a possible solution to the free-rider problem discussed in Chapter 6. A

Table 8.1 Advantages and disadvantages of toehold

Advantages	Disadvantages
Puts pressure on target to negotiate.	Bid intentions revealed. Target put 'in play' and target price driven up.
Improves chances of securing majority control in a bid.	If 10% or more purchased for cash within 12 months, bid may have to be for cash at the highest price paid (see Chapter 6 on the Code).
A large toehold may deter potential rival bids and prevent high bid premium.	If bid fails, bidder stuck with unwanted investment.
If outbid, the stake could be sold at a profit (see Case Study 8.5).	If it exceeds 20%, merger accounting not available (see Chapter 10).
Cash underwriting of offer less expensive, since toehold already bought.	

Note: Percentages refer to proportions of target voting shares.

toehold allows the bidder to enjoy the post-acquisition value creation accruing to the related shares and thus provides an incentive to make takeover bids. Of course, the benefits of toehold must exceed the target search and bid costs. The larger the toehold, the greater is the added value from the acquisition accruing to the bidder.

The implications of toeholds for the probability of a subsequent bid either by the toeholder or by a third party, for the probability of a successful bid and for the bid premium have been discussed by several researchers using the game theory and information economics frameworks. Shleifer and Vishny (1986) predict that a toehold increases the probability of a subsequent bid and reduces the premium in such a bid. Hirshleifer and Titman (1990) examine the relation between toehold, bid premium and the probability of success in a tender offer. Their model predicts that toehold will have a positive impact on success probability. A negative relation between toehold and average bid premium in takeovers is also implied.

In contrast to the previous two models, Jegadeesh and Choudhury (1988) argue that a toehold is used by the bidder to signal the post-acquisition value of the target. A large toehold signals high value. This model predicts that as toehold increases the subsequent bid premium also rises. The empirical evidence for these models is discussed below.

Bid tactics

The objectives of bid tactics are as follows:

- To win control of the target.
- To minimise the control premium paid to target shareholders.
- To minimise transaction costs.
- To smooth post-acquisition integration.

The transaction costs include: professional fees paid to advisers and specialist consultants; printing and advertising; fast-track merger screening fee paid to the OFT; and document charges to the City Panel. For cash underwritten offers, the underwriting fee could be substantial. Stamp duty and value-added tax may also be payable.

CASE STUDY 8.5 Hasbro loses the doll war but makes a dollop of money on toehold

Hasbro, the American maker of the Sindy doll, launched a bid in May 1994 for J.W. Spear, the British Scrabble board game maker. At bid announcement, Hasbro had a 26.7 per cent stake in Spear, built up since 1990. Mittel, the American Barbie doll maker, was then lined up as a white knight by Robert Fleming, Spear's merchant bank adviser. A bidding war ensued, with the offer price going up from Hasbro's £9 per share to the final Mittel bid of £11.50. At this price, Hasbro's toehold was worth over £16 million, whereas it had paid £4.2 million. Although the large toehold did not help Hasbro win the war, it made Hasbro richer.

Source: *Financial Times*, 13.7.1994.

In the case of a bid for a UK public company, except in very unusual cases, the bid must be concluded within 60 days from the posting of the offer document. As noted in Table 6.2, there are other deadlines to be met within this timetable. While the bidder may carefully plan the opening moves in the bid game, subsequent moves are determined by the target responses. To some extent these responses may have been foreseen. But the bidder must still be alert, adaptive and nimble in counteracting the target responses.

Responsibilities of bidder directors

Under the General Principles and Rules of the Code, directors are responsible for the conduct of a bid. They should act in the interests of their shareholders, employees and creditors (see Chapter 6). Under the law directors have a fiduciary duty to act in the best interests of their company. They should ensure that the bid is conducted in accordance with the law and the Code. They should maintain a high standard of integrity in providing information relating to the bid.

Where the board is split, the dissenting director/s may have to seek independent legal or financial advice and also inform the company's financial advisers. Since directors will be in possession of price-sensitive information about the bid, their dealings in the securities of the bidder and the target need to be carried out and disclosed in accordance with the Code, the insider dealing laws and the rules of the London Stock Exchange (see Chapter 6 for a discussion of these).

In bidder companies, a campaign committee including some executive and non-executive directors may often be formed and responsibility for the day-to-day conduct of the bid may be delegated to the committee. However, the board as a whole still remains responsible. 'Delegation does not mean abdication' (PRONED, 1988: 6).

Negotiating a friendly bid

A bid may be friendly, hostile or opportunistic. In a friendly bid, the bidder wins the support of the target management, which then recommends the bid for acceptance by the target shareholders. In a hostile bid, such a recommendation is not forthcoming and the two companies have to slug it out. A friendly bid is less expensive, since it can be concluded sooner, less risky because of the greater access to information about the target in 'due diligence' (see below), and smoother than a hostile bid. This smoothness is conducive to a more successful post-acquisition integration. Where the target management is an essential part of the bidder's post-acquisition strategy, a hostile bid must be counted out.

A hostile bid, of course, demands of the bidder much greater tactical dexterity and staying power, since it is likely to last longer. Often a company plays a white knight to a target under siege. Such a white knight role is in most cases unpremeditated. The value creation logic is then concocted and the white knight may end up paying too much for the target (Banerjee and Owers, 1992). Another, less exalted variety of bidder is the grey knight, a rival to the hostile bidder and, for that reason, probably regarded by the target management as the lesser of the two evils. Again, the grey knight bid may have been provoked by the first hostile bid, a more defensive motive than one which affirms the merit or logic of the bid.

In general, a bidder seeks to obtain the recommendation of the target management. In approaching the target with a friendly overture, the bidder must assess the target management response. This assessment includes an appreciation of the key players in the target in terms of the following:

- Personalities.
- Motivations for sale, e.g. retirement, lack of management depth or lack of resources to develop target business.
- Relation to the target, e.g. are they founder–managers with a sentimental attachment to the firm and its workforce?
- Desire for independence.
- Post-acquisition expectations, e.g. whether they expect to continue to play a role of similar status and authority as now.
- Stake in the target.
- Preference for payment currency, cash or shares.

Not all of the above considerations may be relevant to a public company target. Many vendors, especially the directors of family firms, may be more concerned with the post-acquisition plans of the bidder for the firm, its managers and workforce than with the size of bid premium being offered.

Hostile bid tactics

A hostile bid requires a battle plan detailing the various lines of attack, outflanking moves and counterattacks. An important element of the plan is surprise. In this respect, the initial advantage certainly lies with the hostile bidder, and surprise is more easily achieved in a voluntary bid without pre-bid stake building than in a mandatory bid in which the bidder has already built up a 30 per cent stake. Timing of the various moves, such as revision of the offer terms, must be made in accordance with the bid timetable laid down by the Code.

In a hostile bid, the bidder has to rely on external advisers to a much greater extent than in a friendly bid. In particular, the services of merchant banks with special expertise in hostile bids, lawyers, PR consultants and stockbrokers who can convey and influence the market sentiment in favour of the bid will be indispensable. The role of the merchant bank adviser is of the utmost importance under the City Code (see Chapter 7 on the role of advisers).

Lines of attack

The various lines of attack that a hostile bidder may, in general, follow are outlined in Table 8.2. The first move of talking to the target is often made to coincide with any unpropitious or vulnerable time for the target. The target may have just announced or be just about to announce poor profits or even losses. It may be in the middle of a restructuring programme with depressed earnings. The target may be in a cyclical industry and presently at the bottom of that cycle.

Subject to the constraints of the Code, the bidder must fine-tune the time of release of new information, revision of offer terms, extension of the closing date and market purchases, so as to put the maximum pressure on the target management and shareholders. An early release of information may give the target the chance and time to respond robustly. Early market purchases may signal that the bidder is not confident of winning the bid. Analysis of target shareholder profile is important in choosing the appropriate medium for communication, in effective presentation of arguments for the bid and in tailoring the consideration. Recent examples of the effective or ineffective use of these lines of attack are provided in Case Study 8.6.

Empirical evidence on bid strategies

Evidence for the impact of bidder's toehold on the returns to target shareholders is somewhat ambiguous. Franks (1978) reports that toehold has little impact for his small sample of brewing industry takeovers, whereas in Franks and Harris (1989) target shareholders gain from bidder's toehold. The latter result is consistent with the Jegadeesh and Choudhury (1988) model prediction. Sudarsanam *et*

Table 8.2 Lines of attack in a hostile bid

Line of attack	Nature of attack
The advisory team	Select advisers with experience of hostile bids well ahead of bid.
Strong bid rationale	Justify bid rationale and clearly articulate benefits to bidder and target shareholders.
Timing (see Chapter 6 on the Code rules and Table 6.2)	Announce bid when target is vulnerable. Post offer document early to reduce target response time. Revise offer terms after Day 39. Release own results by Day 46. Choose offer closing date to maximise pressure on target shareholders. Choose when to 'shut off' cash alternative (see Chapter 11).
Denounce target's performance	Attack target's flawed strategy, inept management, poor past performance, unrealistic profit and dividend forecast. Highlight any 'hocus-pocus' in target's accounts to reduce its credibility.
Lobby target shareholders	Present bid case to institutional shareholders. Try for irrevocable acceptances from large shareholders.
Market purchases (see Chapter 6 for the Code rules)	Buy in the market up to 10% within offer price. Otherwise, offer price has to be raised/cash alternative has to be offered.
Public relations	Lobby politicians to minimise adverse political fall-out. Project virtues of bid in the press. Communicate bid benefits to employees, their pension fund trustees and trade unions to win support for bid.
Offer terms (see Chapter 11 on payment methods)	Tailor consideration to suit target shareholder profile. Include cash alternative. Underwrite cash alternative to raise credibility of offer.

al. (1993) provide evidence that toehold reduces the returns to target shareholders, consistent with the prediction of Shleifer and Vishny (1986).

For a sample of over 200 contested bids in the UK during 1983–9, Sudarsanam (1994) finds that bidder's toehold has no significant influence on the outcome.

CASE STUDY 8.6   Bid tactics and their impact

The advisory team
Before making its hostile bid for Arthur Bell in 1985, Guinness assembled
a high-powered team of advisers, including a merchant bank, two
stockbrokers, a public relations firm and a leading advertising agency. In
contrast, Bell assembled its team rather late and chose a merchant bank
with less experience of big hostile bids. Guinness won the bid after a
bitter fight (*Acquisitions Monthly*, January 1986).

Strong bid rationale
Launching Enterprise Oil's bid for Lasmo, Graham Hearne, Enterprise's
chairman, argued that the two companies would benefit from increased
size, since oil was 'a game for the big boys'. Many institutional
shareholders of Lasmo were unimpressed with this rationale and
attributed it to empire building. The bid failed (*Financial Times*, 2.7.1994).

Timing
Hanson Trust announced its hostile bid for Powell Duffryn (PD) in 1985,
three weeks after PD had reported a fall in profits as a result of the
miners' strike. Although its timing was good, Hanson still lost due to its
subsequent tactical errors (*Acquisitions Monthly*, January 1986).

Denounce target's performance
Kingfisher, the high street retailer, justified its hostile offer for fellow
retailer Dixons on the grounds that the latter's approach to retailing was
flawed, its profits would not recover under the present management,
and it needed Kingfisher's management skills to restore profitability
(offer document, 12.12.1989). The bid was referred to the MMC.

Lobby target shareholders
IMI made a hostile bid for Birmingham Mint in October 1990. It made
presentations to target shareholders and received the feedback that a
higher-priced offer would be successful. It also bought the 15.8 per cent
stake in the target held by a fund manager (*Acquisitions Monthly*, April
1991).

Market purchases
On the last closing date of its £745 million bid for Pleasurama, Mecca had
received acceptances including small market purchases of only 45 per
cent. Over the following two days, however, Mecca bought 10 per cent
more in the market to declare the bid unconditional (*Acquisitions Monthly*,
January 1989).

Public relations
The battle for Bell described above also involved assuaging any hostility
based on Scottish nationalism aroused by the bid for a Scottish company
by a non-Scottish firm. To pacify these sensitivities, Guinness engaged a

media consultant and Scottish merchant bankers to make the bidder's case and held press briefings in Scotland.

Offer terms
Kalon's offer for Manders in August 1992 consisted of a share offer with a partial cash alternative, but the latter was not underwritten. In response, Manders attacked the lack of a full cash alternative, and implied that Kalon had failed to underwrite because of the reluctance of the financial institutions (Manders defence circular, 14.8.1992).

However, the presence of large institutional block shareholders helps the hostile bidder. This probably reflects the success of shareholder lobbying. The most decisive factor in favour of the bidder, though, is the method of payment. Consideration in the form of pure equity or equity plus cash favours the target and reduces the chances of a successful bid. If consideration includes cash, the bidder stands a better chance of winning. Given the problem of valuing a securities exchange offer (see Chapter 11) an equity offer often evokes a strong attack from the target management. A cash offer reduces the scope for such attack. Jenkinson and Mayer (1991) also provide evidence, from a smaller sample of 42 contested UK bids, that a cash offer is more effective than an equity or mixed offer in facilitating a successful bid.

Table 8.3 shows the average returns gained by target and bidder shareholders in the announcement month in UK mergers between 1955 and 1985, after adjusting for risk. It appears that both groups of shareholders gain from being offered either cash or cash as a component. Other studies from the USA and the UK also report that shareholders of both bidders and targets gain more from a cash bid than from a share exchange offer (see Chapter 11). The lower returns from equity offers may explain the Sudarsanam (1994) result that equity reduces the chances of a successful hostile bid.

Empirical evidence on bid strategies from the USA

The empirical evidence on the relations among toehold, bid premium and takeover outcome is mixed. Hoffmeister and Dyl (1981) find that bid premium has little impact on the bid outcome whereas Walkling (1985) reports a positive impact in line with Hirshleifer and Titman (1990). In Walkling and Edminster (1985), there is evidence

Table 8.3 Average returns to shareholders in
UK mergers, 1955–85 (%), classified by
payment method

	Target	Bidder
All cash	30.2	0.7
All equity	15.1	−1.1
Cash or equity	27.6	0.7
Cash and equity	23.8	0.3
Convertible	11.7	1.8
Convertibles and equity	10.1	−0.4

Source: Franks *et al.* (1988).

of a decline in the average bid premium as bidder's toehold
increases. Stulz *et al.* (1990) find that bidder's toehold reduces the
wealth gains to target shareholders. Both these results are consistent
with the Shleifer and Vishny (1986) and Hirshleifer and Titman
(1990) models.

Cost of bids

Takeover bids, especially hostile bids, are very expensive affairs for
bidders as well as targets. In addition to the fees paid to the
advisers, there are other transaction costs, such as fees paid to the
Panel, the OFT and the Stock Exchange, and costs of printing,
mailing and advertising. If the cash alternative is underwitten, then
the bidder pays the underwriting and arrangement fee to the
merchant bank and the sub-underwriters. All these make up the
direct costs of a bid, but there are also opportunity costs. The latter
include, in the case of a failed hostile bid, loss of face, a strategy in
shambles and diminished credibility in future bids. The smell of
defeat lingers on. In the case of a successful bid, the opportunity
costs may be in the form of departure of target management, fear
and anxiety among staff, and their reduced morale (see Chapter 4).
Opportunity costs also include the corporate resources such as top
management time diverted to the prosecution of the bid.

Some idea of the direct costs of a hostile bid is provided in the
recent failed bid by Enterprise Oil for Lasmo, the oil exploration
company. This was a particularly acrimonious and no-holds-barred
battle, and Case Study 8.7 provides a breakdown of the costs to the
protagonists. Enterprise, which bought 10 per cent of Lasmo shares
just before the failure of its bid, also wrote down the investment by

£18 million (*Financial Times*, 9.9.94). The total costs of the bid to Enterprise were £25 million. The costs in some other recent hostile bids are shown in Case Study 8.8. As a proportion of bid value, these costs range from less than 1 per cent to about 4.4 per cent.

CASE STUDY 8.7 Lasmo and Enterprise fight a costly punch-up (fees in £m)

	Lasmo (target)	Enterprise Oil (bidder)
Financial advisers	16	4
Legal advisers	4	2
Accountants	4	0.50
Public relations	0.50	0.25
Petroleum consultants	0.25	
Sundry expenses	0.25	0.25
Total	25.00	7.00

Final revised value of bid: £1.6 billion.

Source: *Acquisitions Monthly*, August 1994.

CASE STUDY 8.8 Direct costs of hostile bids

Year	Target	Bidder	Bid value (£bn)	Cost (£m)	Outcome
1985	Distillers	Guinness	2.50	110	S
		Argyll		48	F
1986	Woolworth	Dixons	1.80	12	F
1987	Dee	Barker & Dobson	2.00	3	F
1988	Carless	Kelt Energy	0.21	9	S
1989	Consolidated Gold Fields	Minorco	3.50	20	F
1992	Manders	Kalon	0.11	2	F
1993	Owners Abroad	Airtours	0.29	9	F

Note: Bid value and cost figures are rounded. S = successful bid; F = failed or abandoned bid.
Sources: Press reports and company annual accounts.

Overview

We have described the important elements of takeover bid strategies. Depending upon whether the bid is friendly or hostile, these strategies differ. Researching the target for its strengths and weaknesses is the foundation of an effective bid strategy. The advantages and disadvantages of different types of bid strategy have been discussed. The internal organisation for an acquisition, the A team and its functions have been described. The role of external advisers and their relation to the A team have been highlighted. Several examples from recent UK bids on the effectiveness of alternative bid strategies have been provided. Evidence of the high direct and indirect costs of hostile bids has been given.

References and further reading

Banerjee, A. and J.E. Owers (1992) 'Wealth reduction in white knight bids', *Financial Management*, Autumn, 48–57.

British Institute of Management (1986) 'The management of acquisitions and mergers', Discussion Paper 8.

Franks, J. (1978) 'Insider information and the efficiency of the acquisition market', *Journal of Banking and Finance*, **2**, 379–93.

Franks, J. and R. Harris (1989) 'Shareholder wealth effects of corporate takeovers: the UK experience 1955–85', *Journal of Financial Economics*, **23**, 225–49.

Franks, J., R. Harris and C. Mayer (1988) 'Means of payment in takeovers: results for the United Kingdom and the United States', in A.J. Auerbach (ed.), *Corporate Takeovers: Causes and Consequences*, University of Chicago Press.

Grossman, S. and O. Hart (1980) 'Takeover bids, the free-rider problem and the theory of the corporation', *Bell Journal of Economics*, **11**, 42–64.

Hirshleifer, D. and S. Titman (1990) 'Share tendering strategies and the success of hostile takeover bids', *Journal of Political Economy*, **98**, 2, 295–324.

Hoffmeister, J. and E.A. Dyl (1981) 'Predicting outcomes of cash tender offers', *Financial Management*, Winter, 50–8.

Jegadeesh, N. and B. Choudhury (1988) 'Optimal pre-tender offer share acquisition strategy in takeovers', working paper, Anderson Graduate School of Management, University of California.

Jenkinson, T. and C. Mayer (1991) *Takeover Defence Strategies*, Economic Research Associates Ltd, Oxford.

PRONED (1988) *Takeover Bids: A guide for directors*, Promotion of Non-executive Directors, London.

Rock, M. (1987) *Mergers and Acquisitions Handbook*, McGraw-Hill.

Shleifer, A. and R. Vishny (1986) 'Large shareholders and corporate control', *Journal of Political Economy*, **94**, 31, 461–88.

Stulz, R., R.A. Walkling and M.H. Song (1990) 'The distribution of target's ownership and the division of gains from successful takeovers', *Journal of Finance*, **XLV**, 3, 817–33.

Sudarsanam, P.S. (1994) 'Determinants of outcome in contested UK bids: defensive strategies, shareholding structure and method of payment', paper presented to the European Financial Management Conference, Maastricht, June.

Sudarsanam, P.S., P. Holl and A. Salami (1993) 'Shareholder wealth gains in mergers: empirical test of the synergy and agency effects', paper presented to the Midwest Finance Association, USA, April.

Walkling, R. (1985) 'Predicting tender offer success: a logistic analysis', *Journal of Financial and Quantitative Analysis*, **20**, 4, 461–78.

Walkling, R. and R. Edminster (1985) 'Determinants of tender offer premiums', *Financial Analysts Journal*, **27**, 27–37.

9

Target valuation

Valuation of the target in an acquisition is an important part of the process of determining the consideration to be offered to the target shareholders. The value that the bidder places on the target sets the maximum or 'walk away' price that the bidder can afford to offer the target shareholders. The value of the target from the bidder's point of view is the sum of the pre-bid stand-alone value of the target and the incremental value the bidder expects to add to the target's assets. The latter may arise from improved operation of the target or synergy between the two companies. Added value may also come from profitable target asset disposals, as in a bust-up takeover.

Valuation of the target requires valuation of the totality of the incremental cash flows and earnings. The expected incremental value may be reflected in the earnings and cash flows of both the target and the bidder in the post-acquisition period. The incremental earnings and cash flows may include those arising from reduced corporation tax liability and 'pension holidays'.

Valuation of a target is based on expectations of both the magnitude and the timing of realisation of the anticipated benefits. Where these benefits are difficult to forecast, the valuation of the target is not precise. This exposes the bidder to valuation risk. The degree of this risk depends on the quality of information available to the bidder, which, in turn, depends upon whether the target is a private or a public company, whether the bid is hostile or friendly, the time spent in preparing the bid and the pre-acquisition audit of the target.

There are a number of models employed by firms to evaluate targets. These may be broadly divided into those based on (1) earnings and assets and (2) cash flows. The earnings and assets-based models are less information intensive than the cash flow models, and less rigorous. In this chapter we describe how these models can be applied in target valuation.

Earnings and asset-based valuation models

With these models, the earnings or assets of the target are estimated after taking into account any changes which the acquirer plans to make to the operations and asset structure of the target in the post-acquisition period. The estimated earnings or assets are capitalised into target value using an appropriate benchmark earnings or assets multiplier. The choice of this benchmark multiplier is very important and can present problems where the target is a private company or a multibusiness firm.

Price/earnings ratio

Price/earnings ratio (PER), also known as the earnings multiple, expresses the relationship between a firm's earnings for equity and its equity market capitalisation.

$$\text{Price/earnings ratio} = \frac{\text{Market value of equity}}{\text{Earnings for equity}}$$

$$= \frac{\text{Share price}}{\text{Earnings per share (EPS)}}$$

During takeover bids, the PER is often cited by both offerors and targets to indicate whether the price being offered is generous or inadequate (see Case Study 9.1).

Investors generally employ two alternative definitions of the PER: the historic and the prospective. The historic PER relates current market value of equity to the earnings of the most recent accounting year. Prospective PER relates the current market value of equity to the earnings expected to be reported at the end of the current accounting year. In Case Study 9.1, Kingfisher used the prospective PER to demonstrate what a generous offer it was making. Prospective PER requires a forecast of prospective earnings. Kingfisher used the average forecast of stockbrokers for Dixons. The earnings multiple implied in the Kingfisher offer represented a premium on

CASE STUDY 9.1 *Kingfisher uses the price/earnings ratio to value Dixons*

Kingfisher plc made a bid for Dixons plc in 1989. The cash offer of 120 pence per share for Dixons' ordinary share capital amounted to £461 million. Kingfisher's offer document justifies this price: 'Our offer represents a multiple of between 14 and 19.7 times recent available forecasts of leading stockbrokers for prospective earnings for the current financial year and a significant premium over UBS Philips & Drew Securities Limited's forecast of the Stores Sector multiple of earnings for the year to April 1990 of 12 times.'

Source: Kingfisher offer documents.

the pre-bid value of Dixons at £414 million a week before the bid announcement.

A second interesting aspect of the use of PER by Kingfisher is that the Stores Sector average multiple provides a benchmark for assessing the adequacy of the offer. Further, Kingfisher's offer represents a premium over the valuation of Dixons based on the sector average PER.

The PER implied by the Kingfisher offer is much above the benchmark PER. The difference reflects the control premium the bidder has to pay to induce target shareholders to tender their shares. This control premium is in general paid out of the added value that the bidder expects to create from the acquisition target.

Interpretation of the PER

The PER is a function of four factors:

- The level future equity earnings of the firm.
- Investors' expected return for equity investment in the firm, which in turn rests on the riskiness of the firm's earnings.
- The expected return on the investments made by the firm.
- The length of time the firm can earn returns on its investments in excess of the investor-required return.

Where a firm makes a return on its investments equal to the investor-expected return, the net assets of the firm do not grow. For example, suppose the firm raises £100 equity from investors expecting a 10 per cent return, and invests in projects yielding a profit after tax of £10. It pays out the profit to shareholders as dividend. Its net assets both before and after the investment will be £100. The investment has not added to the firm's growth. On the other hand, if the investment yields a profit of £20 and the firm pays out £10 as dividend, the firm's net assets increase by £10 to £110: that is, a 10 per cent growth.

Growth comes from the firm's ability to invest in projects yielding higher returns than the investors' required return. This ability depends upon the competitive advantages the firm possesses: for example, a low-cost production process, product differentiation through branding, exclusive access to a distribution network, or privileged access to raw materials. The growth phase does not last for ever and is terminated by the emergence of competitors. However, the longer the competitive advantage can be maintained, the greater the value of the firm to its shareholders (see Chapter 3).

The value of a firm comprises two components:

Value of firm = Level earnings capitalised at the investor-required return + Value of 'growth' earnings

Level earnings are the stable earnings of the non-growing firm. The historic PER capitalises last year's earnings and the prospective PER the forecast earnings for the current year. Neither explicitly allows for growth in earnings. However, the above value relationship shows that a growth firm will be valued higher than a firm with only level earnings in the future, and will command a higher PER. It can also be shown that the higher the risk attached to the earnings of a firm, the higher is the investor-required return, and the lower the value of those earnings. Thus the PER will be lower for more risky earnings streams.

Estimating target value using the PER model

Application of the PER model proceeds in the following steps:

1. Examine the most recent profit performance of the target firm and the expected future performance under the current target management.
2. Identify those elements of revenue and costs which will be raised or lowered under the acquirer management.

3. Re-estimate the target's future, post-acquisition earnings for equity shareholders on a sustainable basis. These earnings are known as sustainable or maintainable earnings.

4. Select a benchmark PER.

5. Multiply the sustainable earnings by the benchmark PER to arrive at a value for equity.

Past performance of the target firm

In examining the recent profit and loss accounts of the target, the acquirer must carefully consider the accounting policies underlying those accounts. Particular attention must be paid to areas such as deferred tax provision, treatment of extraordinary items, interest capitalisation, depreciation and amortisation, pension fund contribution and foreign currency translation policies. Where necessary, adjustments for the target's reported profits must be made, so as to bring those policies into line with the acquirer's policies. For example, the acquirer may write off all R & D expenditure, whereas the target might have capitalised the development expenditure, thus overstating the reported profits.

Re-estimating the target earnings

This goes beyond adjustments needed to bring the two companies' accounting policies into harmony. Re-estimation reflects the improvements in the target operation which the acquirer plans to make after the acquisition. For example, the combined operation of the two firms may be expected to lead to higher prices or lower cost of sales, thus improving the gross profit margin. Reduction of sales and administration costs resulting from the acquisition may lead to improved net profit margins.

The acquirer's post-acquisition management plans for the target, based on the acquisition logic, determine the extent of cost saving or revenue enhancement. The assumptions behind the plans, such as higher output prices, lower input costs or reduced selling and administration costs, must be carefully vetted and must reflect the genuine capabilities of the two firms and not just wishful thinking. The costs of achieving the planned operational efficiencies must be allowed for in estimating the purchase price. For example, rationalisation of production or sales force may lead to redundancy costs or relocation costs.

In estimating the future earnings for equity shareholders, the capital structure – that is, the proportion of debt and equity in financing the acquired firm – is an important consideration due to the tax deductibility of interest on debt. Where the target firm is going to be funded differently from its pre-acquisition capital structure, the equity shareholders' earnings will be different. In general, an increase in gearing will increase those earnings.

Since equity earnings are estimated post-tax, the impact of accumulated trading losses must be taken into account in estimating the corporation tax on profits. In the UK there are strict rules for offsetting past losses against future profits, and these rules are discussed below. Provided the conditions are satisfied, past losses reduce the effective rate of corporation tax.

Some of the adjustments that the acquirer has to make to the target earnings, such as redundancy costs and tax savings due to accumulated tax losses, are of a transitory nature. Since the PER model requires an estimate of sustainable earnings, one solution to the estimation problem is to identify and value the transitory components separately. Their value can then be incorporated in the purchase price.

Selecting the benchmark PER

As seen in the case of the Kingfisher bid for Dixons (Case Study 9.1), there are alternative PER benchmarks available:

- The target's prospective PER at the time of the bid.
- The PER of firms comparable to the target.
- The target's sector average PER.

In choosing the benchmark, we must ensure its comparability in terms of risk and growth. It is the risk–growth configuration of the target post-acquisition and not its historic profile which forms the basis of comparison. The benchmark is normally adjusted to reflect this expected configuration. Such an adjustment is often a matter of subjective judgement, since the relation between PER and risk and growth is, in practice, only imperfectly understood. Sustainable earnings estimated in the previous step are then capitalised at the adjusted benchmark PER to give a target value.

Determining the purchase price

Estimation of the sustainable post-acquisition earnings of the target involves a concomitant appraisal of the investment needed to sustain those earnings. This appraisal helps the acquirer identify those target assets which are not needed and can be disposed of, as well as the new investment to be made, such as new plant and equipment. The proceeds of such disposals reduce the purchase price (see Case Study 9.2). Similarly, a pension fund surplus in the target employees' pension scheme may be refunded, with the effect that the purchase price is reduced. The rules governing the disposition of such surpluses are discussed below.

Where rationalisation is contemplated by the acquirer, the associated costs must be added to the purchase price if they have been excluded from the computation of sustainable earnings. It must be remembered that profits on asset disposals and refund of pension fund surpluses are subject to corporation tax, and rationalisation costs are tax deductible. The cost of new investments must be added to the purchase price.

CASE STUDY 9.2   Hanson's disposals pay for its acquisition

Hanson Trust acquired Imperial Group, the tobacco, brewery and food conglomerate, in 1986 for £2.5 billion. By the end of that year, Hanson had raised £2.34 billion by way of disposal of the brewery and food businesses. It retained the tobacco business, a mature cash generative business which, on its own, was valued at over £1 billion in 1990. Hanson pulled off a similar feat with SCM of the USA, with disposals of $1.6 billion exceeding the purchase price of $930 million in the same year, 1986.

Source: *Financial Times*, 18.9.1991.

Example of valuation using the PER model

Target plc is the subject of a takeover bid from Bidder plc. Both Bidder plc and Target plc operate a number of car dealer franchises, but in different parts of the UK. Bidder's rationale for the merger is as follows:

- The two companies' operations are complementary in terms of dealerships of different manufacturers and geographical spread.
- The merger will help each company diversify its product range and geographical coverage.
- The increased size of the merged firm will help increase its bargaining power and improve its purchasing terms *vis-à-vis* the manufacturers.
- Bidder can improve the profitability of Target through improved management and selling techniques.

Table 9.1 Income statement of Target plc (£m)

Turnover	150.00
Cost of sales	138.00
Gross profit	12.00
General and administration expenses	7.50
Associate company loss	0.50
Operating profit	4.00
Interest payable	1.00
Corporation tax @ 33%	1.00
Earnings for ordinary shareholders	2.00

Table 9.2 Balance sheet of Target plc (£m)

Fixed assets		
Plant, property and equipment	30.00	
Investment in associate	3.00	33.00
Current assets		
Stocks	12.00	
Debtors	11.00	23.00
Total assets		56.00
Current liabilities		
Accruals	2.00	
Creditors	16.00	18.00
Long-term loans		9.00
Ordinary shareholders' funds		29.00
Net asset value per share (pence)		290

Any added value from the acquisition that Bidder hopes to achieve must stem from this rationale. Target's forecast income statement and its forecast balance sheet for the next accounting year end 1996 without the takeover by Bidder are shown in Tables 9.1 and 9.2 respectively. These are assumed to have been derived from Target's historic financial statements and the incumbent management's plans for Target. In practice, these plans are unlikely to be publicly disclosed.

The forecast earnings of Target in Table 9.1, when multiplied by the company's prospective PER, yield its stand-alone value. It may be assumed that the pre-bid market value of Target is also its stand-alone value. For its shareholders to gain from the acquisition, Bidder needs to run Target better than the latter's incumbent management, and enhance its value from the stand-alone level.

Bidder expects to make the following changes after acquisition, with impact on the revenues, costs and assets of Target:

- Increase both volume and sales. Forecast revenue growth is 8 per cent per annum.

- Reduce cost of sales. Forecast operating margin (profit before interest and tax/sales) is 4 per cent, raised from the current 2.67 per cent.

- Sell off loss-making associate investment at book value.

- Sell Target's head office premises.

- Improve fixed asset turnover and reduce new fixed asset expenditure to 17 per cent of incremental sales from about 20 per cent, the present ratio of fixed assets excluding investment in associate to sales.

- Reduce new working capital investment to 4 per cent of incremental sales from about 4.7 per cent, the present working capital-to-sales ratio (Working capital = Stocks + Debtors − Creditors).

Although some of the planned improvements of Target will benefit Bidder and add to its own earnings and, therefore, its valuation, in this example all the benefits are attributed to Target and incorporated in its earnings.

Table 9.3 provides the pro forma income statement for Target under Bidder's management. The projected post-acquisition profit for Target is much higher than the pre-acquisition profit. Target's prospective PER before the bid is 10. The average PER of its direct competitors is 12 and the sector average is 9.

In choosing among the alternative benchmark PERs, Bidder evaluates the underlying growth expectations and riskiness of Target, its competitors and the average firm in the sector. Such an evaluation is done using traditional financial statement variables or stock-market-based historic returns and risk measures. From a careful evaluation, Bidder concludes that Target's risk and growth profile is better than that of the sector average firm. Bidder is also confident that its post-acquisition plan for Target will raise its performance to that of its competitors. Thus the appropriate benchmark PER is 12.

Bidder estimates that, in order to achieve the projected level of sustainable earnings, it has to invest in new show rooms, an inventory control system and a new dealer network. This capital expenditure is projected at £9 million. Additional working capital

Table 9.3 Pro forma income statement of Target under Bidder (£m)

Turnover	162.00
Cost of sales	147.42
Gross profit	14.58
General and administrative expenses	8.10
Operating profit	6.48
Interest payable	1.00
Corporation tax @ 33%	1.81
Profit for ordinary shareholders	3.67

Table 9.4 Value of Target to Bidder (£m)

Value of the sustainable earnings from the PER model (prospective earnings of £3.67m in Table 9.3 × 12)	44
Plus	
Associate company divestment	3
Sale of Target head office	6
Pension surplus refund	1
Less	
New fixed asset investment	9
Additional working capital investment	2
Redundancy costs	2
	41

investment to sustain the higher level of sales is £2 million. Thus total new investment is expected to be £11 million. This investment, to be spread over the following five years, is stated at its present value (see Table 9.5 below). Since Bidder's post-acquisition plan involves rationalisation, the expected redundancy costs are £2 million.

Bidder plans to divest the loss-making associate company investment for the book value of £3 million. Further, Target's current head office will be closed and its functions transferred to Bidder's head office. The head office property is, therefore, redundant and will be disposed of for £6 million after any capital gains tax. Bidder anticipates an after-tax refund of £1 million from the pension surplus of Target. The maximum, walk-away price that Bidder can, therefore, pay Target is made up as shown in Table 9.4.

Target's pre-acquisition value was £20 million (forecast earnings of £2 million in Table 9.1 times 10). Thus from Bidder's view, potential added value from the acquisition is £21 million. Any control premium that Bidder has to pay must not exceed this added value, and must fall short of it if Bidder shareholders are going to gain from the acquisition.

Limitations of the PER model

The PER model estimates the post-acquisition earnings for the target for a single period, and assumes that this level will be maintained. There is no explicit recognition of the time pattern of earnings growth. For example, operating profit margin may increase from the current 2.67 per cent to the projected 4 per cent over a five-year period. Moreover, the model does not explicitly consider the investor-perceived risk of the target firm's earnings. Problems also arise in the selection of the benchmark PER, as indicated above. Despite these limitations, the PER model provides a valuation based on the capital market consensus view of the value of earnings. It is widely used by the investment community and makes for ease of communication during a bid, as illustrated in the Kingfisher case.

Asset-based valuation

This model is based on the relationship between the assets of a firm and its market value. The best known of the asset-based models is the Tobin's Q, which is the ratio of the market value of a firm to the replacement cost of its assets. The replacement cost of an asset is the cost of acquiring an asset of identical characteristics, such as the production capacity of a plant.

$$\text{Tobin's } Q = \frac{\text{Market value of a firm}}{\text{Replacement cost of its assets}}$$

For example, if the market value of a firm is £500 million and the replacement cost of its assets is £250 million, its Q is 2. Why does a firm have a Q greater than one?

The excess of market value of a firm over its replacement cost suggests that the firm is in possession of certain intangible assets, such as future growth opportunities. The excess value may also be regarded as the value of the option to exploit these opportunities. The value of a firm is thus made up of two components:

Firm value = Replacement cost of assets + Value of growth options

This relationship is similar to the one between firm value, the value of level earnings and the value of growth earnings we discussed above.

Tobin's Q has been used in the acquisition context to spot undervalued companies. In the early 1980s, many firms were selling at Q values below one: that is, at a discount to their assets at replacement cost. This discount was seized upon by many predators who bid for those undervalued companies. *Business Week* captioned one of its articles 'The Q-ratio: fuel for the merger mania' (24.8.1981), reflecting the spirit of the times.

Tobin's Q can also be used as a valuation tool in the same way as the PER. Selection of a benchmark Q is, however, much more difficult than in the case of the PER. The asset structures of firms could differ considerably, even if they are in the same business. Moreover, evaluation of the underlying growth options is not easy. Growth options facing different firms in the future are not always identical. For example, two oil exploration and production companies operating in different parts of the world may have different growth opportunities. In some other sectors such as property, although valuation of the firm's individual assets can be done more easily, there is nevertheless the problem of valuing the growth options.

There are other limitations in the use of Tobin's Q for valuation purposes. In the UK, assets reported in company accounts are valued not at replacement cost, but mostly at historic cost. Although frequent revaluations allow reported firm asset values to approximate to their replacement cost, this practice is not consistently followed by all firms, since revaluation under current accounting rules is not mandatory. Thus asset figures reported by UK companies are a mixture of historic and current cost values.

As regards the numerator of the Q ratio, market value of the firm is the sum of the market values of all the financial claims on the firm, such as equity and debt. Since corporate debt in the UK is generally not traded, market value of debt is difficult to ascertain. Often analysts use the sum of the market value of equity and the book value of debt, but this is only an approximation to the firm market value.

An approximation to the Q widely employed in practice is the ratio of the market value of equity to the net asset value of the firm, the net assets being the proportion of the firm's assets which can be ascribed to the equity shareholders. This ratio is known as the 'market to book value' or, simply, the valuation ratio. For Target, this ratio under its pre-acquisition management is 0.69, derived from the stand-alone market value of Target at £20 million and its net worth of £29 million in Table 9.2. This ratio level suggests that Target's assets are seriously undervalued by the stock market, thus offering Bidder the scope for enhancing the valuation ratio.

Discounted cash flow model

The discounted cash flow (DCF) model is applied in the following steps:

1. Estimate the future cash flows of the target based on the assumptions for its post-acquisition management by the bidder over the forecast horizon.
2. Estimate the terminal value of the target at forecast horizon.
3. Estimate the cost of capital appropriate for the target, given its projected post-acquisition risk and capital structure.
4. Discount the estimated cash flows to give a value of the target.
5. Add other cash inflows from sources such as asset disposals or business divestments.
6. Subtract debt and other expenses, such as tax on gains from disposals and divestments, and acquisition costs, to give a value for the equity of the target.
7. Compare the estimated equity value for the target with its pre-acquisition stand-alone value to determine the added value from the acquisition.
8. Decide how much of this added value should be given away to target shareholders as control premium.

In preparation for the forecast of target cash flows under the bidder's management, the historic cash flow statements of the target must be examined. As with the sustainable earnings forecast discussed earlier, the cash flow forecast is based on assumptions about the changes to the operation of the target to be introduced by the bidder. In particular, these assumptions relate to the value drivers.

Value drivers and cash flow forecast

Value drivers are those key revenue, cost or investment variables which determine the level of a firm's cash flows, and hence its value to the shareholders. Rappaport (1986) identifies five key value drivers:

- Forecast sales growth in volume and revenue terms.
- Operating profit margin.
- New fixed capital investment.
- New working capital investment.
- The cost of capital.

The bidder's post-acquisition management plan normally aims at altering the above value drivers, so that additional value can be created from the acquisition. Alteration of the value driver levels depends upon the value creation logic underlying the acquisition. Changes in the driver levels are often interdependent. For example, higher sales growth may be achieved only by increasing expenditure on marketing, advertising or product development, or by additional investment in fixed assets and current assets. These changes in the value drivers are then translated into a forecast of cash outflows and inflows.

Operating cash inflows, arising from the operations of the firm, are after (corporation) tax cash flows but before payment of interest on borrowing that has been used to finance the target. Cash outflows are due to additional fixed capital and working capital investments. After-tax operating cash flows net of investment cash outflows are called free cash flows (FCF) (see Chapter 2 on FCF).

Target cash flows are generally forecast for the next five to ten years. In general, the longer the forecast horizon, the less accurate the forecast. Whatever the forecast horizon, the terminal value of the target at the end of that period based on free cash flows thereafter also needs to be forecast. Often this terminal value is based on the assumption of perpetual free cash flows based on the same level of operations as in the last year of the forecast period. The level perpetual cash flows are then capitalised at the cost of capital to yield the terminal value.

The forecast free cash flows when discounted provide the acquirer with the value of the target as a whole. From this firm value, debt is subtracted to give the equity value.

The cost of capital is the weighted average cost of capital (WACC), estimated from the target's pre-acquisition costs of equity and debt. If, after the acquisition, the risk profile of the target changes, perhaps due to product or market diversification of the target, the cost of equity and of debt will change. The pre-acquisition cost of capital has, therefore, to be adjusted to reflect this change in risk.

Further, if the post-acquisition capital structure for the target differs from its pre-acquisition structure, the WACC has to be adjusted for the difference. Thus,

$$WACC = K^e\ E/V + (1 - T^c)\ K^d\ D/V + K^P\ P/V$$

where K^e = cost of equity;
K^d = cost of debt;
K^P = cost of preference shares;
E = market value of equity;
D = market value of debt;
P = market value of preference shares;
T^c = corporation tax rate;
V = $E + D + P$, the value of the firm.

Estimating the weighted average cost of capital

This requires estimation of the costs of the various components of long-term capital, including equity, preference shares and debt. As regards equity, earning yield (earnings/share price) and dividend yield (dividend/share price) do not fully reflect the opportunity cost of equity to the shareholder. The capital asset pricing model (CAPM) may be used to estimate the historic cost of equity for the target. The CAPM estimates the investor-required return as the sum of a risk-free rate and a risk premium based on the overall market risk premium and the risk of the stock in relation to the market. This risk is known as the systematic risk, and a measure of that risk is known as beta.

Expected return on stock = Risk-free rate + Market premium × Beta

Market premium = Expected return on the market − Risk-free rate

Beta = Sensitivity of stock return to market return

$$= \frac{\text{Covariance of stock with market returns}}{\text{Variance of the market return}}$$

Beta is estimated by an econometric procedure using historic share price data. For public companies, betas are also readily available from investment advisory services in different countries, such as Value Line in the USA, and Risk Measurement Service of the London Business School in the UK. For a private company, the beta of a similar public company may be used. The risk-free rate is in practice the return on a short-dated, say 90 days, government Treasury bill. The market is generally proxied by a broad-based stock market index such as Standard & Poor's in the USA and the Financial Times All Share Index in the UK.

The pre-acquisition expected return on equity for the target needs to be adjusted for a possible change in the target beta after the acquisition. This adjustment, necessitated by changes in the underlying operating characteristics of the target due to the acquisition, is somewhat subjective, since the relation between the operating characteristics of a firm and its betas is not definitively understood.

The cost of debt is more difficult to estimate, since debt is often non-traded. The actual interest paid in the case of variable interest borrowing is a good approximation to the true cost of debt. But with fixed rate debt, the coupon may not fully reflect the actual cost. Similar problems may arise in the case of preferred stock. Thus in either case the estimated cost of capital may be an unsatisfactory approximation to the real cost.

Having estimated the individual components of cost of capital, we then weight them by the proportion of each type of capital in the capital structure of the target. The relevant capital structure is the post-acquisition capital structure contemplated by the bidder.

Determining the purchase price

The value of target free cash flows to the bidder is:

$$TV_a = \sum \frac{FCF_t}{(1 + WACC)^t} + \frac{V_t}{(1 + WACC)^t}$$

where TV_a = target value after the acquisition;
FCF_t = free cash flow of target in period t;
V_t = terminal value of target at t.

The total value of the target to the bidder may also include the proceeds of sale of assets and divestments, reorganisation costs or pension fund surplus refunds discussed earlier. These sale proceeds and pension fund surpluses must be calculated on an after-tax basis. From the total value, the debt and preferred stock of the target must be subtracted to yield the target equity value to the bidder. The actual purchase consideration paid to the target shareholders must fall short of this value if the bidder shareholders are to receive any gains from the acquisition.

Table 9.5   Valuation of Target equity using forecast free cash flows (£m)

	1996	1997	1998	1999	2000	2001
Sales	162.00	174.96	188.96	204.07	220.40	220.40
Operating profit	6.48	7.00	7.56	8.16	8.82	8.82
−Corporation tax	2.14	2.31	2.49	2.69	2.91	2.91
−Additional fixed assets	2.04	2.20	2.38	2.57	2.78	0.00
−Additional working capital	0.48	0.52	0.56	0.60	0.65	0.00
Free cash flow (FCF)	1.82	1.97	2.13	2.30	2.48	5.91

Corporate value of Target = Present value of FCF	39.67
+ Divestment of associate	3.00
+ Sale of Target head office	6.00
+ After-tax refund of pension fund surplus	1.00
− Redundancy costs	2.00
− Long-term loans	9.00
Value of Target equity to Bidder	38.67

DCF valuation of a target – example

Table 9.5 projects the free cash flows for Target over the five years following the acquisition in 1995. It assumes that the operating cash inflows from year 6 will be constant and at the same level as in year 5. No new investment in fixed assets or working capital is needed after year 5. The terminal value of Target at the end of year 5 is, therefore, the capitalised value of this level perpetuity of free cash flow at the post-acquisition WACC of Target. The forecast assumes the following values for the five value drivers:

Expected sales growth   = 8% per annum for 1996 to 2000
Operating profit margin   = 4% of sales
Additional fixed capital   = 17% of incremental sales
Additional working capital = 4% of incremental sales
Cost of capital (WACC)   = 11%

It is further assumed that Target expends the depreciation provision each year to maintain its operating capacity at the pre-acquisition level. In the example, the depreciation provision is therefore not added back to operating profit in deriving the FCF or to fixed asset investment.

The estimated Target value of £38.67 million compares with the pre-bid market value of £20 million, which is assumed to be also its stand-alone value. Thus the added value expected from the acquisition is £18.67 million. This is the maximum control premium that Bidder can afford to pay to Target shareholders. This maximum will be reduced by bid costs, which could be substantial if the bid were to become hostile (see Chapter 8 on bid costs).

Sensitivity analysis of the DCF valuation

Given the uncertainty surrounding the forecast process, it is sensible that the acquirer examines how sensitive the target value is to any variation in the assumptions. This kind of analysis highlights those critical value drivers which the acquirer needs to focus on. In particular, the assumptions behind the critical drivers need to be robustly justified. Forecasting their post-acquisition levels also demands greater accuracy. The impact of changing some of the value driver forecasts while maintaining the others is illustrated in Table 9.6. The value of the acquisition appears most sensitive to improvement in operating profit margin and increase in the discount rate.

The values to Bidder of Target derived from the PER model, £41 million (Table 9.4), and the DCF model, £38.67 million (Table 9.5), are in our example fairly close. However, such closeness depends on the assumptions underlying each model. Indeed, each model can be used to test the sustainability of the assumptions in the other model. For example, assuming that the PER model valuation is correct, the assumptions about the value drivers in the DCF model can be re-examined.

Of the two models, the DCF model is much more information intensive, but also much richer in its analysis. It allows for a detailed

Table 9.6 Sensitivity of Target value to value drivers

1% increase in	Change in equity value (£m)
Sales growth rate	0.44
Operating profit margin	12.60
Fixed asset investment	−0.52
Discount rate	−4.19

sensitivity analysis. While the problems of forecasting free cash flows and estimating the cost of capital remain, the DCF model is conceptually and analytically more sophisticated.

Valuation of private companies

While the principles of valuation of private companies are the same as for public companies, an important difference is that for private company targets we do not have the benchmark valuation provided by the stock market. Use of the PER model or the discounted cash flow model requires that we locate a stock market proxy for the private company. This proxy must be as similar as possible to the target. Often the proxy is matched by industry or sector and size to the target. The proxy's PER or its cost of capital may then be used to value the target.

Even where the proxy is well matched to the target in terms of industry and size, the proxy PER needs to be discounted for the potential non-marketability of target shares before it can be applied to the target. Similarly, the cost of capital has to be raised to compensate for this additional risk.

Compared to a public company which is often widely researched by investment analysts, information about the private target may be sparse. Forecasting the future cash flows is thus a more difficult exercise. Offsetting this disadvantage is the fact that private company bids are almost always friendly, with easier access to the target's management information.

Impact of tax on target valuation

In the past, some of the acquisitions were driven by tax factors. For example, a target with accumulated trading losses (called tax losses) which could be offset against the acquirer's profits would be an attractive target. The acquirer could reduce the tax liability for the group after acquisition. Because of subsequent changes in the tax law in the UK, use of tax losses is now subject to strict conditions.

The trading losses can be carried forward only for offset against future profits of the same company. That is, there is no immediate transfer of losses and profits between the target and the acquirer after the acquisition. Further, there should be no major change in the target's trade in the period three years before and three years after the change of ownership. The practical implication of this rule is that the acquirer has to run the same business of the target as before, turn around that company, and then use the tax losses to reduce future tax liability.

A similar 'no major change' rule applies to the use of unrelieved advanced corporation tax (ACT) in the target. It can be carried forward to shelter a future mainstream corporation tax liability in the target, provided there is no major change in its trade or business three years before and three years after the acquisition (see Case Study 9.3). More recent tax law provisions in the UK also restrict the carry back by the target of losses and unrelieved ACT incurred after a change of ownership to the pre-change periods (Scott, 1994).

Accumulated capital losses of a target cannot be set against a chargeable capital gain (i.e. a gain liable to capital gains tax, CGT) made by another member of the group. It is also difficult to buy a target with accumulated capital losses, and transfer to it from the acquirer assets pregnant with capital gain, thus offsetting the gain against the losses. In pricing a target, the buyer therefore has to examine very carefully whether the potential tax benefits can be reliably factored into the valuation.

Acquisitions and employee pension funds

In arriving at the purchase price for a target, the buyer has to take the following into consideration:

- Any surplus or deficit in the target company's employee pension scheme.
- All pension commitments to be transferred, including those which, though not guaranteed under the scheme, had become an established custom.
- The cost of providing the agreed pension benefits.

The assets being transferred as part of the pension scheme to the buyer should cover all pension liabilities. Any shortfall will increase the cost of the acquisition. Any surplus of assets may be repaid to the acquirer, or the acquirer may be able to reduce or suspend future pension contributions to the scheme. The latter is known as a pension contribution holiday. The pension scheme may provide that a surplus should first of all be used to increase the benefits to the employee members of the scheme, thus reducing the size of the refund to the company (see Case Study 9.4).

CASE STUDY 9.3   GKN seeks to avoid ACT

In February 1994, GKN, an engineering and industrial services group, made a £496 million bid for Westland, a British helicopter manufacturer. Although a British company, GKN made substantial profits overseas and had accumulated a large unrelieved ACT. This problem arose because of the relatively low level of UK-based profits on which the company was paying its mainstream corporation tax. Any increase in UK-based profits would, therefore, allow GKN to absorb the unrelieved ACT, with a resultant increase in its reported profits. One way to increase the UK share of GKN's profits was to acquire a UK company with substantial profits from the UK. Westland fitted this need. Many analysts judged that the ACT benefit was a more compelling reason for the bid than any industrial synergy which GKN was putting forward. It was estimated that the acquisition would reduce GKN's effective corporation tax rate by 5 per cent.

Source: *Financial Times*, 10.2.1994.

CASE STUDY 9.4   Hanson tries to cream off pension surplus

In 1985 the Imperial Group plc was anticipating a hostile bid from Hanson Trust. To protect the employee pension scheme against a possible Hanson attempt to transfer the surplus, and to discourage the bid, the rules of the pension scheme trust were amended. The first amendment closed the fund to new members in the event of any party acquiring control of Imperial. The second provided that pensions should be increased by at least 5 per cent or the retail price index rise, whichever was the smaller. Hanson's bid succeeded in 1986 when the fund had a surplus of £130 million. Hanson attempted to transfer the Imperial employees to another scheme within the group, thereby gaining access to the surplus, and threatened to limit pension increases to 5 per cent. In the case which followed, the court held that, in making changes to a pension scheme, a company should act in good faith and not just in its own interests.

Source: *Financial Times*, 5.12.1990.

Overview

This chapter has described different techniques for the valuation of target companies. In particular, the earnings-based, asset-based and cash-flow-based models have been described and their application illustrated. All valuation models suffer from varying degrees of imprecision and unreliability. Many of the assumptions underlying these models are subjective and somewhat arbitrary. Thus, using a range of values from alternative models for target valuation is prudent and sensible. Having priced the target, the bidder has to decide on the method of payment. One of the important considerations in choosing the method is its impact on the reported profits of the group after the acquisition. This impact depends on the accounting rules used to account for the acquisition. We discuss acquisition and merger accounting in the next chapter, and the method of payment in Chapter 11.

References and further reading

Brealey, R. and S. Myers (1991) *Principles of Corporate Finance*, McGraw-Hill.

Mulcahy, R. (1994) 'Pension aspects of acquisitions', in *Company Acquisitions Handbook*, Tolley Publishing Co.

Rappaport, A. (1986) *Creating Shareholder Value*, Free Press.

Rees, W. (1995) *Financial Analysis*, Prentice Hall.

Scott, T. (1994) 'Tax planning', in *Company Acquisitions Handbook*, Tolley Publishing Co.

10

Accounting for mergers and acquisitions

When mergers and acquisitions take place, the combined entity's financial statements have to reflect the effect of the combination. In many countries, accounting regulations require that the accounts of companies which are members of a group be prepared in the form of group accounts. In the UK, group accounts have to be prepared in the form of a consolidated set of accounts, as if the parent company and its subsidiaries constituted a single entity. Consolidated accounts are prepared in accordance with the Companies Act 1985, as amended by the Companies Act 1989 and the Financial Reporting Standard (FRS) 2.

In the year of the business combination, the consolidation of the new subsidiary with the parent is carried out using different sets of accounting rules depending upon the nature of the combination: that is, whether it is treated as a merger or as an acquisition. The two sets of rules are known as merger accounting and acquisition accounting. The choice of the accounting method can have a dramatic impact on the combined entity's post-combination financial performance and condition, as reflected in its consolidated accounts. Foreseeing such an impact, companies may structure their acquisition deals in such a way as to qualify for their preferred method of accounting.

Thus, accounting rules may influence not only the presentation of post-combination performance, but also the financial structure of the deal resulting in the combination. In this chapter, we set out the merger and acquisition accounting rules, the disadvantages and advantages of each from the acquirer's point of view, creative accounting in the acquisitions context, and the current efforts at reforming the accounting rules for business combinations.

Accounting rules for business combinations

A business combination can be classified as either: (1) an acquisition (also called a takeover) or (2) a merger. In an acquisition, the acquiring company purchases the interests of the acquired company's shareholders in their company. The latter cease to have any interest thereafter. In a merger, the two groups of shareholders continue to maintain their interest in their own companies, but also have an interest in the other company: that is, they pool their interests. Hence the American terms 'purchase' and 'pooling' respectively for an acquisition and a merger.

In the UK, accounting rules for acquisitions and mergers are derived from both the Companies Act 1985 and the Statement of Standard Accounting Practice (SSAP) 23, 'Accounting for Acquisitions and Mergers'. For their accounting years commencing after 22 December 1994, UK companies have to comply with the new Financial Reporting Standards, FRS 6 (Acquisitions and Mergers) and FRS 7 (Fair Values in Acquisition Accounting). Pending transition to the new standards, SSAP 23 is still relevant. In this chapter, we discuss this standard first and then outline the changes introduced by FRS 6 and FRS 7.

SSAP 23 provides a test for determining whether a combination is a merger or an acquisition. Where the business combination is effected almost entirely by a share-for-share exchange, it is defined as a merger. In contrast, in an acquisition there is a transfer of ownership of the acquired company, and substantial resources leave the group as consideration for that transfer. Thus a combination financed substantially by cash would amount to a purchase or acquisition. Depending on whether or not a combination satisfies the SSAP 23 test, it will be accounted for as a merger or an acquisition. However, where the combination satisfies the test for merger, it can still be accounted for as an acquisition. In other words, merger accounting is not mandatory.

SSAP 23 is concerned with the way the combination will be represented in the holding company's accounts and in the consolidated accounts. Table 10.1 sets out the differences between merger

Table 10.1 Differences between merger accounting and acquisition accounting under SSAP 23

(a) In holding company accounts

Merger accounting	Acquisition accounting
Investment in subsidiary recorded at nominal value of issued shares.	Recorded at fair value of acquisition.
No share premium arises.	Share premium normally recorded.

(b) In consolidated accounts

Merger accounting	Acquisition accounting
Subsidiary's pre-merger reserves included in group reserves and available for dividend payment.	Excluded from group reserves and not so available.
Group accounts reflect profit of subsidiary for full merger year.	Only profit from date of acquisition.
Subsidiary assets consolidated at pre-merger book values.	They are at fair value.
Does not allow provisions for future losses/reorganisation costs.	Allows.
Goodwill not recognised.	It is.
Previous year's accounts restated as if merger in effect then.	Prior year's figures not restated.

and acquisition accounting in both holding company and consolidated accounts.

The presumption behind merger accounting is that the shareholders of the merging companies pool their interests and continue to retain their interests in their companies, albeit now jointly. Merger accounting seeks to preserve this continuity. This principle of continuity also means that the profits and accumulated reserves of the two firms can be pooled without regard to the date of the merger. It is as though the two firms had always existed together under joint ownership. For this reason, the prior year accounts are restated for comparison.

In the case of acquisition accounting, the rule that the prior year accounts are not restated may often lead to a sudden increase in the acquirer's assets and profits, thus painting a flattering picture of dramatic growth. This merely reflects the fact that in the year of acquisition and thereafter the reported accounting results include those of two companies, whereas in the previous year they include only the acquirer's.

SSAP 23 defines fair value as being based on an arm's-length transaction. Since merger accounting presumes that the merger is not such a transaction, the assets of the companies or the payment for the deal need not be stated at fair values. On the other hand, an acquisition is regarded as an arm's-length purchase deal, and both the acquired assets and the purchase consideration are recorded at fair values. A consequence of this is that the difference between these fair values needs also to be recognised. Where the consideration includes shares, the difference between the fair (market) value and the nominal value of the shares issued must be recognised as share premium.

The excess of fair value of consideration over the fair values of the separately valued assets is called goodwill. Goodwill represents the value of the acquired firm to the acquirer over and above the values of the individual assets of the firm, and is an intangible asset. Goodwill is essentially derived from certain competitive advantages the firm has over its rivals. It consists of the firm's reputation, excellence of research and development or after-sales service, quality of management, locational advantage, market power, etc.

Merger and acquisition accounting – example

The above rules are applied to the case of the business combination between Big Fish plc and Small Fry plc. The combination results from a successful offer for Small Fry by Big Fish. Small Fry becomes the wholly owned subsidiary of Big Fish. The details of the offer and the pre-offer balance sheets of the two companies are given in Table 10.2. Table 10.3 shows the consolidation of Small Fry's accounts into Big Fish's under merger accounting and acquisition accounting.

In Table 10.3, the share premium is the excess of the market value of Big Fish shares (£1225 million) over their nominal value (£700 million). Goodwill is the excess of the fair value of Big Fish's offer of £1225 million over the net assets of Small Fry after revaluation of its fixed assets of £1020 million.

In this example we note the following points of difference between the two methods of accounting:

- Acquisition accounting gives rise to goodwill of £205 million and a share premium of £525 million, and increases the value of the acquired fixed assets by £190 million.

Table 10.2   Big Fish offer for Small Fry

Offer details: Big Fish issues 700 million shares in a one-for-one share exchange offer. Nominal value of both shares, £1. Market value of Big Fish share at the unconditional date, 175 pence per share. The fair value of the fixed assets of Small Fry, £750 million. The balance sheets of the companies (£m) are:

	Big Fish	Small Fry
Fixed assets	820	560
Net current assets	330	270
	1150	830
Share capital	800	700
Profit and loss account	350	130
	1150	830

- Merger accounting increases the group profits of Big Fish from £350 million to £480 million, since the profits of Big Fish and Small Fry are pooled.

These differences have important implications. With acquisition accounting:

- Goodwill now has to be 'dealt with'. Accounting for goodwill is the subject of SSAP 22, which is discussed below.
- The share premium account has a restricted use. Big Fish cannot easily use it as a means of writing off goodwill, and needs the permission of the court to do so.
- The increase of £190 million in the value of fixed assets compared to the merger accounting figure increases the annual depreciation charge and potentially reduces reported profits in the post-acquisition period.
- Big Fish cannot access the £130 million reserves of Small Fry if it wished to pay a larger dividend to its shareholders, unlike under merger accounting.

All of these appear to make acquisition accounting a less attractive choice than merger accounting for acquirers. To prevent the abuse of

Table 10.3 Holding company and consolidated balance sheets of Big Fish Group (£m)

	Holding co.	Small Fry	Group
(a) Merger accounting			
Fixed assets	820	560	1380
Investment in Small Fry	700		
Net current assets	330	270	600
	1850	830	1980
Share capital	1500	700	1500
Profit and loss account	350	130	480
	1850	830	1980
(b) Acquisition accounting			
Goodwill			205
Fixed assets	820	750	1570
Investment in Small Fry	1225		
Net current assets	330	270	600
	2375	1020	2375
Share capital	1500	700	1500
Share premium	525		525
Revaluation surplus		190	
Profit and loss account	350	130	350
	2375	1020	2375

merger accounting, SSAP 23 sets up rather strict conditions for the use of merger accounting. These conditions are as follows:

- The offer leading to the business combination must be made to holders of all equity shares and for all voting shares not already held by the offeror.
- The offeror must secure at least 90 per cent of equity and voting rights.
- Before the offer, the offeror's holding in the target company should not exceed 20 per cent of equity and voting rights.
- Equity should be not less than 90 per cent of the consideration. Thus the cash part of the consideration cannot exceed 10 per cent.

The spirit behind these conditions is that only when pooling and continuity of interests are genuinely maintained should merger accounting be used. However, in practice, companies and their advisers have devised ways of observing the letter but not the spirit of the merger accounting rules. More about these devices later.

Merger relief

An important court judgment in 1980 (*Shearer* v. *Bercain*) outlawed merger accounting, including the recording of the shares issued as consideration at nominal value, and required the recording of share premium on those shares. However, an amended Companies Act 1985 provides the following under certain conditions:

- The parent company can record its investment in the subsidiary at either fair or nominal value of consideration shares.
- If the parent records the shares at fair value, the excess over nominal value can be credited to a merger reserve account instead of a share premium account.

The relief is from having to record the share premium. The conditions for this relief to be available are as follows:

- The offeror must secure 90 per cent of equity of the offeree.
- At least part of the consideration given by the offeror must be in the form of equity shares.

Merger accounting and merger relief compared

Although seemingly similar, the two sets of conditions differ in significant detail. Table 10.4 compares the two. In practice, merger relief has been more often combined with acquisition accounting than with merger accounting, making the former more flexible from the acquirer's point of view. In Table 10.3, Big Fish could have credited the share premium of £525 million to a new merger reserve.

Accounting for goodwill

As we have seen, acquisition accounting gives rise to goodwill. In theory, goodwill can be negative: that is, the fair value of considera-

Table 10.4 Merger accounting and merger relief conditions compared

Merger accounting	Merger relief
Offer must secure 90% of equity and voting shares.	90% of equity shares.
Consideration to include at least 90% as equity.	No minimum but at least some equity.
Pre-offer holding not to exceed 20%.	No such restriction.
Applies only when interests pooled.	Applies to both pooling and purchase.
No share premium recognised.	Merger reserve created.

tion can fall below the fair value of the net assets purchased. This represents a smart, bargain buy for the acquirer, and the accounting rules apply to negative goodwill as well. In practice, negative goodwill is rare, so we will concentrate on positive goodwill. We must remember that goodwill 'emerges' as a residual figure, as the excess of fair value paid by the acquirer over the fair value of assets acquired (see Table 10.3 for the calculation of goodwill).

The fair value of consideration, such as cash, equity or debt security, is far more easily ascertainable than the fair value of assets received. The latter, as current accounting rules stand, is also assessed from the acquirer's point of view. This means that there is scope for manipulation of the fair value of the assets and, hence, of the estimated goodwill.

Goodwill in acquisitions is accounted for under SSAP 22. Under both accounting rules and CA 1985, goodwill that a firm has built up through its trading and operations (the home-grown goodwill) cannot be recognised on the balance sheet of the company as an asset. The reason for this is the extreme uncertainty in valuation of such goodwill. On the other hand, goodwill in acquisitions is relatively easily valued by comparison of fair values of consideration and assets. Further, it is argued, to retain purchased goodwill as an asset while keeping out the home-grown variety is inconsistent.

SSAP 22 provides alternative treatments of purchased goodwill:

- Immediate write-off to reserves.
- Capitalisation and amortisation through the profit and loss account.

The preferred method in SSAP 22 is the former. Under the standard, goodwill can be written off to the following reserves:

- Revenue reserves, e.g. accumulated retained profits.

- Merger reserve (this may be prohibited under current Accounting Standards Board (ASB) proposals: see below).

- Share premium account, with the permission of the court.

The disadvantage of the amortisation procedure from the acquirer's point of view is that the annual goodwill charge reduces the reported post-acquisition profit, and most companies appear to dislike this result. The disadvantage of immediate write-off to retained profits is that it may reduce the potential dividend-paying capacity of the company as perceived by investors. Immediate write-off, by reducing the reserves and, hence, the shareholders' funds, also raises the debt/equity ratio and the perceived financial risk of the acquirer. The problems arising from immediate write-off may be alleviated if the company can create a merger reserve to which the goodwill is immediately written off. Hence the popularity of acquisition accounting in conjunction with merger reserve accounting.

The Big Fish acquisition of Small Fry illustrates the alternative treatments of goodwill (see Table 10.3). Big Fish has the following options:

- Keep goodwill on its group balance sheet (i.e. capitalise) and amortise it over, say, twenty years with an annual charge and reduction in profits of £10.25 million.

- Write off the whole £205 million to the share premium account with the court's permission.

- Write off the whole £205 million to the merger reserve created instead of the share premium account.

For companies preferring not to have their reported 'bottom line' (earnings per share) hit, the third method offers the most flexible and attractive choice.

SSAP 22 allows the acquirer to take into account future trading losses and reorganisation costs that the acquirer expects to incur in managing the acquired company *after* the takeover. The acquirer can make provisions for such losses and costs which reduce the fair value of the assets acquired and increase the goodwill figure. These losses and costs are only the acquirer's subjective estimates and, therefore, are open to manipulation.

The advantage of manipulating these costs and losses upwards is that the depreciation charge in respect of the acquired tangible assets in future periods will be reduced and the reported profits of the group inflated. Further, excess provisions can be released into the profit and loss account directly, again inflating the post-acquisition group profits. SSAP 22 even allows the estimation of these losses and costs a year after the acquisition. Some acquirers have used such 'hindsight' to increase the goodwill, which is then written off to reserves (see Case Study 10.1). Others have reported increased profits by releasing the excess provisions.

CASE STUDY 10.1   Acquirer develops hindsight and 'earns' goodwill

Booker plc acquired Fitch Lovell plc (FL) in 1990 and used acquisition accounting. It made fair valuation of FL's assets at the time of acquisition, but warned that this valuation was not precise. In its 1991 accounts, Booker stated that it had completed the integration of FL and the fair value assessment. This reduced the fair value of the assets acquired by £21.2 million and increased goodwill by the same amount.

Source: Booker plc company accounts.

Criticism of SSAP 22, SSAP 23 and merger relief

The present accounting rules for acquisitions and mergers have been criticised on several grounds. First, merger accounting is not mandatory when the merger accounting conditions are satisfied. Acquirers have, therefore, used a 'pick-and-mix' approach. Even when merger accounting conditions are fulfilled, acquisition accounting has been used. Second, acquirers have structured their acquisition deals in such a way that they apparently qualify for merger accounting while the spirit of those rules is violated. Two techniques which have been employed to this end are vendor placing and vendor rights issues. Third, the rules allow too much laxity in the way acquirers account for goodwill. Fourth, merger relief, contrary to the intention behind its creation, has been mostly combined with acquisition accounting. Fifth, the discretion to make provisions has been abused by acquirers to manipulate their post-acquisition earnings.

Vendor placing and vendor rights arrangements combine the advantages of merger accounting with the need to satisfy the cash preferences of the vendors: that is, the shareholders of the acquired company. In vendor (consideration) placing, the acquirer, whose shares must be listed, offers its shares to the target company's shareholders in exchange for their shares in that company. At the same time, the acquirer arranges for its own merchant bank or other intermediary to place these shares in the market if the target shareholders so desire.

While the vendors receive cash, it is not paid out by the acquiring company. The target shareholders take the cash from the placing and walk away. There is no real merger of interests. Nevertheless, SSAP 23 allows merger accounting under the circumstances. In a vendor placing, new, normally institutional, shareholders displace the target shareholders. The existing shareholders find their shareholdings diluted. This dilution may be avoided in a vendor rights offer.

In a vendor rights offer, the placing agreement provides that the acquiring company's shareholders have an option to buy back the consideration shares. After the vendor rights issue, cash has been transferred from the acquiring company shareholders to the vendors. This method is similar to a conventional rights issue. However, under SSAP 23, a rights issue followed by a cash consideration bid would not qualify for merger accounting. The mechanics of a vendor rights issue are illustrated in Case Study 10.2.

The creative use of provision accounting can often lead to some

CASE STUDY 10.2   *Vendor rights in an acquisition*

In February 1985, Systems Designers International (SDI), a UK consultancy firm, bought Warrington, a private US company, whose shareholders preferred cash rather than SDI's shares in payment. The price included substantial goodwill, whose write-off to reserves was precluded because of SDI's small reserves. If goodwill were amortised, SDI's earnings per share would fall significantly.

Samuel Montagu, SDI's financial adviser, suggested a vendor rights offer. Under this arrangement, SDI would make a share exchange offer to the target. Samuel Montagu would offer cash to Warrington shareholders, but would recoup its outlay by offering the shares it bought to SDI's own shareholders by way of a vendor rights issue. SDI could then use merger accounting to overcome the goodwill problem.

Source: Paul Rutteman, *Accountancy*, August 1987.

CASE STUDY 10.3   Provision accounting in acquisitions

Coloroll acquired John Crowther in 1988 for £215 million in cash and shares. Immediately before the acquisition, Crowther had in April 1988 net assets of about £70 million. Thus there was an apparent goodwill of £145 million. However, in Coloroll's accounts for the year to March 1989, the total cost of the deal was raised by £75 million for incidental costs, stock and debtor write-offs, redundancy and reorganisation provisions, and other items. The net assets of Crowther were further written down by £4 million to £66 million. After making these adjustments, the estimated goodwill was:

£224m = Original goodwill (£145m) + Various costs and provisions (£75m) + Net asset value reduction (£4m)

This goodwill compares with the value of consideration of £215 million.

Source: Smith (1992: ch. 4).

bizarre results, as shown by Coloroll's acquisition of John Crowther in Case Study 10.3. Goodwill acquired by Coloroll exceeded the price paid to John Crowther! Part of this goodwill resulted from the large provisions that Coloroll made in respect of the anticipated reorganisation of Crowther.

The benefit to Coloroll of this simultaneous provisioning and increase in goodwill was twofold: the provision was used subsequently to pay for reorganisation costs, thus avoiding a charge to the post-acquisition profit and loss account which would have reduced the reported profits; and the goodwill could be, and indeed was, written off to reserves, and therefore did not affect the reported post-acquisition profits. If the accounting rules had required amortisation of goodwill, the incentive to inflate goodwill would have been less.

Accounting methods in practice

Although, as we have seen above, merger accounting seemingly offers some advantages over acquisition accounting, UK acquirers have in the past overwhelmingly chosen acquisition accounting, as indicated in Table 10.5. Acquisition accounting with merger relief dominates. Only in 54 out of 211 cases where the acquirer qualified

Table 10.5 Accounting methods in UK acquisitions, 1980–90

Acquirer uses	Qualified for merger accounting?	Acquisitions	
		Number	%
Merger accounting	Yes	54	11
Acquisition accounting with merger relief	Yes	137	28
Acquisition accounting without merger relief	Yes	20	4
Acquisition accounting with merger relief	No	127	26
Acquisition accounting without merger relief	No	155	31
Total		493	100

Source: Salami and Sudarsanam (1994).

for merger accounting did it actually employ that procedure. Higson (1990) reports for his sample of 373 UK business combinations over 1976–87 that less than a third of those acquirers which qualified for merger accounting actually employed it.

There are several possible reasons for the relative popularity of acquisition accounting. The availability of merger relief has given acquirers much flexibility in coping with the problems of goodwill and fair valuation of assets and consideration. Moreover, the ability to make provision for reorganisation and other costs under acquisition accounting has enabled acquirers to lever up the post-acquisition profits. According to one estimate, about 40 per cent of UK acquirers made acquisition provisions. A striking example of provision accounting was BTR, which made provisions for £380 million on its acquisition of Hawker Siddeley in 1991. This amounted to almost a quarter of the purchase price (*Accountancy*, October 1994).

Recent developments in the UK

The new Financial Reporting Standards issued in September 1994, FRS 6 and FRS 7, attempt to tackle some of the criticism made against SSAP 23 and SSAP 22. FRS 6, on accounting for mergers and acquisitions, defines a merger and an acquisition, makes merger accounting mandatory and reduces the scope for such 'clever dodges' as vendor rights. Under FRS 6, a business combination satisfying the following five conditions should be accounted for by merger accounting:

- None of the combining parties is portrayed as either acquirer or acquired. This suggests a genuine pooling of interests.
- Post-combination management is based on the consensus of the combining parties. This provides that the combination serves the interests of all combining parties.
- No party is so large as to dominate the combined entity. This requires a combination of near equals.
- Non-equity consideration is only an immaterial part of the fair value of the total consideration paid. This ensures that material resources do not leave the group and that continuity of ownership is maintained.
- None of the parties retains interest in only a part of the combined entity: that is, becomes a minority interest. This again suggests a genuine pooling of interests.

Other combinations should be accounted for by acquisition accounting. Thus merger accounting has become mandatory, narrowing the scope for the pick-and-mix approach witnessed in the past.

Under FRS 7, on fair values in acquisition accounting, assets and liabilities of the acquired entity should be measured at fair values at the date of acquisition, reflecting the conditions at that date. The standard prohibits provisions for reorganisation costs and future operating losses. Costs of reorganisation and integration of the acquired business should be dealt with as post-acquisition costs. FRS 7 also provides guidelines for measuring the fair values of monetary and non-monetary assets and monetary liabilities.

Some major UK companies have fiercely opposed FRS 7 on the ground that a proper valuation of the acquired business requires the expected future costs of reorganisation and future operating losses to be assessed at the time of acquisition and incorporated in the valuation. While this argument has some merit, the new standard does reduce the scope for acquirers to manipulate the provisions and inflate their future profits. It is for the latter reason that FRS 7 has received much support from the users of accounts in the investment community (*Accountancy*, October 1994).

ASB's discussion paper on goodwill and intangible assets considers two alternative methods of accounting for goodwill: capitalisation and amortisation over a predetermined period, such as twenty years, or capitalisation and write-off only when there is permanent diminution in value. The latter proposal, which finds favour with a lot of UK companies, is, however, at odds with the International Accounting Standard (IAS) 22, which requires capitalisation and amortisation over a predetermined period.

Accounting for business combinations in other countries

In the USA, the Accounting Principles Board Opinion 16 governs the accounting of pooling (mergers) and purchase (acquisitions). There is no counterpart of merger relief in the USA. The US rules do not provide the same flexibility as the UK rules, since pooling (merger) accounting is mandatory if all the conditions for merger accounting are satisfied. Many American companies have complained that the UK rules, especially the freedom to write off goodwill immediately to reserves, rather than amortise as in the USA, have given British companies an unfair advantage in winning takeover bids. A research study by Ivancevich (1993) provides some evidence that UK firms have in fact paid higher premia for US targets, leading to larger goodwill.

On the Continent, there is a wide variety of practices in accounting for mergers and acquisitions and for goodwill (Alexander and Nobes, 1994: ch. 12). Although merger accounting is allowed under the Seventh Directive of the European Commission, the method is rarely employed in most European countries. In France, goodwill amortisation ranges from ten- to forty-year periods. In Germany, goodwill is amortised over five, fifteen or more years, but some companies write off goodwill against reserves immediately. In Spain, goodwill is capitalised and amortised over five years. In the Netherlands, there are no legal provisions or authoritative accounting rules for mergers and acquisitions. Goodwill can, however, be written off immediately or amortised over a maximum of ten years (Choi and Mueller, 1992: ch. 3).

Overview

In this chapter, we have described the accounting rules for reporting acquisitions and mergers. Essentially these rules are concerned with (1) the valuation of the consideration paid by the acquirer, the valuation of the assets, and the estimation of goodwill, and (2) the treatment of goodwill and the need to make provisions for future losses and reorganisation costs. The UK rules provide for merger accounting or acquisition accounting of a given business combination.

These rules have been seen to allow acquiring companies to 'pick and mix' different aspects of these rules, so that they can present the post-combination earnings in the best possible light. However, the more recent UK accounting standards have attempted to tighten the rules for the choice of accounting method, and have made merger accounting mandatory. This will go some way towards reducing the opportunity for creative accounting. In other countries, there exists a wide variety of accounting rules for business combinations.

As we have seen, choice of accounting method for a particular business combination depends upon the choice of payment method. The latter depends on other, non-accounting factors as well. We turn to these in the next chapter.

References and further reading

Alexander, D., and C. Nobes (1994) *A European Introduction to Financial Accounting*, Prentice Hall.

Choi, F.D.S., and G. Mueller (1992) *International Accounting*, Prentice Hall.

Higson, C. (1990) *The Choice of Accounting Method in UK Mergers and Acquisitions*, The Institute of Chartered Accountants in England and Wales.

Ivancevich, D.M. (1993) 'Acquisitions and goodwill: the United Kingdom and the United States', *International Journal of Accounting*, **28**, 156–69.

Salami, A., and P.S. Sudarsanam (1994) 'Interaction between financing and accounting policy: the case of corporate acquisitions', paper presented to the American Accounting Association Annual Conference, New York.

Smith, T. (1992) *Accounting for Growth*, Century.

Stedman, G. (1993) *Takeovers*, Longman.

11

Paying for the acquisition

It is clear from our discussion in Chapter 6 of takeover regulation in the UK that in certain circumstances the bidder is obliged to make a cash offer or attach a cash alternative to an all-share exchange offer. This means that the payment method is partly determined by the nature of the bid being made, and by the share purchases made by the bidder prior to the bid. Payment currency, whether cash, shares or debt securities, is, however, a matter of importance to the bidder for other, non-regulatory reasons.

These reasons include the choice of accounting policy which the bidder wishes to employ to account for the acquisition, the availability of finance to make a cash offer, tax considerations, the bidder's liquidity position and its gearing. The choice of payment currency is made by the bidder as a trade-off among these, often competing, factors.

This chapter describes the characteristics of alternative payment methods, and their advantages and disadvantages from the bidder's and target shareholders' points of view. The recent innovations in acquisition financing, such as leveraged buyouts and deferred consideration, are also described. Different payment methods generate different levels of benefits to the bidder and target shareholders. Empirical evidence on the use of different payment currencies in actual takeovers, and their impact on the returns to shareholders of bidders and targets, is provided.

Methods of payment for acquisitions

The principal methods of payment are shown in Table 11.1. Cash is the most common method of paying for acquisitions, followed by share exchange offers, as shown by the historic pattern of payment methods in Table 11.2. The data include acquisitions of both independent companies and subsidiaries of companies. Several interesting patterns emerge from this historic series of payment methods:

- Cash was used in at least 50 per cent of the acquisitions in all years but 1972, 1983 and 1985 to 1987.
- Share exchange was used in 50 per cent or more of the cases only in 1972, 1983 and 1985 to 1987.
- In 1987, when the stock market crashed, cash was used in 35 per cent and shares in 60 per cent of the acquisitions, but in 1988, following the crash, cash was used in 70 per cent and shares in only 22 per cent of cases.
- Use of fixed-interest securities was in most years below 10 per cent of cases, the highest use being 23 per cent in 1972.

It appears that a bidder's choice of payment method between cash and shares is sensitive to the stock market condition. Shares seem

Table 11.1   Principal methods of payment for acquisitions

Bidder offers	Target shareholders receive
Cash	Cash in exchange for their shares
Share exchange	A specified number of the bidder's shares for each target share
Cash underwritten share offer (vendor placing)	Bidder's shares, then sell them to a merchant bank for cash
Loan stock	A loan stock/debenture in exchange for their shares
Convertible loan or preferred shares	Loan stock or preferred shares convertible into ordinary shares at a predetermined conversion rate over a specified period
Deferred payment	Part of consideration after a specified period, subject to performance criteria

Table 11.2 Payment methods in UK acquisitions, 1972–92

Year	Total (£m)	Cash (%)	Ordinary shares (%)	Fixed-interest securities (%)
1972	2532	19	58	23
1973	1304	53	36	11
1974	508	68	22	9
1975	291	59	32	9
1976	448	72	27	2
1977	824	62	37	1
1978	1140	57	41	2
1979	1656	56	31	13
1980	1475	52	45	3
1981	1144	68	30	3
1982	2206	58	32	10
1983	2343	44	54	2
1984	5474	54	34	13
1985	7090	40	52	7
1986	15 370	26	57	17
1987	16 539	35	60	5
1988	22 839	70	22	8
1989	27 250	82	13	5
1990	8329	77	18	5
1991	10 434	70	29	1
1992	5939	63	36	1

Note: Total = total expenditure on acquisitions and mergers.
Source: 'Acquisitions and Mergers in the UK', *Central Statistical Office Bulletin*, London, May 1993.

more likely to be used in bull markets. There are other factors which may influence the choice of payment method. Accounting, tax and financial strategy considerations may be relevant to this choice. The accounting considerations have been dealt with in Chapter 10. Tax and bidder's financial strategy are considered next.

Tax aspects of payment currency

In considering the impact of taxation on the form of payment to target shareholders, the bidder has to take into account both the possible capital gains tax liability at the time of the takeover and the income tax liability on the dividends or interest paid by the acquirer after the acquisition. The tax issue must also be tackled within the acquirer's own tax strategy, since interest on loan stock is normally corporation tax deductible, whereas dividends are not.

Capital gains tax at acquisition

In general, when a target shareholder accepts cash in exchange for his or her shares, he or she becomes immediately liable for capital gains tax (CGT). However, where the shareholder is a CGT-exempt fund, such as a pension fund, charitable trust, unit or investment trust, this problem does not arise. Further, in the case of individual shareholders, there are three concessions in UK tax rules which may mitigate or even eliminate the CGT burden.

First, capital gains are indexed for inflation. Therefore, the real gains on which CGT is charged may not be large. Second, there is annual CGT relief (in 1994/5 it is £5800). Third, CG can be offset against realised capital losses on other shares in the shareholder's portfolio, so that the net impact may be reduced.

Where the target company is a 'personal company' of the selling sharcholder (i.e. he or she holds 5 per cent or more of the voting rights), and where he or she has held such rights and also has been a full-time director, manager or employee of the target throughout the ten years prior to the sale of the company to the acquirer and is past 55 years of age, the shareholder is entitled to a retirement relief of up to £0.25 million of capital gains. Of the next £0.75 million of gains, only 50 per cent are subject to CGT. There are scaled-down reliefs for periods between one and ten years.

Where the proceeds of sale are reinvested in a 'qualifying investment', the whole of the capital gains is tax free. The qualifying investment is an unquoted company carrying on a qualifying trade, as defined by the Finance Act 1994. Thus the potential CGT burden can be considerably mitigated by these various reliefs.

If the consideration consists of shares in the acquirer, the receiving target shareholders are normally entitled to what in effect is a 'roll-over' of the capital gains until the time the consideration shares are disposed of. Thus, in a share exchange offer, CGT does not crystallise immediately. This provides the target shareholders with some flexibility as to the timing of realisation of the consideration shares and of the resultant CGT burden. For this roll-over relief to apply, special clearance from the Inland Revenue is necessary when the selling shareholder or persons connected with him or her hold more than 5 per cent of the target shares. This clearance is to ensure that the share exchange is not an avoidance scheme.

If the consideration is a straightforward loan stock, it is likely to be classified as a 'qualifying corporate bond', which entitles the recipient to 'hold-over' rather than 'roll-over' relief. The distinction between the two is that, under hold-over relief, capital gains accrued by the target shareholder up to the time of the takeover are 'frozen', are carried forward and then become liable for CGT when the loan stock is eventually disposed of.

The disadvantage of hold-over is that such accrued gains cannot be reduced by the subsequent capital loss on the loan stock. If the acquirer is of doubtful credit rating and fails, the qualifying corporate bond holder is still liable for CGT on the frozen gains. Unless the acquirer is a financially strong company, target shareholders will be reluctant to accept qualifying corporate bonds which are not guaranteed. However, the tax law clearly defines qualifying corporate bonds, and certain types of loan security do not fall within that definition. For example, convertible loan stock is not a qualifying bond. So the bidder can overcome the hold-over disadvantage by an appropriate choice of loan security.

Deferred consideration is extremely rare in public company takeovers, and has played a limited part in acquisitions of companies in the services sector. The tax implications for deferred consideration schemes are dealt with below, after the nature, motivation and general terms of such schemes have been outlined.

Income and corporation tax after acquisition

The advantage of issuing loan stock as consideration is that the interest on it is corporation tax deductible. Thus, the acquirer is able to reduce its tax liability. The target company shareholder who accepts loan stock is, however, subject to income tax on the interest he or she receives.

If the consideration is either ordinary shares or preference shares, dividends on them are paid out of profits after corporation tax. The paying company is liable to advanced corporation tax (ACT) at 25 per cent of the cash dividend paid. For individual shareholders subject to the basic rate of income tax at 25 per cent, no further tax is payable, whereas the higher-rate 40 per cent taxpayer will be liable to pay an extra 25 per cent of the dividend.

Dividends have a certain advantage to corporate shareholders and tax-exempt funds. For the former, the dividends received are not subject to any further corporation tax, and the ACT they must pay when they distribute dividends to their shareholders is reduced to the extent of the ACT credit they receive from the acquirer. For tax-exempt institutional shareholders, the ACT is refunded and increases their returns. Thus a share exchange consideration may have substantial attractions to a large body of target shareholders.

Impact of bidder's financial strategy

A company's financial strategy has many strands. Maintaining a reasonable gearing ratio is one of them. Ensuring adequacy of lines of credit from banks is another. Taking advantage of any tax provisions to reduce the cost of capital is also relevant. Finally, timing of security issues to exploit favourable market conditions is an important consideration. The choice of payment currency for an acquisition is based on a trade-off of these often conflicting criteria, which are discussed below.

Where the bidder has an already-high gearing ratio, issue of loan stock to pay for the acquisition is less attractive than a share exchange offer, which will reduce that ratio. Moreover, the operating cash flows of the combined entity and its cash flow or earnings cover for the debt interest must be sufficient and sustainable. These considerations also apply when the bidder raises bank finance to make a cash offer. In either case the source of loan finance differs, but the related obligations are the same. Gearing as an influence on acquisition financing is emphasised by Williams Holdings (see Case Study 11.1).

Issue of loan stock or drawing on the firm's credit lines may cause the acquirer to breach loan covenants stipulating a maximum debt-to-equity ratio or a minimum interest cover. Such a breach is a source of potential financial distress for the acquirer. Of course, the tax deductibility of debt provides the acquirer with an opportunity

CASE STUDY 11.1 Williams Holdings says no to high gearing

Williams Holdings (WH) made a £703 million share offer for Racal in 1991. At that time, WH's gearing was about 30 per cent and it had unused bank credit lines of £600 million. Although the gearing was low, WH was unwilling to increase it to finance the bid. Mr Nigel Rudd, chairman of WH, said, 'I do not like debt. That is the way to go bust.'

Source: *Financial Times*, 18.9.1991.

to enhance the earnings per share (EPS) for its existing shareholders, and thereby the value of the company. This rationale drove some of the high-leverage buyouts of the 1980s, which we discuss later in this chapter.

Earnings dilution in a share exchange

A share exchange, in contrast to a loan stock or a leveraged acquisition, imposes its own 'cost', in that the enlarged shareholder base can lead to a decline in EPS in the year of acquisition or for several years thereafter. Let us assume that Bidder plc (B) makes a share exchange offer for Target plc (T). The two companies have the pre-bid data shown in Table 11.3.

B offers 1.5 of its own shares for each T share. The exchange ratio (ER) is 1.5. The number of B shares after acquisition will be 20 million of the old shares plus 30 million of the new shares. The combined earnings of B and T are £4 million. Thus the EPS will be 8 pence compared to B's EPS of 10 pence before the bid. Thus its earnings are diluted by 20 per cent.

Assuming the share value of B does not change, the bid premium that B offers to T shareholders is 200 per cent:

(B share value × Exchange ratio) − Pre-bid value of T share
£2   ×   1.5   −   £1

B may avoid dilution by offering one B share for each T share. The post-acquisition EPS will then be 10p. In this case, the bid premium is 100 per cent. Bidders making a share offer are often at pains to reassure their own shareholders that dilution will not happen or will be temporary (see Case Study 11.2).

Table 11.3 Pre-bid data for Bidder plc and Target plc

Company	EPS (p)	PER	Share price (£)	No. of shares (m)	NI (£m)	Market capitalisation (£m)
Bidder	10	20	2	20	2	40
Target	10	10	1	20	2	20

Note: EPS = earnings per share; PER = price/earnings ratio; NI = net after-tax income for ordinary shareholders.

CASE STUDY 11.2 *Bidder allays fears over earnings dilution*

When Tesco made its £248 million cash bid, with a share alternative, for William Low, revising it from an earlier £154 million offer, Tesco's share prices fell amid fears of earnings dilution. Tesco's chairman reassured shareholders that the acquisition would have a 'negligible impact' on earnings per share in the current year, and a positive impact in future. He went on to say that analysts who had suggested an earnings dilution underestimated how much Tesco could improve the performance of Wm Low.

Source: *Financial Times*, 4.8.1994.

Can B afford such a high premium as 200 or 100 per cent? The answer to this question lies in the view that the stock market is likely to take of the virtues of the acquisition. This view is expressed in terms of the earnings multiple after the acquisition: that is, the post-acquisition PER. This is the rate at which the EPS of the combined entity (BT) will be capitalised to give the market value of that entity. A bidder has to take into account this post-acquisition value in determining the ER.

For any given value of expected post-acquisition PER, it is in the interest of the target to bargain for as high an ER as possible. The bidder's incentive is to keep the ER as low as possible. However, there is usually a range of ERs over which both can gain, both can lose, or one can gain at the expense of the other. These possible outcomes are shown in Table 11.4 for three alternative expected post-acquisition PERs of 10, 15 and 20 for B's acquisition of T.

The gain or loss to each shareholder group is:

For B: Gain $= (N_B/N_{BT}) \times V_{BT} - V_B$

For T: Gain $= \{(N_T \times ER)/N_{BT}\} \times V_{BT} - V_T$

where N_B and N_T are the pre-bid numbers of shares in B and T, and V_B and V_T are their pre-bid market values. N_{BT} and V_{BT} are the corresponding figures for the post-acquisition firm, BT.

V_{BT} = Post-acquisition PER of BT × BT's combined earnings

For example, if $PER = 20$ and $ER = 0.5$, $V_{BT} = £80m$ and

Table 11.4 Relationship between post-acquisition price/earnings ratio (PER) and the exchange ratio (ER) in share offer (data as per Table 11.3)

Pre-bid market value of B = £40m and T = £20m.
BT's combined earnings = £4m.

ER	Company	Post-acquisition value of B and T at PER (£m)		
		10	15	20
0.5	B	26.6	40.0	53.3
	T	13.4	20.0	26.7
1.0	B	20.0	30.0	40.0
	T	20.0	30.0	40.0
1.5	B	16.0	24.0	32.0
	T	24.0	36.0	48.0

N_B = 20m, N_T = 20m, N_{BT} = 30m, then B's and T's shares of V_{BT} are £53.3m and £26.7m. Gain to B = £13.3m and gain to T = £6.7m.

It will be recalled from Chapter 9 that a company with a high PER is valued highly due to high expected future earnings growth or low risk or both. The forecast PER applied by the stock market determines the value of BT. At a PER of 15, this value is £60 million, the same as the sum of the pre-bid values of B and T. This suggests that the acquisition does not create added value for the shareholders. It has a neutral value creation impact.

At a forecast PER of 10, the same as Target's pre-bid PER, BT's value will be £40 million, implying that the acquisition is actually value destroying by £20 million. The combination of B and T leads to negative synergy. On the other hand, with a PER of 20, the same as B's pre-bid level, BT's value will be £80 million. The added value from the acquisition is £20 million. It can be seen that this added value comes from the capitalisation of T's earnings at 20 not at 10.

Boot strapping

The phenomenon whereby shareholder value increases by the application of the bidder's higher PER to the target's earnings is known as boot strapping. Is boot strapping based on the bidder's pious hope or on stock market inefficiency or on the market's expectation of synergy? Unless the stock market is convinced of the strategic value creation logic of the acquisition, a PER of 20 is unlikely to be applied. Assessment of such logic was discussed in Chapter 3. What does capitalisation at 20 mean? It means that the market expects that the earnings growth of the target after acquisition will match that of the bidder: that is, it will be twice as fast as in the pre-bid period. If this growth is not achieved, boot strapping will be a short-lived delusion and BT's value will decline.

Sharing acquisition gains between bidder and target

The exchange ratio, ER, determines how the overall added value at any PER will be shared between B and T shareholders. From Table 11.4, we can see that, for any given PER, the bidder can avoid losing by choosing an appropriate maximum ER. Similarly, by negotiating for a minimum ER, T can also avoid losing. For example, with a PER of 20, B will lose if ER is 1.5. At 15, it loses with an ER higher than 0.5. On the other hand, T loses when PER is 10 and ER is 0.5.

The case of $PER = 15$ and $ER = 0.5$ is an interesting one, since neither B nor T loses. 15 is the average between the PERs of B and T. An ER of 0.5 is the ratio of T's share value to B's share value. Thus when the bidder expects no synergy, it cannot afford a higher ER than a simple ratio of the target's to the bidder's share price, in order to prevent loss of value from the acquisition. This means that no bid premium is paid to the target. The bidder can justify a bid premium only if the acquisition produces some synergy, and if this synergy is credibly translated into a higher PER than the average of the pre-bid PERs.

The various combinations of expected post-acquisition PER and bidder's choice of ER are shown in Figure 11.1, derived by Larson and Gonedes (1969). The 'Bidder' line represents the maximum ER that the bidder can afford for a given forecast PER. The 'Target' line represents the minimum ER acceptable to target shareholders if they are not to lose from the acquisition. For the acquisition to be beneficial to both B and T shareholders, it must lie in the first quadrant of Figure 11.1.

Valuation risk and payment currency

In negotiating the payment currency, the bidder and target have different and opposing incentives. If B finds it difficult to value the target, offers cash and, post-acquisition, discovers some skeletons in T's cupboard, as did Ferranti (see Case Study 7.8), the entire loss

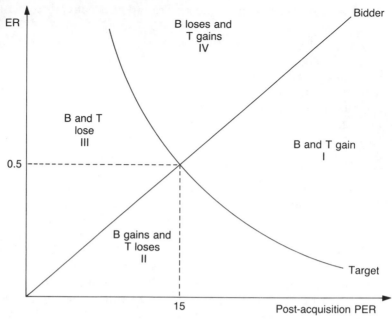

Source: Larson and Gonedes (1969).

Figure 11.1   Impact of PER and ER on the wealth gains of Bidder and Target shareholders.

falls to B's shareholders. If B had offered a share exchange, T shareholders would have stayed on to share the loss. Thus, the downside of the valuation risk is mitigated by a share exchange.

On the other hand, if B is confident that post-acquisition PER will be 20, in a share exchange with an ER of 0.5, T will end up with a gain of £6.7 million. If B could make a cash offer with a bid premium of only, say, £4 million, it would appropriate the extra value for its own shareholders. Thus if B expects good times to roll after the acquisition, it has the incentive to offer cash.

T shareholders also have contradictory incentives. They also face the valuation risk that B is already overvalued or that B will mess up the acquisition. In this event, they will prefer cash to avoid the downside risk. But they forgo the upside potential which they would enjoy if they accepted a share exchange and stayed on to enjoy the good times. This leads to the rather perverse situation that just when B offers paper, T wants cash and vice versa.

The valuation risk arises from what the economists call information asymmetry: that is, each side believes that the other side knows something more. One way of alleviating this problem of mutual distrust is for B to be more generous with the exchange ratio. As we have seen, this may result in perceived earnings dilution and even value loss for B's shareholders. It is for this reason that share exchange offers are often greeted with bidder's share price decline, as exemplified in Case Study 11.3.

CASE STUDY 11.3   *Bidder's share price falls on share offer*

T. Cowie made a hostile bid for Henlys, a fellow motor trader, in July 1992. The initial 1 for 2 share exchange offer was later revised to 7 for 10. An alternative offer of 1 Cowie share plus 40p cash for every 2 Henlys shares was also added. The bid failed, but throughout the offer period, Cowie's share price declined, thus reducing the bid value to Henlys shareholders. Some Henlys shareholders said that 'a larger cash element would have been more persuasive'. When the bid failed, Cowie shares reversed their decline.

Source: *Financial Times*, 28.8.1992.

Financing a cash offer

It will be recalled that, when a bid falls within Rule 9 or Rule 11 of the Code, a cash offer or a cash alternative must be made available to the target shareholders (see Chapter 6). A bidder making a cash offer can finance it from one or more of the following sources:

- Internal operating cash flow.
- A pre-bid rights issue.
- A cash underwritten offer, e.g. vendor placing or vendor rights.
- A pre-bid loan stock issue.
- Bank credit.

Use of a pre-bid loan stock issue or bank credit gives rise to a leveraged bid or leverage buyout (LBO). It has been used in recent years as a way of financing a management buyout (MBO) (see Chapter 15). The bidder's internal operating cash flow is perhaps the cheapest and easiest source, since it avoids both the transaction costs of raising finance and the delay in doing so. However, except for relatively small acquisition targets, a bidder is unlikely to have enough internal cash flow.

A conventional rights issue is often made by firms with a well-defined acquisition programme. When Sheffield Insulation made an agreed £53 million bid for WMS Group, the cash consideration of £47 million was raised by a rights issue (*Acquisition Monthly*, December 1993). The cash underwritten offer is somewhat similar to a rights issue, but it may be more flexible in that the underwriting can be made conditional upon the bid succeeding. Thus if the bid fails, the bidder is not left with a surplus of cash.

The Code allows the underwritten cash alternative to a UK share offer to be 'shut off' earlier. Normally, it is shut off after the first closing date: that is, Day 21 (see Chapter 6). Since underwriting expenses are related to the period over which the underwriting commitment is kept open, the cash underwritten offer may be cheaper than a rights issue. Moreover, some 'core' underwriters are also paid a success-related commitment fee, which further reduces the cost of the cash underwritten alternative (*Acquisitions Monthly*, October 1987).

Another advantage of a cash underwritten offer is that the early shut-off can add to the pressure on target shareholders to accept the offer, and thus improve the chance of a successful bid. Further, such an offer is much more tax efficient from the target shareholders' perspective, since shareholders with different exposures to potential CGT liability can choose either the cash or the paper offer, so as to minimise their tax liability. As observed in Chapter 10, a cash underwritten offer also allows the bidder to use merger accounting, whereas a rights issue does not. Further, it serves as a signal to the market that the bid is supported by financial institutions.

Leveraged cash financing

One of the most important considerations in this form of financing is the ability of the bidder to service the debt obligations: that is, periodic interest payments and capital repayment. The bidder may rely on two alternative sources of cash flows for this purpose:

- Operating cash flows.
- Cash proceeds from sales of the target's assets.

A careful forecast of the future operating cash flows from the target under the bidder's management must be made to assess the debt-servicing capacity. Where the bidder expects to asset-strip the target in order to realise immediate cash flows to pay off the debt, careful consideration must be given to the CA 1985 provisions (section 151) prohibiting a public company from providing financial assistance to purchase its own shares. Where the target becomes a wholly owned subsidiary, this prohibition may not apply. Where the target is a private company, subject to certain conditions, target assets may be used to finance the acquisition (Stedman, 1993: ch. 22).

The high gearing that results from this method of financing may be of concern to the bidder. There have been numerous cases of highly leveraged acquisitions causing the decline and downfall of acquirers. One attraction of leverage is that the related interest payment is tax deductible, thus enhancing future EPS. This compares well with a share offer or a cash offer financed by a rights issue. Leveraged buyout is discussed in more detail in Chapter 15.

Financing with loan stock

This differs from the leveraged cash offer in that the loan stock is the consideration for the bid and is offered to the target shareholders. They swap their shares in the target for the loan stocks of the bidder. As noted earlier, such a loan stock may be construed as a qualifying corporate bond, with a certain tax disadvantage compared to a share offer. Nevertheless some deferral of CGT is achieved. Further, the transaction cost of a direct loan stock is lower than that of a leveraged cash buyout.

To the target shareholders, a loan stock minimises the problem of information asymmetry, since, as in a cash offer, they are assured of a definitive sum on redemption of the stock. For some target shareholders, accepting loan stock may mean an unwanted shift of their portfolio weighting against equity. Further, acceptance of loan stock means loss of control over their company.

Financing with convertibles

Use of convertibles in acquisition financing is less common than that of straight loan stock. Convertibles may be preferred stock (CPS) or loan stock (CLS). They represent a bundle of two underlying securities – the straight preferred or loan stock, and an option on the shares of the company. Valuing a convertible is rather complex, and may be done with a mathematical model such as the Black–Scholes option pricing model. Case Study 11.4 shows the use of convertibles in one of the largest takeovers in the UK in 1986. Under UK tax rules, a convertible is not a qualifying corporate bond. Target shareholders can, therefore, 'roll over' their capital gains and avoid immediate CGT.

CASE STUDY 11.4   *The battle of the convertibles for Imperial*

Hanson Trust and United Biscuits (UB) were locked in a fierce battle for Imperial Group (Imp). On 17 February 1986, Hanson raised its hostile offer to £2.32 billion and was immediately upstaged by UB with a revised £2.56 billion bid. Both included convertibles in their offer:

- *Hanson's offer*: For each Imp share, 1 Hanson share plus 153p cash *or* 1 share plus 153p nominal of 10% new CLS *or* 1 share plus 153p nominal of 12% loan notes *or* an underwritten cash alternative of 293p. The mixed paper offer was worth 301p.
- *UB's offer*: 5 ordinary shares plus 5 CPS plus 275p in cash for every 6 Imp shares. The CPS was underpinned by a cash alternative of 100p per convertible. UB's offer was worth 332p.

Source: Dimson and Marsh (1988: 171–2).

Deferred consideration financing

As discussed earlier, both bidders and target shareholders face valuation risk in negotiating a price and the payment currency in a takeover. One way of mitigating this risk is to make the consideration payable to the vendors contingent upon the future performance of the target under their own management. In the 1980s this method, called 'earn-out', was used to finance a number of private company deals involving service companies like advertising agencies. In such companies, the value of the company often depends on the intangible asset of human creativity and the flair of one or two individuals. Valuing such companies, therefore, is immensely difficult.

In an earn-out, consideration to the vendor is made up of the following:

- An immediate payment in cash or shares of the acquirer.
- A deferred payment contingent upon the target turned subsidiary achieving certain predetermined performance levels.

The performance level may be expressed in terms of sales revenue or pre-tax profits.

The structure of a typical earn-out acquisition is as follows. B acquires the shares of a fellow TV programme maker, C, under an earn-out deal. C's 1995 pre-tax profits are £1.5 million. B estimates that future pre-tax profits of C will be £2.5 million in 1996, £3 million in 1997 and £3.5 million in 1998. B will make an initial payment of £10 million and an earn-out payment in cash at the end of 1998. The earn-out formula is twice the excess of pre-tax profits over £2 million from 1996 to 1998. Maximum earn-out payment will be £6 million. The total consideration is as follows:

Initial payment	£10 million
Earn-out period	3 years
Maximum earn-out payment	£6 million in cash
Total consideration	£16 million

A recent earn-out deal is described in Case Study 11.5.

The earn-out element may be paid in shares or loan notes as well as cash. The tax position of the vendors under the UK rules with regard to the deferred element is somewhat complex. The tax law makes a distinction between ascertainable and unascertainable contingent payment. If the amount is fixed and known at the time of the acquisition, that amount is immediately liable for CGT.

CASE STUDY 11.5 Sage chooses earn-out

Sage, an accounting software company, enhanced its market position and product portfolio when it acquired in July 1994 Multisoft Financial Systems, a leading supplier of accounting and business software, developing a new range of software for client/server networks which were being introduced in large companies. Sage paid the vendors £4 million in cash immediately and agreed to make an additional payment based on Multisoft's sales performance up to September 1995. The maximum earn-out payment agreed was £2.5 million.

Source: *Financial Times*, 15.7.1994.

If the payment is contingent upon future profit levels, it is not ascertainable. In this case, the right to receive that payment (called chose in action) is treated as an asset and the value of that right is included as part of the consideration for the shares and thus becomes liable for CGT immediately. Where the earn-out payment is paid in shares of the acquirer, the right to receive those shares is treated as if shares have been received, provided the transaction has a commercial justification. In this event, the vendor may claim roll-over relief for any accrued capital gains with the approval of the Inland Revenue.

Earn-outs are not free of problems. The culture shock of transformation from owning and managing an independent company to running a subsidiary under the control of a larger firm may be quite traumatic. For the buyer, an earn-out is a way of retaining the vendor's talents. However, the vendor may lack motivation or try to maximise short-term profits to the detriment of the long-term interests of the buyer. These and other advantages and disadvantages are given in Table 11.5.

The earn-out agreement must carefully spell out how profits will be measured to avoid problems of interpretation. The vendor may also be concerned that when the earn-out payment is due the buyer

Table 11.5 Advantages and disadvantages of earn-out

Advantages	Disadvantages
(a) For acquirer	
Vendor's talents retained.	Conflict of motives between vendor and buyer.
Valuation risk reduced.	Vendor given autonomy and buyer's integration plan delayed.
'Buy now and pay later' reduces financing need.	Vendor, after becoming rich, may lack motivation.
Provides hedge against warranty and indemnity claims.	Management succession after earn-out may cause problems.
(b) For vendor	
Increases personal wealth.	Loss of control.
Career opportunities may be brighter.	Pressure for short-term results.
Buyer can fund future growth of business.	Culture shock of working in a large, 'bureaucratic' company.

might be unable to pay. So the vendor will look for some security to ensure payment. Despite these problems, a survey of earn-outs in the UK has found that both acquirers and vendors are largely satisfied. Hussey (1990) surveyed 27 acquirers and 33 vendors. He found that 87 per cent of the acquirers regarded their earn-out deals as mainly or highly successful. While most vendors considered the personal wealth gain as important, they also regarded job challenge and job satisfaction as important motivating factors.

Empirical evidence on the impact of payment method

Franks *et al.* (1988), in their extensive study of payment methods and their impact on shareholder returns for the UK and the USA for the period 1955–85, report a negligible use of convertibles in the UK, but a significant use in the USA. They find that shareholders of target companies earn a risk-adjusted return of 30 per cent in all cash offers and 15 per cent in all share offers in the month of bid announcement (see Chapter 13 for methodology). For the bidder shareholders, the returns are 0.7 and −1.1 per cent respectively. The returns for 'cash or equity' for the same month are close to all-cash offers, and for 'cash and equity' offers the returns are higher than in pure equity offers.

Salami (1994) finds similar results for a later sample of over 500 UK acquisitions during 1980–90, as shown in Figure 11.2 for targets. For the bidders, cash and equity offers generate little abnormal return, although in mixed offers combining equity and cash, bidder shareholders experience negative returns. The relative superiority of cash offers in the returns to shareholders is also observed in other countries (see Franks *et al.*, 1988, for the USA; Eckbo and Langohr, 1989, for France). Many other US and UK studies have reported broadly similar results for cash and equity offers.

Overview

This chapter has examined the alternative methods of financing an acquisition. Historically, cash has been generally the most popular method, although when the stock markets are high there is a shift to share exchange offers. Use of debt securities is not very popular.

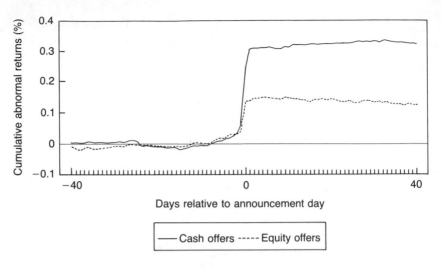

Figure 11.2   Cumulative abnormal returns for targets by method of payment, 1980–90 (market-adjusted method).

The choice of payment currency depends upon a variety of considerations, including the tax implications, concern about earnings dilution, and the impact on financial risk. Deferred payment as a way of overcoming some of the problems associated with a cash or share offer has been discussed, and its own shortcomings have been highlighted. The payment currency often has a significant influence on the outcome of contested bids. Target companies, as part of their defensive tactics, attack the method of payment. These defensive tactics and others are discussed in the next chapter.

References and further reading

Dimson, E., and P. Marsh (1988) *Cases in Corporate Finance*, John Wiley.

Eckbo, E., and H. Langohr (1989) 'Information disclosure, method of payment and takeover premiums', *Journal of Financial Economics*, **24**, 363–403.

Franks, J., R. Harris and C. Mayer (1988) 'Means of payment in takeovers: results for the UK and the United States', in A.J. Auerbach (ed.), *Corporate Takeovers: Causes and consequences*, University of Chicago Press.

Hussey, R. (1990) 'Maintaining the honeymoon time' and 'Problems and priorities when you look after baby', *Accountancy Age*, 1 and 8 March.

Larson, K.D., and N.J. Gonedes (1969) 'Business combination: an exchange ratio determination model', *Accounting Review*, October, 720–8.

Salami, A. (1994) 'Determinants and financial consequences of the method of payment in corporate acquisitions', unpublished Ph.D. thesis, City University Business School, London.

Stedman, G. (1993) *Takeovers*, Longman.

12

Defences against takeovers

In Chapter 8, we described the various strategies and tactics that a bidder could deploy in winning control of the target firm. In this chapter we discuss how the target management can counter these. When target company managers decide to resist a bid for their company, the chances of successful resistance depend upon the defences available, the regulatory and shareholder constraints on their use, and their cost. In the UK, the City Code imposes very stringent constraints on the target management's choice of defensive strategies and tactics. Despite these constraints, target managements do employ a variety of strategies and tactics, and some have been pretty effective too. We discuss the range of these strategies.

The defensive strategies deployed in the UK are in contrast to those available in other countries. We document the practices in some of those countries. We also report the available empirical evidence on the use and effectiveness of defensive strategies. Evidence on the impact of bid resistance on the wealth position of target shareholders is presented.

Bid resistance motives

Managers of companies which become the targets of bids have to decide whether to accept them on a friendly basis or resist them. For either course of reaction there is a variety of motives. Managers may honestly believe that remaining independent is the best way to serve the interests of their shareholders and other constituencies, such as

196

employees and local communities. Managers may regard resistance as a tactical posture to extract the maximum bid premium from the bidder for the benefit of the shareholders. Less unselfishly, they may resist because they fear losing their jobs, status, power, prestige and other psychological perquisites of their jobs when taken over. Available evidence on management turnover in targets after takeover suggests that this fear is not wholly misplaced.

Acceptance of a bid by managers may again be because it secures them a better deal in the post-acquisition dispensation. The target management may be allowed an acceptable degree of autonomy. They may be allowed to keep their power and perks. They may even be elevated to the parent's board as a reward for their meekness in accepting the overwhelming logic of the bid, and their loyalty in recommending the bid to the target shareholders. Less selfishly, managers may consider takeover by the favoured bidder the best option available to the target. In practice, it is difficult to disentangle the selfish from the disinterested motive.

From the target shareholders' point of view, bid resistance may be a mixed blessing. While resistance raises the bid premium and the returns, it also reduces the chance of the hostile bid succeeding. Thus for the target shareholders, the optimal course is to provide enough incentives to their managers to resist to the point where the bid premium is maximised without endangering the chance of a successful bid. Devices such as 'golden parachute' are designed to achieve this optimal result.

Bid defence strategies

The best form of defence is being prepared. Eternal vigilance is indeed the price of independence for a company which is a probable takeover target. However, the best-laid strategic defensive plans might go awry and the company, having become a target, needs battlefield tactical plans. One can thus divide defensive strategies into pre-bid and post-offer categories. Each of these categories of defence encompasses an extensive range of weapons.

Pre-bid defences

Pre-bid defences that may be set up by the potential target fall into two broad categories. Internal defences are those decisions/actions to alter the internal structure or nature of operations of the firm.

External defences are actions taken to influence outsiders' perceptions of the firm, and to provide early warning signals about
potential predators. These various defences are listed in Table 12.1.

If hostile bids are driven by the desire to create shareholder value,
the best defence available to a firm is to ensure that its operations
and strategies deliver cost efficiencies, high profit margins and high
earnings per share. This in itself may not be enough to increase the
market valuation of the firm.

The firm must engage in a consistent programme of educating the
shareholders, analysts and media that its policies are indeed value
enhancing. Where the company experiences setbacks due to the
economic cycle or the restructuring it has undertaken, it must make
a credible case to the analysts and investing institutions that the
setbacks are indeed temporary. The use of investor relations
consultants in this context is discussed in Chapter 7. The company
needs to keep a close watch on unusual share price movements or
share purchases to see whether any potential predator is building up
a toehold. As noted in Chapter 6, section 212 of the Companies Act
1985 enables the company to flush out the true owners behind the
nominees.

Some of the defensive actions listed in Table 12.1 are not available
in all countries. For example, in the UK, the London Stock Exchange
does not allow companies with dual-class shares (i.e. with differen-
tial voting rights) to be listed, although there are still a small number
of old listed companies with such a share structure. Trust House
Forte's (THF) bid for the Savoy, the famous hotel company, was
blocked in the 1980s because of the dual-class share structure. It
acquired 68 per cent of the equity, but only 42 per cent of the votes
in the Savoy.

Poison pills are relatively common in the USA. They refer to
shareholder rights plans which confer upon the target shareholders
the right to subscribe at a heavy discount to shares in the target
(flip-in pill) or to the shares of the successful bidder (flip-over pill).
The aim of these toxic arrangements is to increase the cost of the
acquisition. Poison pills of this kind are unknown in the UK, where
the term is used to denote any arrangement to raise the cost to a
potential bidder.

Equally rare in the UK is a staggered board of directors, only a few
of whom are replaced each year. Thus the acquirer may have to wait
several years before it succeeds in shaping the board 'in its own
image'. A golden parachute is a contract to compensate the
management for loss of office in the event of a takeover of the firm.

Table 12.1   Pre-bid defensive strategies against hostile takeovers

Action	Result
(a) Internal defences	
Improve operational efficiency and reduce costs.	Improved EPS, higher share prices and firm value.
Improve strategic focus by restructuring, divestment, etc.	Improved EPS and higher firm value. Asset stripping by bidder difficult.
Change ownership structure, e.g. dual-class shares, high gearing, share buy-back, poison pill.	Control by bidder difficult. Scope for LBO limited.
Change management structure or incentive, e.g. staggered board, golden parachute.	Predator control delayed and bid cost increased.
Cultivate organisational constituencies, e.g. unions and workforce.	Useful alliance against bidder; share support from pension funds/ESOPs.
(b) External defences	
Cultivate shareholders and investors, e.g. use investor relations advisers to inform about company's performance, prospects and policies.	Ensures loyalty and support during bid of key shareholders.
Inform analysts about company strategy, financing policies and investment programmes.	Share undervaluation risk reduced and bid cost raised.
Accept social responsibility to improve social image.	Public hostility to predator roused.
Make strategic defence investment, e.g. joint venture/mutual shareholding in fellow targets.	Predator control blocked.
Monitor the share register for unusual share purchases; force disclosure of identity of buyers.	Early warning signal about possible predators.

Note: EPS = earnings per share; LBO = leveraged buyout; ESOP = employee share ownership plan.
Source: Sudarsanam (1991).

Under Rule 21 of the Code, such a contract, except in the ordinary course of business, requires shareholder approval.

In the UK, employee share ownership plans (ESOPs) were introduced only a few years ago. An ESOP is an arrangement involving an employee benefit trust, which, with financial assistance from the employer, acquires substantial quantities of employer shares or securities for subsequent allocation to employees. Companies can use an ESOP to see shareholding accumulate in comparatively friendly hands. In the event of a hostile takeover, an ESOP may play a crucial role in defence (Reid, 1990: 26). Under UK company law, however, use of an ESOP as a poison pill is not permitted (Carnell, 1990). In the USA, ESOPs were used in takeover defence in the 1980s.

With a highly leveraged capital structure, control of the company can be maintained with a relatively small equity holding. High gearing, with possible restrictive covenants on existing debt, may discourage a heavily leveraged buyout (LBO, see Chapter 11), since post-acquisition asset disposals to raise the cash to pay off the acquisition-related borrowing will be constrained. Thus financial engineering is unlikely to be profitable for the bidder.

Share repurchase also leads to increased gearing and often to higher EPS and net asset value per share, with a possible increase in the share price of the company. Moreover, it reduces the number of shares which could fall into the hands of predators. Repurchase during a bid requires the approval of the shareholders under Rule 37 of the Code.

Post-offer defences

In the UK, under the Code, the offer period is in most cases limited to 60 days from the posting of the offer document by the bidder, adding urgency to the target's tactics (see Table 6.2). Further, Rule 21 of the Code imposes upon the target management the obligation to get the approval of their shareholders for any frustrating action, which is defined widely to include the following:

- Issue of shares, or options or securities convertible into shares.
- Disposal or acquisition of assets of a material amount – normally 10 per cent of the target's assets.
- Contracts made except in the ordinary course of business.
- Golden parachutes arranged at the onset of a bid or when it is imminent.

Table 12.2 Post-offer defences against hostile takeover bids

Defence	Description and purpose
First response and pre-emption letter	Attack bid logic and price; advise target shareholders not to accept.
Defence document	Praise own performance and prospects; deride bid price and logic, form of finance and predator's track record.
Profit report/forecast	Report or forecast improved profits for past/current year to make offer look cheap.
Promise higher future dividends	Increase returns to shareholders; weaken predator's promise of superior returns.
Asset revaluation	Revalue properties, intangibles and brands; show bid undervalues target.
Share support campaign	Look for white knight or white squire; enlist own employee pension fund or ESOP; attempt to block control.
Regulatory appeal	Lobby antitrust/regulatory authorities to block bid.
Litigation	To enforce antitrust rules or force disclosure of nominee shareholders.
Acquisition and divestment	Buy a business to make target bigger or incompatible with bidder; sell 'crown jewels'; organise a management buyout; bid cost higher and bidder strategy thrown into disarray.
Unions/workforce	Enlist to lobby antitrust authorities or politicians and to attack bidder's plans for target.
Customers/suppliers	Enlist to lobby antitrust authorities or to show relations with them will be jeopardised if predator wins.
Red herring	Attack predator on peripheral matters.
Advertisement	Media campaign to discredit bid.

Source: Sudarsanam (1991).

Despite the above constraints, a range of tactics is still available in contested bids, as shown in Table 12.2. In addition to Rule 21 of the Code, other rules of the Code are also relevant to the target's defensive strategy. Rule 19 requires that each document issued to shareholders must satisfy the highest standard of accuracy, and that the information contained must be adequately and fairly presented. Advertisements must in most cases be cleared by the Panel and must avoid arguments and invective.

Profit forecasts are required by Rule 28 to be compiled with scrupulous care, and the target's financial adviser and accountant must ensure that they are so prepared. The reporting accountant's consent to the forecast must accompany it. The Panel monitors these forecasts long after the end of the bid, to see whether there was any deliberate distortion of the forecasts in the light of information available at the time the forecasts were made (see Case Study 6.2). Similarly, under Rule 29, asset valuations must be supported by an independent valuer. The actual use of the various defensive strategies in some of the hostile bids in the UK is described in Case Study 12.1.

Impact of defensive strategies

The chances of a successful defence against a hostile predator are more than even. In a sample of 238 contested bids covering the period 1983–9 and accounting for about 24 per cent of all bids for UK public companies, 147 (62 per cent of sample) successfully defended themselves. However, of these only 112 (47 per cent of sample) remained independent, with 35 falling to the embrace of white knights (Sudarsanam, 1994). Table 12.3 reports the frequency of use of 23 defensive strategies based on the same sample. Blocking is the use of any device, eg recapitalisation, to raise obstacles/cost to the bidder.

CASE STUDY 12.1   *Post-offer defensive strategies in UK hostile bids*

Note: The first company in each pair was the target. The year of the bid is in parentheses.

Divestment: In Hogg Robinson (HR) v. TSB (1987), HR proposed demerger of its insurance and travel agency businesses. The demerger was opposed by TSB, but approved by the shareholders. The bid failed.

Acquisition: In Barrow Hepburn (BH) v. Yule Catto (YC) (1986), BH announced a bid for Tor Coating and issued shares in consideration amounting to 12 per cent of its enlarged capital. YC condemned the acquisition, which won BH shareholder approval. YC bid failed.

White squire (WS): In Standard Chartered Bank (SCB) v. Lloyds Bank (1986), a leading Hong Kong business customer of SCB bought a strategic stake in SCB. The bid failed.

White knight (WK): In Martin the Newsagent (MN) v. W.H. Smith (1984), Guinness made a successful WK bid for MN.

Antitrust lobbying: In Arthur Bell v. Guinness (1985), Bell sought an MMC reference, but the OFT did not recommend one. Guinness won the bid.

Litigation: In Consolidated Goldfields (CGF) v. Minorco (1988), CGF appealed to US courts alleging violation of Federal securities and antitrust laws. Its American associate also filed an antitrust suit against Minorco which effectively killed the bid.

Political lobbying: In Rowntree v. Nestlé (1988), the Swiss chocolate company, there was heavy lobbying of MPs and ministers to win a reference to the MMC, but it was unsuccessful. The bid was won by Nestlé.

Suppliers: In Woolworth (W) v. Dixons (D) (1986), Woolworth was a high-street retailer of, among other things, confectionery, whereas Dixons was an electrical retailer. Many confectionery manufacturers like Cadbury and Rowntree, fearing loss of outlets for their products, opposed the bid.

Red herring: In Dee Corporation (D) v. Barker & Dobson (BD) (1987), D sacked its banker, Citibank, for its part in financing the leveraged bid.

Good news: In Britoil v. British Petroleum (1987), Britoil announced new oilfield discoveries.

Statistical test of the effectiveness of these strategies indicated that only the following strategies made a significant positive contribution to a successful defence (Sudarsanam, 1994):

- Entry of a white knight.
- Lobbying friendly shareholders.
- Support of the unions.
- Litigation.

Divestment had a significantly negative impact on defence. Advertising also did not help the targets in their defence, although its impact was not statistically significant. It appears that advertising during bids containing perhaps too much rhetoric and hyperbole lacks credibility. The remaining strategies, such as profit forecasts or

Table 12.3 Frequency of use of defensive strategies in the UK contested bids

Strategy	Times used	Frequency (%)
Knocking copy	157	66
Profit forecast	106	45
Increased dividend	102	43
Antitrust lobbying	79	33
Friendly shareholders	62	26
Profit report	51	21
White knight	46	19
Divestment	40	17
Regulatory appeal	36	15
Asset revaluation	32	13
Good news	29	12
Acquisition	29	12
Blocking	23	10
Red herring	22	9
Political lobbying	18	8
Union support	16	7
Pre-emption letter	15	6
White squire	13	6
Litigation	13	6
Customer support	12	5
Advertising	10	4
Management change	10	4
Bidder shareholder appeal	6	3

Source: Sudarsanam (1994). Based on a sample of 238 contested bids.

increased dividend announcements, made no difference to the outcome of hostile bids.

Cost of defence

Predictably, defending against a hostile bid can be an expensive affair. Targets in hostile bids incur both direct and indirect costs. Indirect costs are the value or opportunity cost of management time and the corporate resources devoted to defence. Direct costs are the fees paid to professional advisers and other costs. Table 12.4 provides an estimate of these costs for a typical bid valuing the target at £30 million, such costs amounting to 1.6 per cent of bid value. As a proportion of bid value, these costs may range from 1.6 per cent for large to 2 per cent for small bids (TOI Corporate

Table 12.4 Direct defence costs in hostile bids in the UK

(a) Breakdown of costs for a £30 million target (£000)

Merchant bank fees	320
Stockbroker fees	75
Accountant's fees	35
Solicitor's fees	35
Public relations	5
Printing	2
Miscellaneous	1
	473

(b) Direct defence costs in recent hostile bids

Target	Bidder	Year	Bid (£bn)	Costs (£m)
Plessey	GEC	1985	1.2	7.5
Woolworth	Dixons	1986	1.5	18.0
Pilkington	BTR	1986	1.2	9.7
Dee Corporation	Barker & Dobson	1987	2.0	14.4
RHM	GFW	1988	1.7	10.0
Manders	Kalon	1992	0.1	1.9
Owners Abroad	Airtours	1993	0.3	4.9

Sources: TOI Corporate Services, *Acquisitions Monthly*, January 1994; and company accounts and press reports.

Services, *Acquisitions Monthly*, January 1994). Costs in specific bids vary depending on the complexity of defence. The lower part of Table 12.4 provides evidence of direct costs in some recent hostile bids. For mega bids of £1 billion or more, the costs appear to be about 1 per cent.

Takeover defence outside the UK

Hostile bids are most prevalent in Anglo-Saxon countries. These countries differ among themselves in the regulation of takeover bids (De Mott, 1988). The defences available to target companies in hostile bids, therefore, also differ. In countries on the Continent and in Japan, hostile bids are very rare. The reasons for the absence of hostile bids are both cultural and institutional. Here we take a brief overview of the takeover defences in the USA and some Continental countries to give the reader a flavour of the differences among countries.

Takeover defence in the USA

Between the USA and the UK there are some similarities but also major differences in takeover regimes. In the USA, tender offers are regulated under the Williams Act (WA) 1968 by the Securities and Exchange Commission (SEC). WA imposes obligations on both offerors and targets, and prevents secret accumulation of large stakes by requiring disclosure of purchases when they take the shareholding in the target company to above 5 per cent.

WA defines when a tender offer commences and sets out the information to be disclosed, including the source of funds and the purpose of the offer. Tender offers must be kept open for twenty business days and extended by ten days if offer terms are amended or a competing offer emerges. The 'best price' and 'all holders' rule requires that the bidder buys the tendered shares at the best price during the offer, and that the tender must be open to all shareholders. WA prohibits an offeror from purchasing the shares subject to the offer, except pursuant to the offer itself. WA also makes illegal any fraudulent act including insider trading in connection with a tender offer.

WA imposes obligations on targets as well. It requires the target to inform its shareholders of its position on a tender offer within ten days. A target must disclose conflicts of interest, golden parachutes, the reasons for its recommendation, the identity of advisers and their compensation terms. Targets must refrain from materially misleading statements.

Since in the USA companies are incorporated under state laws, these laws have considerable impact on takeover defences. After the takeover binge of the 1980s, many states have amended their laws to shift the balance of power against the predator and in favour of the target management. State laws may in some cases render takeovers difficult to accomplish. They may permit the use of certain defensive devices by target companies. In addition, companies may be allowed to include in their charters provisions ('shark repellents') which frustrate or delay hostile bids.

Some states, such as Indiana, have legalised discriminatory poison pills and allow managements to consider non-shareholder interests in responding to hostile takeovers. Some defences are built into the

Table 12.5 Pre- and post-offer defences in the USA

Pre-offer	Post-offer
Staggered board of directors	Targeted repurchase (greenmail)
Super majority approval of merger	Standstill agreement with potential predator
Fair price requirement	Litigation
Issue of poison pill securities	Asset restructuring
Dual-class recapitalisation	Liability restructuring

Source: Ruback (1988).

target company charters and approved by shareholders, whereas others do not require such approval.

Ruback (1988) identifies a number of pre-offer and post-offer defences that target managements in the USA have used. These are shown in Table 12.5.

Super majority approval by, say, 75 per cent of the shareholders, makes consummation of merger very difficult. The requirement to extend a fair price to all shareholders makes the bid more expensive than a two-tier offer in which those who accept the offer earlier receive a higher price and those who tender late receive less. With a standstill agreement, the potential predator whose holding has been bought out in a greenmail agrees not to bid for an agreed period of, say, ten years.

The above defensive strategies encompass many others. Asset restructuring covers asset lock-up, sale of 'crown jewels' and 'Pacman defence'. Liability restructuring includes recapitalisation to increase leverage, ESOPs and stock lock-up. In an asset lock-up, the target agrees to sell to a friendly buyer those parts which the predator might covet in the event of a bid. In a Pacman defence, the target turns on the predator and makes a counterbid. A stock lock-up involves the issue of shares to a friendly party, so as to prevent the predator from gaining a controlling stake.

If an acquisition falls within the scope of the Hart–Scott–Rodino Antitrust Improvement Act 1976 (HSR Act), the bidder has to file its premerger notification on announcing the tender offer. The HSR Act imposes a waiting period of 30 days before the bidder may accept the tendered shares. The proposed acquisition may be challenged on antitrust grounds by the Federal Trade Commission (FTC) or the

Department of Justice under Section 7 of the Clayton Act. The target can sue to obtain injunctive relief to restrain an acquisition that would violate Section 7.

Takeover defences on the Continent

There are substantial differences between Continental European countries and the UK or the USA in the defences available to target companies. In general, hostile takeovers are much more difficult to win because of the panoply of effective defences that targets can deploy. The differences arise from philosophical, cultural and statutory factors. There is a clear distinction between the Anglo-Saxon tradition, where the shareholders' interests predominate over the interests of other stakeholders, and the Continental tradition.

In the Continental tradition, these stakeholders often have an equal claim. In many Continental countries, the board of directors have a responsibility to their company rather than to their shareholders. The former requires that directors take account of the interests of shareholders, employees, customers and the local communities in making their decisions. This broader responsibility is reflected in both company statute and corporate practice. For example, the Dutch company law reflects the philosophy that 'the balance of power should not unduly favour the shareholders. It must also take into account the interests of other stakeholders such as employees' (Peter Verloop, *Acquisitions Monthly*, 1991).

In a report on barriers to takeovers in the European Community, Coopers & Lybrand (1989) classified such barriers into structural, technical and cultural barriers. They are barriers to an easy transfer of management and ownership, and are so defined from an essentially UK point of view, in which, as embodied in the Code, the shareholders are the final arbiters of the merits of a bid. The term 'barriers' is, therefore, used to denote a rule, an arrangement or attitude which limits or obstructs this freedom and right of shareholders.

While a detailed examination of the barriers is made in Chapter 16, here their role as defences against unwelcome bids is highlighted. These barriers consist of legal and regulatory rules, institutional arrangements and cultural attitudes. The degree to which they are strong and impede takeovers varies from one country to another. Employees are given varying rights in different countries in the context of takeovers. In Denmark, Germany, Luxembourg and the Netherlands, they are represented on supervisory boards, and therefore have a say in determining whether a bid will be accepted.

In France, employee representatives may attend board meetings, but without voting powers. Trade unions do not have to be consulted about a merger, but in companies with more than 50 employees they can attend meetings between employers and employees. Workers' councils are consulted about bids, but have no power to block them. In Germany, such councils have rights regarding working conditions and hiring and firing (Franks and Mayer, 1990: 206). In all countries, employees have some redundancy rights.

One share one vote (OSOV) is not a principle adhered to in all countries. Issue of non-voting shares is common. In France, listed companies may limit transferability of shares by contract or by articles of incorporation. Shareholders who have held shares for a specified period may also be entitled to double votes in France. Among all the EU countries, managements in the Netherlands have the greatest freedom to issue shares with limited voting rights.

Dutch companies can issue priority shares which confer on the holders a substantial degree of control over the issuing company. Often these shares are issued to an institution whose directors may include the managing or supervisory directors of the issuing company itself. Preference shares with limited financial but full voting rights may be issued to a trust office, whose main purpose is to serve the interests of the company and its business. Non-voting depository receipts, which separate the voting rights from the financial rights, are also issued. An administration office holds the shares, exercises the voting rights and issues the depository receipts. Binding appointment of directors can be made either by a change in company statutes or by vote of the priority shareholders. Ordinary shareholders are then deprived of the ability to appoint their own directors (Kabir *et al.*, 1994).

Kabir *et al.*'s recent empirical study of the use of defensive strategies by 177 Dutch companies has found that 79 firms issued priority shares, 70 issued depository receipts, 64 made binding appointments and 7 firms restricted the voting rights. Only 16 firms remained unprotected by any of these defensive measures. Recent changes to the Amsterdam Stock Exchange rules, however, set limits to the extent and number of defensive actions that listed companies can take (Carrington and Pessôa de Araújo, 1994: ch. 6).

In countries like France, Germany and the Netherlands, the management can limit the voting rights to a maximum ranging from 5 to 15 per cent. The original intention behind this discretion was to protect small shareholders from others who acquire a large minority stake and thereby exercise virtual control over the company.

CASE STUDY 12.2   Limiting voting rights as a takeover defence

Hostile bid for Feldmühle Nobel of Germany
In 1988 the Flick brothers (known as Mick and Muck) made a tender offer for 50 per cent of Feldmühle Nobel (FN). FN was born of the restructuring of Feldmühle, sold by their uncle to Deutsche Bank (DB) for DM5 billion. DB sold the investment portfolio of Feldmühle and recovered the price it had paid. It floated the remaining businesses as FN for DM2 billion. DB's representative also became chairman of Feld-mühle's supervisory board. DB was particularly keen to preserve the independence of its own creation. It therefore advised Feldmühle's management to follow its own example and restrict voting rights to no more than 5 per cent.

BSN of France moves against hostile stake building
In 1992 BSN feared that Agnelli, the Italian holder of 5.8 per cent of the shares in BSN, might make a hostile bid. It therefore proposed restricting the voting rights of any shareholder to a maximum of 6 per cent, or 12 per cent if they had double voting rights. BSN argued that the restriction was necessary to avoid the threat of an investor exercising disproportion-ate influence over the company by buying a minority stake.

Source: *Financial Times*, 21.6.1988 and 25.6.1992.

However, this ability to limit the voting rights has often been used to fend off hostile bids, as shown in Case Study 12.2.

Large or 'structure' companies in the Netherlands are required to have supervisory boards which wield tremendous powers to dismiss managing directors, adopt annual accounts and veto certain important management decisions. The directors of the supervisory board have responsibility to shareholders, but the interests of the company can override this responsibility. As a result, Dutch public companies are better protected from hostile takeovers than their counterparts in most European countries.

In Continental countries, managers also enjoy a high degree of protection. In Germany, the management board of directors is appointed by the supervisory board for a fixed term of up to five years. During that time, they can only be removed for clear breaches of duty. Removal of the supervisory board members requires the approval of 75 per cent of the votes of shareholders.

The corporate governance structure plays an important role in Germany, where only a small proportion of public companies, about 600, are listed on the stock exchange. The banks play a crucial role as lenders, equity holders and share depositories. Shareholders

CASE STUDY 12.3   Role of banks in German takeovers

- In the Feldmühle bid, Deutsche Bank held 8 per cent, but with the proxy votes which it cast, the bank was able to thwart the Flick brothers.

- In the Krupp bid for Hoesch, DB chaired the supervisory board of Hoesch and supported the bid, even though it was opposed by the head of the management board.

- In the Pirelli bid for Continental, DB again chaired the supervisory board and voted a large number of proxy shares. It was closely involved in shaping Continental's attitude to the bid. It opposed the bid, but supported merger talks between the two companies. When the head of the management board opposed the merger, DB was instrumental in removing him.

Source: Franks and Mayer (1994).

often deposit their shares with banks which then exercise the proxy votes on behalf of these shareholders. Although shareholders can direct the depositories to vote according to their wishes, in practice, the proxy votes are determined by the banks' own preferences.

Although German banks own less than 10 per cent of voting shares in public companies, their shareholding in combination with the proxy votes can be decisive. Further, German banks also have representation on the supervisory boards, sometimes as chairmen. Franks and Mayer (1994) note that banks' power is especially strong in companies with widely dispersed shareholding, precisely the companies where a hostile bidder has a good chance of success by appealing direct to small shareholders. The power of banks to restrict or allow takeovers is demonstrated in Case Study 12.3.

The above examples show that defences against hostile bids for Continental companies can be formidable. These are reinforced by the unfavourable attitude of German companies and shareholders to hostile bids. The adversarial nature of hostile bids is perhaps anathema to the more consensual Continental tradition. This is reflected in the fact that German companies avoid making hostile bids for companies in other countries.

Overview

This chapter has outlined the various strategies available to target company managements in the UK, and has provided some empirical evidence on their effectiveness. The different strategies have been illustrated from actual UK bids in which they were deployed. The direct transactional cost of takeover defence has been indicated. No information on the indirect cost – that is, the cost of management time spent in defence and the cost of poor managerial decisions made due to that diversion – is available. Some comparative information on defence strategies available to targets in the USA and the Continental countries has been provided by way of contrast. The next chapter provides an assessment of acquisitions by evaluating the empirical evidence.

References and further reading

Carnell, D. (1990) 'ESOP: Opportunities knock', *Accountancy*, February, 105–7.

Carrington, N., and B. Pessôa de Araújo (1994) *Acquiring Companies and Businesses in Europe*, Chancery Law Publishers.

Coopers & Lybrand (1989) *Barriers to Takeovers in the European Community*, Department of Trade and Industry, HMSO, London.

De Mott, D.A. (1988) 'Comparative dimensions of takeover regulation', in J. Coffee, L. Lowenstein and S. Rose-Ackerman (eds.), *Knights, Raiders and Targets*, Oxford University Press.

Franks, J., and C. Mayer (1990) 'Takeovers', *Economic Policy*, April, 189–231.

Franks, J., and C. Mayer (1994) 'The ownership and control of German corporations', working paper, London Business School.

Herzel, L., and R.W. Shepro (1990) *Bidders and Targets: Mergers and acquisitions in the US*, Basil Blackwell.

Kabir, R., D. Cantrijn and A. Jeunink (1994) 'Takeover defenses, ownership structure and stock returns: an empirical analysis with Dutch data', working paper, Tilburgh University.

Reid, D. (1990) *ESOPS: Employee share ownership plans in the UK*, Butterworths.

Ruback, R. (1988) 'An overview of takeover defence economy', in A. Auerbach (ed.), *Mergers and Acquisitions*, Chicago University Press.

Sudarsanam, P.S. (1991) 'Defensive strategies of target firms in UK contested takeovers', *Managerial Finance*, **17**, 6, 47–56.

Sudarsanam, P.S. (1994) 'Less than lethal weapons: defence strategies in UK contested takeovers', *Acquisitions Monthly*, January, 30–2.

13

Assessing the success of acquisitions

The cover page of *International Business Week*, 3 June 1985, carried the question, 'Do mergers really work?'. In its cover page of 21 April 1988, *Financial Weekly* asserted, 'Hostile bids don't work'. The magazine then followed up this caption with another 'Bids – the mania returns', in its 21 July 1988 issue. The rhetorical question and similar proclamations reflect the widespread perception that mergers are not successful and are often driven by irrational impulses. To what extent is this perception based on carefully assembled evidence? Who are the winners and losers in mergers and acquisitions?

The outcome of acquisitions and mergers is of considerable interest to all the stakeholders in the merging firms. These include shareholders, managers, employees, the consumers and the wider community. All these groups may be affected to different degrees by the changes brought about by the merger. In this chapter, we assess the 'success' of mergers from different perspectives. The methodological problems in making this assessment are indicated, and broad conclusions from the major empirical studies are outlined. The survey of empirical evidence is not exhaustive, and the interested reader can pursue this subject with the suggested further reading.

Defining success

A merger involves the coming together of two companies – the acquirer and the acquired. In each company there is a range of stakeholders, including the shareholders, managers, employees, consumers and the community at large. The antitrust authorities, such as the Office of Fair Trading (OFT) and the Monopolies and Mergers Commission (MMC) in the UK, and the European Commission acting under the Treaty of Rome or the Merger Regulation (see Chapter 5), are the custodians of the interests of consumers and the community at large, and regulate mergers and acquisitions. The MMC's brief that mergers which operate against the public interest should be disallowed embodies this role.

In this chapter, we are concerned with assessing the success of mergers from the perspectives of shareholders, managers and employees. As we have seen, the interests of these three groups do not always coincide. One group can win at the expense of the others. For example, a takeover can lead to high shareholder returns, but loss of managerial jobs. This conflict often drives managerial resistance to takeover bids (see Chapter 12). Similarly, acquisitions are often motivated by efficiency considerations and rationalisation of the operation of the two companies involved, with a consequent redundancy among the workforce or loss of pension rights. We look at these groups in turn.

Acquisitions and shareholders

According to modern finance theory, managers' decisions are aimed at enhancing shareholder wealth. How do acquisitions stand up to this test? If we can show that shareholders are better off – that the value of their shares has increased as a result of the acquisition – then this test is satisfied. While conceptually simple, the test in practice poses a number of problems.

First, we need a benchmark against which the value increase must be judged. Second, the time scale for assessing the wealth increase needs to be established. With a cash bid, this is not a concern, since the target shareholders accept cash and thus 'freeze' their gains. With a share exchange, what is an attractive deal at the time of the takeover may turn out to be a disaster. For the acquiring company shareholders, the long term is important whatever the payment currency.

Researchers have tried to tackle the benchmark problem, but without complete success. This is due to the absence of unambiguously and incontrovertibly good yardsticks. As regards the time scale, we need to look at shareholder wealth experience both at the time of an acquisition and for several years afterwards. The benchmark problem is much more serious for long-term performance measurement, since it is compounded when an inappropriate benchmark is used over a long period.

Measuring shareholder wealth changes

The common approach to this is the so-called abnormal returns methodology, which compares the returns to shareholders of both bidders and targets during a period surrounding the takeover announcement, to 'normal' returns from a period unaffected by the 'event'. The event is the takeover announcement in the present instance, but it could be any other, such as divestment, rights issue or dividend payment. This genre of measurement technique is therefore called 'event study' methodology. The period surrounding the event which is observed is called the event period or 'event window'.

The abnormal return, AR, due to the acquisition event is therefore

$$AR = R - E(R) \tag{1}$$

where R is the actual return measured during the event period and $E(R)$ is the benchmark return expected in the absence of that event. Measuring R is a fairly simple matter and requires the calculation of share price changes and dividends paid during the event period. Estimating $E(R)$ is much more sophisticated.

In the research literature, $E(R)$ is estimated using share price and dividends data from the 'estimation period', which is assumed to be uncontaminated by the event, so that an unbiased benchmark can be set up. For example, if a takeover is announced today, the benchmark could be estimated from data relating to one or two years ending, say, two months before the announcement. In the case of studies using monthly data, the estimation period is often five years, ending a few months before the announcement.

Estimating the benchmark returns

One of the commonest models employed in the literature is the 'market model', a relationship between an individual stock's return and the return on 'the market':

$$R_{it} = \alpha_i + \beta_i R_{mt} + e_{it} \tag{2}$$

where R_{it} and R_{mt} are the returns during t (a day or a month) on company i's stock and on a broad-based stock market index such as the UK's Financial Times All-Share Index or the American S & P Index, proxying for 'the market'. α is the intercept and β is beta, also called the systematic risk. e_{it} is a random error which averages out to zero. The model's parameters, α_i and β_i, are estimated by running a regression of R_{it} on R_{mt} over an appropriate estimation period. The estimated parameters are then used to calculate normal return $E(R_i)$ for each company i and the abnormal return as follows:

$$AR_{it} = R_{it} - E(R_i) \tag{3}$$

$$AR_{it} = R_{it} - \{\alpha_i + \beta_i R_{mt}\} \tag{4}$$

If the takeover event is expected to create additional value for the shareholders of i, then AR will be positive. It will be zero if the effect of the takeover is neutral. To test whether the event has generated positive returns, statistical tests are undertaken with a sample of takeovers.

Most of the early literature has used monthly returns. Since daily share price data are now available more easily, in recent studies they are used to calculate normal and abnormal returns. Although with daily data we can locate the event more precisely than with monthly data, the latter has less volatility and may, therefore, lead to more stable or reliable parameter estimates.

Use of the market model has some estimation shortcomings which reduce its reliability. Two of these interrelated deficiencies are low-volume (thin) trading and size disparity between sample firms and the market proxy. They lead to wrong benchmarks, and many researchers have attempted to use more refined procedures to minimise these problems. Two other models which to some extent avoid one or the other of these problems are the adjusted market model, in which the parameter estimates are corrected for thin trading, and the market-adjusted model, which avoids the necessity of estimating α and β. The latter uses the return on the market R_m as the normal return and does not adjust for risk. A further variant of the methodology is the use of the CAPM (see Chapter 9).

Empirical evidence on shareholder returns

We present this evidence in two steps: the short-term performance and the long-term performance. First the UK evidence and then some comparative international evidence are presented. Table 13.1 shows the abnormal returns to targets and bidders in completed

Table 13.1 Abnormal returns for target and bidder shareholders surrounding
UK takeover announcements

Study, period and sample size	Window	Data	Target (%)	Bidder (%)
Firth (1980); 1969–75; 486 targets	Announcement month	Monthly returns	28	−6.3
Franks and Harris (1989); 1955–85; 1445 targets	Announcement month	Monthly returns	22	0.0
Limmack (1991); 1977–86; 462 targets	Bid period	Monthly returns	31	−0.2
Sudarsanam *et al.* (1993); 1980–9; 171 share offers	−5 to +5 days around announcement Day 0	Daily	21	−2.0

Note: Target returns in all studies and bidder returns in Firth and Sudarsanam *et al.* are significant at the 5% significance level or better.

takeovers reported in four UK studies based on the market model. Limmack (1991) and Sudarsanam *et al.*'s (1993) results are thin trading adjusted. In Limmack, the bid period extends from the beginning of the announcement month to the end of the completion month. Franks and Harris (1989) also report using the market-adjusted and CAPM models. Results based on these alternative models are generally similar for the targets, but more variable for bidders.

It is thus clear that, in the short window surrounding a bid, the target shareholders are the overwhelming winners, whereas the bidder shareholders either lose or scrape through. The combined abnormal sterling gains to the target and bidder shareholders are reported as: −£36.6m (Firth); £2.63m (Franks and Harris) and £5.84m (Limmack). When set against the average bid size, the combined returns are very small indeed. Sudarsanam *et al.* (1993) report a combined return of 3.09 per cent significant at the 5 per cent level.

The post-merger, long-term performance data are available only for the acquirer, since the target companies are most often de-listed. Evidence on post-merger performance is shown in Table 13.2. Franks and Harris's study highlights the problem that different

Table 13.2 Post-merger performance of acquirers

Study, period and sample size	Window	Data	Return (%)
Firth (1980); 1969–75; 434 acquirers	+1 to +36 months	Monthly	−0.0
Franks and Harris (1989); 1955–85; 1048 acquirers	+1 to +24 months	Monthly	−12.6
Limmack (1991); 1977–86; 448 acquirers	+1 to +24 months	Monthly	−4.5

Note: + refers to the month after the bid has been completed.
Returns reported by Franks and Harris and Limmack are
statistically significant at the 5% level.

benchmarks can lead to different conclusions about the impact of
acquisitions on shareholder wealth. With the market-adjusted model
and CAPM, they report 4.8 and 4.5 per cent over the months +1 to
+24, making acquisitions a more attractive proposition for acquiring
company shareholders. The benchmark effect is specifically
addressed by Franks *et al.* (1991) with their study of American
takeovers (see below).

The UK evidence may be summarised as follows:

- Takeovers are at best neutral in overall value creation for the
  shareholders together, and at worst modestly value destroying.
- The target shareholders gain almost exclusively from takeovers.
- There is some evidence of a wealth transfer from the acquirer to
  acquired shareholders. This follows from the negative returns to
  acquirer shareholders and the broad neutrality of the overall
  effect.

That only target shareholders gain does not by itself create the
presumption that acquisitions do not rest on sound value creation
logic. An acquisition can increase the cash flows of the combined
firm compared to the sum of the cash flows of the two pre-
acquisition firms. But these cash flows may not accrue to the benefit
of the acquiring company shareholders if their managers are
overgenerous to the target shareholders. This explanation is consis-

tent with Roll's (1986) hubris hypothesis that managers tend to overpay for their acquisitions because they overestimate their own capacity to create value from those acquisitions.

According to the models we presented in Chapter 9, change in valuation of a company is in general a function of the change in cash flows and earnings. If mergers do create value for shareholders, such added value should reflect the increase in earnings and cash flows of the merged entity compared to those of the pre-merger firms. We next review evidence on the question of whether mergers lead to enhanced earnings and cash flows.

Accounting-based performance evaluation of mergers

Disappointing Marriage: A study of the gains from mergers by Meeks (1977) captures the scepticism which has greeted takeovers. Meeks studied the impact of mergers on the profitability of the merging companies. His study has been followed by many others (Kumar, 1984: ch. 5; Cosh *et al.*, 1980). The basic methodology in accounting-based studies is to compare reported post-merger profits to the weighted average of the pre-bid profits of each of the merging firms. To allow for changes in profits brought about by factors independent of the merger, they are calculated relative to the performance of the companies' own industries, or the performance of a sample of non-merging firms. The results from the above studies are summarised in Table 13.3.

In sum, the verdict of these studies is not wholly adverse to mergers. Moreover, a substantial minority of mergers studied (about 40 per cent) actually improved profitability, even though the average sample performance was negative. What this means is that certain types of merger can be successful. It appears that some acquirers do have the skill, judgement and shrewdness to pick the winners and make them work.

An important problem in making comparisons of profitability between pre- and post-merger firms is that the latter is affected by the way the merger has been accounted for. It will be recalled (see Chapter 10) that acquisition accounting generally gives rise to goodwill, the possible increase in asset values of the acquired firm due to fair value accounting, and the freezing of pre-acquisition reserves. If goodwill is not written off immediately, the net assets base will increase. Since an increase in asset values means higher depreciation and lower profits, the ratio of net profits to net assets may also fall.

Thus acquisition accounting may lead to a fall in after-merger

Table 13.3 Change in profitability of merging firms in the UK over 3 and 5
years after merger (profitability = net income/net assets)

Study, period and sample size	Control sample	Over 3 years	Over 5 years
		after merger	
Meeks (1977); 1964–71; 164	Industry normalised	Significant decline	Significant decline
Kumar (1984); 1967–74; 241	Industry normalised	Significant decline	Decline not significant
Cosh et al. (1980); 1967–70; 225	Non-merged firms	Significant improvement	Significant improvement

Note: The benchmark in each study was the 5-year average profitability
before merger. Sample size is the number of mergers. It is smaller for the
5-year comparison.

profits compared to merger accounting. This bias must be corrected
for in using accounting data to assess merger performance. In the
studies summarised in Table 13.3, Kumar and Cosh et al. did not
adjust for this accounting bias, which may have understated the
post-merger performance of their sample firms. Their results,
therefore, lend even more credence to a positive view of merger
performance.

More recently, researchers, aware of the limitations imposed by
accounting rules, have used operating cash flow as a profit measure.
The first study to make use of cash flow with American data, by
Healy et al. (1992), is discussed later in this chapter. Manson et al.
(1994) replicate the Healy et al. approach for a sample of 38 UK
takeovers completed in 1985 to 1987. They compare the five-year
median operating cash flow of the acquirer to the median cash flow
that could be expected when allowance is made for the erosion of
the pre-merger competitive advantage of either of the merging
firms.

Manson et al. report that mergers lead to improved operating cash
flow, and that the increase in cash flow is positively related to the
total abnormal returns to the two firms during the bid. This suggests
that the stock market correctly anticipates and capitalises the
expected increase in cash flow from the acquisition. While the
particular measure of cash flow (operating rather than cash flows

available for shareholders) employed in this study may be questionable, the study counters the often one-sided accounting view of mergers as failures. The use of cash flow to measure performance also overcomes the weakness of the accrual profit measures used in the earlier studies.

Before we pronounce ourselves entirely satisfied about the value-enhancing merits of mergers, we need more evidence based on large samples. Further, in addition to the focus on operating cash flow, one also needs to consider non-operating cash flow from disposal of non-core businesses, since at least in the 1980s the strategic logic of acquisitions often encompassed selective divestitures to achieve a more coherent focus to the combined business of the acquirer and the acquired firms (see Chapter 9 on the relevance of divestments to target valuation). Exclusive focus on operating cash flow gains is likely to understate the beneficial impact of acquisitions.

Merger type and post-merger performance

Our discussion in Chapter 3 indicated that the value creation potential in a merger depended upon its specific type. Many researchers have investigated whether related mergers in which the merging companies have potential economy of scale or scope perform better than unrelated conglomerate mergers. The evidence to date is inconclusive in terms of returns to shareholders (Sudarsanam *et al.*, 1993). In terms of accounting profitability, Hughes (1993) summarises evidence from a number of empirical studies to show that conglomerate mergers perform better than horizontal mergers. He argues that one reason for this result may be that horizontal mergers generate more serious post-merger integration problems. The impact of merger type on post-merger performance, however, remains to be explored further.

Acquisitions and managers

Acquisitions affect the managers of the acquirer and the acquired companies differently. For the acquirer managers, they offer new opportunities to enhance their company's competitive advantage, operational efficiency and financial performance, thereby increasing shareholder value. They also allow managers scope for maximising their own utility by increasing remuneration and job security. For the acquired company managers, a takeover causes uncertainty and stress because of the expected changes. They now have to adapt to the new bosses and their culture. For many, a takeover may mean loss of power, status and freedom to innovate, or redundancy (see Chapters 4 and 14).

Whether or not all of these dire consequences will be visited upon acquired firm managers depends upon the motivation and the strategic logic of the acquisition. For example, a merger based on expected synergies may not lead to redundancies, whereas one driven by rationalisation in a mature industry is likely to. Similarly, a disciplinary takeover with its presumption of inefficient target management will, almost by definition, result in high turnover of that management.

Franks and Mayer (1994) document that top management turnover is high after a hostile takeover compared to that in friendly takeovers and in non-acquired companies. For a sample of 34 recommended and 31 hostile UK bids, they estimate that 90 per cent of executive and non-executive directors of targets resigned after the takeover, whereas only 50 per cent did so in friendly bids. Both these turnover rates are much higher than for a smaller sample of 10 non-acquired firms.

The acquiring companies' managers, in contrast, are 'sitting pretty'. An immediate advantage of an acquisition is that the firm becomes larger. Acquisition accelerates the growth of a firm compared to organic growth. Managerial remuneration is often positively linked to firm size. Indeed, this may be one of the motivations behind the acquisition. Firth (1991) provides evidence consistent with this managerial self-interest.

For a sample of 171 UK acquisitions in the period 1974–80, Firth finds that acquisitions that are well received by the stock market lead to significant increases in managerial rewards. Even acquisitions with negative abnormal returns at bid announcement appear to reward senior management. Firth concludes that the acquisition process leads invariably to an increase in managerial remuneration, and this appears to be predicated on the increased size of the company.

Acquisitions are not always a one-way ticket to great fortune for acquirer managers. Many of them do make a hash of their acquisitions, as the evidence from the accounting-based studies suggests. Acquisition failure can be horrendously costly to the managers. Some of the more spectacular and frequent acquirers of the go-go 1980s ended up in receivership, and some were subsequently taken over, as shown in Table 13.4. Companies such as the

Table 13.4 Aftermath of high-level acquisition activity

Acquisitive company	Acquisitions since 1985		Fate (January 1991)
	Number	Value (£m)	
British & Commonwealth	20	1422	Receivership
Coloroll	14	403	Receivership
Leisure Investments	10	228	Receivership
Parkfield	34	140	Administration
Ferranti	9	439	Heavily divested
Midsummer Leisure	13	55	Acquired in hostile bid
Parkway	23	68	Taken over
Saatchi & Saatchi	31	584	Financial restructuring
WPP	45	1292	Financial restructuring

Source: A. Blackman, *Acquisitions Monthly*, January 1991.

advertising agencies Saatchi & Saatchi and WPP made big acquisitions in the USA, subsequently went into financial restructuring, and are just emerging from intensive care. Ferranti went into receivership in 1993.

Acquisitions and employees

Acquisitions may have twofold effects on the level of employment in the acquired company, and on the wages, pensions and other rights of employees. In rationalising acquisitions, the acquirer seeks to improve the efficiency and productivity of the target's operations. One of the easiest targets for rationalisation is the head office of the target. With many of its functions taken over by the parent's head office, redundancy of target head office is likely to follow. For example, during Tesco's bid for William Low in July 1994, it was reported that significant job losses were likely among the 300 staff at Wm Low's head office (*Financial Times*, 4.8.1994). Hanson Trust's acquisition strategy seeks to make 'the target's assets work harder', as exemplified in its acquisition of Berec in 1981 (see Case Study 13.1).

In the UK, employment law gives some protection to employees in the context of takeovers, in terms of, for example, unfair dismissal, redundancy terms, change in the terms and conditions of employment, and pension benefits. The rights of employees also

CASE STUDY 13.1   Hanson's rationalisation of Berec

Berec, the manufacturer of Ever Ready batteries, was taken over by Hanson in December 1981. Immediately after the acquisition, Berec's head office, sales and marketing staff was cut from 550 to 75 and relocated. The number of management layers was reduced from nine to three. UK factory staff was cut by 60 per cent.

Source: *Financial Times*, 22.8.1990.

depend on whether shares or businesses of the target are purchased. In the latter case, employees may receive the protection of the Transfer of Undertaking (Protection of Employment) Regulation 1981 (TUPE), which implements the European Community's Acquired Rights Directive (Dawson, 1994). There are similar employment protection rules in many Continental European countries.

US evidence on success of acquisitions

The US literature on acquisitions is voluminous, and the event study methodology has its origin in the USA. Here we present an overview of the research findings relating to mergers and acquisitions in the USA. The US-based research findings are broadly consistent with the above observations concerning the acquisitions performance in the UK context. Jensen and Ruback (1983) summarise the results of thirteen event studies of the impact of acquisitions on shareholder returns, with almost all of them based on pre-1980 takeovers. Jarrell and Poulsen (1989) examine a large sample drawn from three decades. Their results are shown in Table 13.5.

A tender offer in the USA is made directly to the shareholders and, in general, is not recommended. A merger is an offer made to target management, who then recommend it to their shareholders. Hostile tender offers tend to generate higher returns for target shareholders, as we would expect. The returns to shareholders are fairly similar to those available in UK takeovers (see Table 13.1 above).

The long-term performance of acquirers has been a subject of some lively debate in the US literature. Franks *et al.* (1991) argue that the negative long-term returns to acquirer shareholders are due to an inappropriate benchmark (i.e. the market return in the market model in equation (2) above) in the presence of the size effect (see

Table 13.5 Abnormal returns to shareholders in USA surrounding takeover announcements

Study, period and sample size	Event window	Type of offer	Abnormal returns (%)	
			Target	Bidder
Jensen and Ruback (1983); mostly pre-1980; summary of 13 studies	Various	Merger Tender	20 30	0 4
Jarrell and Poulsen[1] (1989); 1963–86; 526	−20 to +10 days	Tender	29	1

Note: [1]Abnormal returns significant at 5% or better.

our earlier discussion on estimating abnormal returns). They use alternative benchmarks which explicitly adjust for size of the acquiring company, and find that acquirers' post-merger performance is neutral.

Agrawal *et al.* (1992), however, rebut this conclusion and provide evidence that Franks *et al.*'s results are not valid across different time periods. Loderer and Martin (1992) broadly confirm Franks *et al.*'s conclusions, although in their study also the returns to acquirers depend upon the period of observation. Before this controversy can be settled, more research needs to be carried out.

Performance evaluation of acquisitions based on accounting measures provides results similar to those in the UK. Ravenscraft and Scherer (1987: ch. 4) conclude that mergers do not improve operating profits. On the other hand, Healy *et al.* (1992), using cash flow rather than accrual profits as performance measure, with a sample of 50 large acquisitions, find that merged firms show significant improvements in asset productivity relative to their industries, leading to higher operating cash flow returns. Moreover, there is a strong positive correlation between post-merger increase in operating cash flows and abnormal stock returns at merger announcements, indicating that expectations of economic improvements underlie the equity revaluations of the merging firms.

Impact of acquisitions on US managers

Walsh (1988) examines the top management turnover after acquisitions for a sample of 55 acquisitions during 1975–9. He matches this against a control sample of 30 non-acquired companies. Over the five years following the acquisitions, 59 per cent of the top management in the acquired companies are removed, whereas with the control sample the turnover is only 33 per cent. The first year's turnover is much more dramatic, with 25 and 6 per cent turnover respectively for the two samples. Neither the type of acquisition (i.e. related, horizontal, conglomerate, etc.) nor the size difference between the acquirer and the acquired could explain the high incidence of top management turnover.

Walsh and Ellwood (1991) extend the above study to investigate the relation between the pre-merger performance of the acquired companies and post-acquisition top management turnover. For a larger sample of 59 acquired companies and 75 non-acquired control companies, Walsh and Ellwood find turnover is 61 per cent for the acquired and 34 per cent for the control sample. Interestingly, there is no link between post-acquisition turnover and the acquired company's pre-acquisition performance measured by the cumulative abnormal returns. This calls into doubt the hypothesis that top management turnover is due to the disciplinary impact of a takeover.

Martin and McConnell (1991), however, provide evidence consistent with the disciplinary model. They classify a takeover as disciplinary if there is top management turnover in the target firm in the two years after the takeover. They examine the five-year pre-takeover performance of the targets in terms of cumulative abnormal returns in both disciplinary and non-disciplinary takeovers. The results are that turnover increases after a takeover. For example, in the fourteen months after takeover, the rate of turnover for the top executive is 42 per cent, whereas the annual turnover in the previous five years is only 10 per cent. Further, targets with high turnover underperform their industry in the pre-takeover period.

In sum, the evidence on management turnover in the US acquisitions confirms that acquisitions do lead to a substantial degree of top managerial job losses, especially in the first year or two. However, ambiguity surrounds the proposition that such turnover represents the disciplinary effect of the takeover, since the relation between turnover and pre-bid performance is not clear cut.

Overview

This chapter has briefly surveyed the empirical evidence on post-merger performance from the points of view of shareholders, managers and employees of merging firms. Evidence from both the USA and the UK has been presented. While there is a consensus that target shareholders gain wealth from mergers, evidence on wealth gains to acquiring company shareholders is not conclusive. Performance evaluation based on accounting measures similarly produces inconclusive results. Acquisitions, however, lead to significant top-level management changes, especially in hostile takeovers. The next chapter provides further evidence on post-acquisition performance based on surveys of acquiring managers, who also supply their own reasoning for acquisition failure.

References and further reading

Agrawal, A., J.F. Jaffe and G.N. Mandelker (1992) 'Post-merger performance of acquiring firms: a re-examination of an anomaly', *Journal of Finance*, **47**, 1605–21.

Cosh, A., A. Hughes and A. Singh (1980) 'The causes and effects of mergers: an empirical investigation for the UK at the microeconomic level', in D.C. Mueller (ed.), *The Determinants and Effects of Mergers*, Oelschlager, Gunn & Hain, Cambridge, Mass.

Dawson, W. (1994) 'Employment responsibilities and objectives', in *Company Acquisitions Handbook*, Tolley Publishing Co.

Firth, M. (1980) 'Takeovers, shareholder returns and the theory of the firm', *Quarterly Journal of Economics*, **94**, 235–60.

Firth, M. (1991) 'Corporate takeovers, stockholder returns and executive rewards', *Managerial and Decision Economics*, **12**, 421–8.

Franks, J. and R. Harris (1989) 'Shareholder wealth effects of corporate takeovers: the UK experience 1955–85', *Journal of Financial Economics*, **23**, 225–49.

Franks, J. and C. Mayer (1994) 'Post merger management change and restructuring', working paper, London Business School.

Franks, J., R. Harris and S. Titman (1991) 'The post-merger share price performance of acquiring firms', *Journal of Financial Economics*, **29**, 81–96.

Healy, P., K. Palepu and R. Ruback (1992) 'Does corporate performance improve after mergers?', *Journal of Financial Economics*, **31**, 135–75.

Hughes, A. (1993) 'Mergers and economic performance in the UK: a survey of the empirical evidence 1950–90', in M. Bishop and J. Kay (eds.), *European Mergers and Merger Policy*, Oxford University Press.

Jarrell, G.A. and A.B. Poulsen (1989) 'The returns to acquiring firms in tender offers: evidence from three decades', *Financial Management*, Autumn, 12–19.

Jensen, M. and R. Ruback (1983) 'The market for corporate control: the scientific evidence', *Journal of Financial Economics*, **11**, 5–50.

Kumar, M. (1984) *Growth, Acquisition and Investment*, Cambridge University Press.

Limmack, R. (1991) 'Corporate mergers and shareholder wealth effects: 1977–86', *Accounting and Business Research*, **21**, 83, 239–51.

Loderer, C. and K. Martin (1992) 'Post acquisition performance of acquiring firms', *Financial Management*, Autumn, 69–79.

Manson, S., A. Stark and H.M. Thomas (1994) 'A cash flow analysis of the operational gains from takeovers', Research Report 35 of the Chartered Association of Certified Accountants.

Martin, K.J. and J.J. McConnell (1991) 'Corporate performance, corporate takeovers and management turnover', *Journal of Finance*, **46**, 2, 671–88.

Meeks, G. (1977) *Disappointing Marriage: A study of the gains from mergers*, Cambridge University Press.

Ravenscraft, D. and F. Scherer (1987) *Mergers, Sell-offs and Economic Efficiency*, Brookings Institution, Washington, DC.

Roll, R. (1986) 'The hubris hypothesis of corporate takeovers', *Journal of Business*, **59**, 2, 197–216.

Sudarsanam, P.S., P. Holl and A. Salami (1993) 'Shareholder wealth gains in mergers: empirical test of the synergy and agency effects', paper presented to the Midwest Finance Association, USA, April.

Walsh, J. (1988) 'Top management turnover following mergers and acquisitions', *Strategic Management Journal*, **9**, 173–83.

Walsh, J. and J. Ellwood (1991) 'Mergers, acquisitions and the pruning of managerial deadwood', *Strategic Management Journal*, **12**, 201–17.

14

Making acquisitions work

In the previous chapter, we reviewed the empirical evidence on the success of acquisitions from different stakeholder perspectives. The picture which emerges from that review is somewhat mixed in terms of profit performance of acquirers and the returns to shareholders of those companies. While, on average, mergers do not seem to deliver the Promised Land, this average picture masks a substantial minority of successful performers. The interesting questions are, therefore, what factors contribute to success and what factors cause failure?

In this chapter, we seek to provide some answers to these questions. The answers are based both on survey evidence of managers' own assessment of success or failure and on their identification of critical success factors. While one can glean a list of these critical success factors from different acquisition experiences of companies, such a list has no universal validity, since each acquisition may have its own idiosyncratic characteristics.

It becomes abundantly clear from the reported surveys that successful acquisitions are distinguished from failed ones in a number of dimensions, ranging from pre-acquisition planning to post-acquisition integration management. Behavioural considerations are as important as hard-nosed strategic and financial analyses. The human factor emerges as a key dimension of both pre-acquisition planning of the deal and the post-acquisition management. These varied issues impinging on the successful outcome of an acquisition are illustrated from actual takeovers in recent years.

Survey evidence on acquisition performance

From time to time, surveys of corporate managers have been carried out to elicit their assessment of the acquisitions they have undertaken in the recent past, and of the factors contributing to their success or failure. A survey has one advantage over the statistical methodology presented in the previous chapter, in that the acquisition decision-makers are asked to make their own assessments of their decisions. Moreover, they are also asked to provide the reasons for their decisions and for the outcomes. These can only be inferred from a statistical study.

However, a survey is also more subjective and often based on small samples. It is in the nature of a confessional and often done some time after the event. It is by no means a 'fly on the wall' account and depends on the quality of recapitulation that the respondents are capable of. Subject to these limitations, a survey provides some useful insights into managerial decision making.

One of the earliest surveys of managers in the context of mergers was undertaken by Newbould (1970). His survey covered managers in 38 public companies which had undertaken mergers during 1967 and 1968. His results showed that, after two years, 17 companies reported no beneficial effects of any kind, and in 21 cases no further benefits were anticipated within five years. Another study (Kitching, 1974), based on interviews with executives, found that 30 per cent of UK acquisitions were 'failures', while a further 17 per cent were described as not worth repeating.

More recent surveys seem to confirm the pessimistic assessment of the above two. Coopers & Lybrand, the accounting and consulting firm, carried out a study in 1992 of the acquisition experience of UK companies. In-depth interviews with senior executives of the UK's top 100 companies, covering 50 deals worth over £13 billion, formed the basis of analysis. The study covers large acquisitions with a minimum value of £100 million by some of the largest companies in the UK during the recession years of the late 1980s and the early 1990s. Some 54 per cent of the acquisitions were regarded as failures by the interviewed executives. This level of perceived failures is consistent with the 49 and 48–56 per cent failure rates reported in earlier surveys in 1973 and 1988 by *Business International* (Coopers & Lybrand, 1993).

Coopers & Lybrand also investigated the causes of failure and success of acquisitions, and the executives' responses are shown in Table 14.1.

Table 14.1 Causes of acquisition failure and success: Coopers & Lybrand study (1993)

Cause of failure (%)	Cause of success (%)
Target management attitudes and cultural difference (85)	Detailed post-acquisition integration plans and speed of implementation (76)
No post-acquisition integration planning (80)	Clarity of acquisition purpose (76)
Lack of knowledge of industry or target (45)	Good cultural fit (59)
Poor management of target (45)	High degree of target management co-operation (47)
No prior acquisition experience (30)	Knowledge of target and its industry (41)

Note: The numbers in parentheses represent the % of interviewees who cited this cause.

Cultural difference reflected the way that the decisions were made in the acquirer and target companies (see Chapter 4 on organisational culture). Some respondents felt that the target managements lacked self-motivation and entrepreneurial instincts. Such managements were also accustomed to a hierarchical decision-making structure, or one in which decisions were made by committees. Hostile bids were thought to have hindered a good cultural fit between the acquired and the acquirer.

Lack of knowledge of the target and its industry was blamed on a poor pre-acquisition audit (see Chapter 7). The warranties received by the acquirer did not in some cases cover the problems found. Lack of adequate pre-acquisition planning led to loss of valuable time in integration. Where such planning had been done, the actual synergies exceeded what were anticipated.

Details of the interviews, the conditions under which they were carried out and the distribution of acquirers and targets in terms of size, industry, etc. are not available for the Coopers & Lybrand study. Nevertheless, its overall conclusion is quite consistent with the results from the statistical studies reviewed in the previous chapter.

A more rigorous questionnaire cum interview-based study into the managerial perceptions of acquisition success and the factors which contribute to it is that by Hunt *et al.* (1987), already referred to in earlier chapters (see Chapter 4). The executives were asked to rate acquisitions on a scale ranging from extremely positive to extremely negative on the following measures:

1. Was the acquisition a success from a business perspective?
2. Was the implementation handled successfully?
3. Is the acquired business in better shape than before purchase?
4. Does the acquired business have better prospects than before purchase?
5. With the benefit of hindsight, would you go through with it again?

The acquiring and acquired company executives' responses were aggregated into an overall index of success. In two-thirds of cases, the ratings of executives from the two companies were the same, but in response to question 5 above, some of the sellers were unwilling to repeat the experience thanks to the trauma of being taken over. The overall assessment is as follows:

Very successful	20%
Successful	35%
So-so	20%
Unsuccessful	17%
Very unsuccessful	8%

Thus, overall, only 55 per cent of the respondents considered the acquisitions they were involved in successful or better, and 25 per cent regarded them as failures. This assessment broadly agrees with that from the Coopers & Lybrand study and from the statistical studies.

Factors contributing to acquisition failure

In Chapter 4 we described the organisational dynamics of the acquisition decision-making and acquisition integration processes. The acquisition decision process is characterised by fragmented perspectives, escalating momentum and expectational ambiguity. The acquisition integration process may also be undermined by a variety of pitfalls, thereby destroying the acquisition's value creation potential.

A number of caveats follow from the above description of the acquisition process:

- Often the failure of a specific acquisition is due to a flawed corporate or business strategy. This means that the company being acquired may have only a superficial strategic fit.
- A good strategic analysis is a necessary but not a sufficient condition of a successful acquisition.
- There must be clarity in the value creation logic underlying any acquisition programme, or a specific acquisition within that programme.
- Value potential in acquisition is realised or destroyed at the implementation stage.
- Integration approaches must be tailored to the target and the value creation logic: that is, absorption, preservation or symbiosis. This determines both the speed and extent of integration.
- There must be some continuity between the teams negotiating a deal and implementing it, so that the aims of the acquisition are preserved. The implementation team must command the respect and credibility of both companies, and must stand up to needless interference in the integration process, especially from various acquirer's departments and functions.
- Any integration plan the acquirer has must be capable of being modified to accommodate ground realities when the process starts.
- The integration process is fraught with uncertainty, fear and anxiety among target company staff, which may lead to withdrawal of their commitment and lack of morale. The acquirer's implementation team must handle these concerns with tact, sympathy and understanding in order to instil confidence and trust between the two companies' personnel.
- The acquirer must communicate its plans and expectations for the acquisition clearly and at the earliest possible moment, so as to allay the anxieties of the target personnel.

Survey evidence on the acquisition process

There is little direct evidence in support of the above paradigm developed by Haspeslagh and Jemison (see Chapter 4). The Hunt *et al.* (1987) survey was not designed to test any of the above propositions. Nevertheless it provides some useful indirect evidence. As regards the acquisition planning stage, we find the following characteristics:

- Acquisition targeting is haphazard.
- The acquisition motive is often emotional rather than cold, clinical and rational. The chairman or chief executive's whims and prejudices often dictate the need for and the pace of acquisition as well as the choice of target. In some cases, machismo and hubris provide the motive force.
- Acquisitions are often opportunistic – an 'it was there and we grabbed it' approach.
- The decision to pursue a target is by no means neat and tidy.

The deal negotiation phase bears the imprint of escalating momentum and expectational ambiguity. Clinching a deal is not a hard-nosed, rational economic process, but one where non-financial factors also play a role. In some deals the two negotiators develop trust and believe they could do business with each other. Thus intuition and judgement play a part.

Negotiating teams are generally small (average size of under three persons) including the chairman, finance director and the managing director of the subsidiary relevant to the acquisition. Bidders, especially the less experienced ones, rely much on their advisers, who have different incentives to close the deal. Sometimes the bidder is hustled into closing a deal by the merchant bank adviser.

Tight secrecy in planning and negotiating is considered necessary to prevent either rivals or the staff of the target finding out about the deal. This secrecy may be one of the reasons for the due diligence audit being somewhat superficial. Even in friendly bids (they made up 80 per cent of the sample), pre-acquisition audit neglects detailed human resources aspects. Financial/legal audit is done in 98 per cent of the acquisitions or more, and engineering/production audit in 40 per cent of the cases.

Management or personnel audit is done in only 37 per cent of the buys. Even in those cases, the audit is less concerned about the target's human resource capabilities than about remuneration, pension rights, etc.: in other words, the pecuniary aspects. The rather limited nature of the audit results in some nasty surprises after the acquisition, even in some friendly deals. Some 35 per cent of the acquirers find dishonest presentation, lax or no management controls and poor management calibre in target companies.

Many acquirer negotiating teams realise that they should engage in credible and honest dialogue, give only those assurances they could deliver after the acquisition, and communicate without ambiguity the benefits to either side from the acquisition. Thus they try to minimise expectational ambiguity.

Evidence on acquisition integration

The Hunt survey also throws light on the approaches to integration adopted by the sample company acquirers. They display a wide variation in their knowledge of the target, partly due to the limited due diligence audit. This unfamiliarity is perhaps also accentuated by the fact that in 88 per cent of the cases the implementation team is different from the negotiating team, although it includes a linkperson appearing in both teams in 85 per cent of the cases. Most of the linkpeople are the managing directors of the acquired businesses. The team often includes someone to follow through when the implementation team has withdrawn.

Only 21 per cent of the acquirers have a clear implementation plan, and another 27 per cent have some 'hazy plan'. Some 52 per cent do not appear to have any plan at all. Two-thirds of the acquirers carry out an audit 'to find out what we had bought'. There is not always a well-thought-out strategy for managing the acquisition, and 'muddling through' is not uncommon. A 'hands on' policy towards the acquired company management is adopted by 58 per cent of the acquirers, and a 'hands off' policy by 42 per cent.

Some 58 per cent of the acquirers take control immediately. However, for 90 per cent of buys, it is 'business as usual' for several weeks as the buyers gradually learn more about the functioning of the acquired firm. The lack of a clear implementation plan and the post-deal audit also mean that, in many cases, the acquirers are adopting a 'wait, watch and go' stance towards implementation, and are also 'learning on the job'.

In many cases the waiting causes uncertainty among the acquired managers and workforce. In 73 per cent of the acquisitions, the chairman or chief executive of the acquirer has a personal meeting or sends a personal letter to the acquired company staff to reassure them of his or her plans.

Many acquirers display much cultural sensitivity and handle the cultural differences between the acquired and acquirer well. In the USA, in particular, the need for socialising with the staff, the need to build up trust and confidence, and the need to honour the ownership instincts of US managers by offering share options are the cultural traditions that British acquirers have to follow. British acquirers also give their US subsidiaries greater autonomy than a US acquirer would have given.

The integration interface is regulated in most cases of US acquisitions by a team including two key individuals, one from each company, acting as a buffer between two cultures, functions and salary levels. Thus this team is performing the gate-keeping role.

The Coopers & Lybrand (1993) study also provides some support for the relevance of the caveats. It emphasises the importance of pre-acquisition audit, including a human element audit, clarity of purpose, good communication and understanding of the cultural nuances of the acquired company.

Critical success factors

Hunt *et al.* (1987) round off their survey by drawing together the common threads and identifying factors which contribute, in the opinions of the acquiring and acquired company managers, to success or failure of the acquisition. They divide these factors into context and buyer behaviour factors. The importance of the context factors, as perceived by the participating managers, is indicated in Table 14.2. A further analysis of the behaviour factors identified as making varying contributions to the success of an acquisition is shown in Table 14.3.

Prior acquisition experience is not absolutely critical. This assessment echoes the Coopers & Lybrand (1993) conclusion that only 30 per cent of managers regard it as contributing to acquisition failure (see Table 14.1). This is not altogether surprising, since some of the spectacular company failures of the 1980s were active acquirers (see Table 13.4). It is the quality of experience that matters, not a high tally of repeated follies. Indeed, a rapid-fire acquisition strategy prevents consolidation and learning from previous acquisitions.

The size of the target and the tone of the acquisition (i.e. hostile or friendly) are quite relevant. A small target may enable the acquirer to be generous to the target company managers and staff, but it could also engender condescension and insensitivity. An acquirer may also pay less heed to the value creation logic because it can afford to in small acquisitions. In hostile acquisitions, the target top management may be the first casualties of battle, but a sensible acquirer can win the loyalty of the remaining staff with new

Table 14.2 Contextual determinants of acquisition success

Contextual factor	Critical	Helpful	Neutral
Pre-acquisition audit	Yes		
Whether target is healthy	Yes		
Prior acquisition experience		Yes	
Relatively small target		Yes	
Friendly not hostile acquisition		Yes	
Clear implementation plan			Yes
Small target + acquisition experience			Yes

Table 14.3 Buyer behaviour determinants of acquisition success

Factors associated with successful acquisitions	%	Factors associated with unsuccessful acquisitions	%
Honourable rhetoric	59	Assurances broken	39
Clear vision communicated	68	No clear vision	67
Buyer management earns credibility and respect	55	Buyer management fails to impress	72
Perceived business benefit to acquirer	64	No perceived business benefit to acquirer	44
Interface well regulated	77	Lax interface	58
Changes with people shape	59	Changes confined to business	61
Incentives and benefits to target staff improved	68	Incentives and benefits to target staff reduced	67

Note: The numbers are the percentages of successful or unsuccessful acquisitions where the factor contributed to the outcome.

incentive structures and a more promising future for the acquired company.

The lack of a clear implementation plan has little influence on the outcome. Determinism, the belief that a pre-acquisition plan is right whatever the realities in the target company, is often inimical to good integration. Open-mindedness and willingness to learn, on the other hand, promote good integration (see Chapter 4). Perhaps the lack of a clear plan facilitates such learning for many successful acquirers.

The two critical factors – pre-acquisition audit and the health of the target company – are interrelated. Indifferent quality of such audit is probably due to the escalating momentum of the acquisition decision process. Neglect of the human audit also appears to contribute to failure. An interesting result of the survey is that many factors considered hitherto critical to successful acquisitions, such as pre-acquisition planning, are indeed not so. One possible reason for this is that the acquirer's weaknesses in some contextual factors can be made up by its behaviour during the negotiation and integration stages. These behaviour factors are discussed next.

The behaviour factors are largely self-explanatory and consistent with the caveats derived from the Haspeslagh and Jemison model. Honesty, sensitivity, competence and willingness to share with the target staff the benefits of the acquisition are the important contributors to success. Truth should not become the first casualty of an acquisition. The need for competent management of the interface is also highlighted by the survey.

Any change that the acquirer brings about in the target must take into account its impact on the people. Again honest dealing and concern for the people are necessary to ensure a willing co-operation and commitment to the change. Whatever the merits of an acquisition on financial and business criteria, it is the people who make it all happen (Hunt *et al.*, 1987: 6).

Acquisitions and the human factor

Mergers and acquisitions are often change events which presage a massive dislocation in the professional and private lives of managers and other staff of the companies, especially those of the acquired company. Both the uncertainty associated with the event and the actual changes it brings about can cause fear, anxiety and stress. Potential sources of merger stress include loss of identity and job security, and changes in personnel and work practices, resulting in cultural incongruence (Cartwright and Cooper, 1993).

The extent of these merger-related negative feelings and their impact on the merger outcome depend on two factors:

- The degree of culture fit which exists between combining organisations, given the 'terms of marriage': that is, whether merger presupposes cultural integration, displacement or preservation of cultural autonomy.
- The impact of the event on the individual: that is, the degree and scale of stress generated by the merger process and its

duration. The long-term stress may have an adverse impact on the physical health, psychological well-being and performance behaviour of the individual.

These two factors are also interrelated, since cultural incompatibility may result in considerable fragmentation, uncertainty and cultural ambiguity, and, consequently, stress (Cartwright and Cooper, 1993).

Cartwright and Cooper (1993) carried out a questionnaire-based survey of the middle managers of two UK building societies being merged, one much smaller than the other. The survey aimed to assess the degree of cultural incompatibility between the two societies, and the extent to which the organisational commitment, job satisfaction, and physical and psychological health of those involved were affected by the merger. The questions related to organisational culture, organisational commitment, job satisfaction, potential stress sources and mental health.

A total of 157 middle managers responded to the questionnaire, a response rate of 52 per cent. The merging partners were regarded as culturally compatible and similar. They were also strategically well matched. Cultural integration was smooth. Nevertheless, the merger was stressful for both groups of managers, especially the smaller society's managers. Overall job satisfaction was maintained.

An important lesson from this study is that cultural congruence is no guarantee that merging company staff will welcome the merger and become committed to its goals. The human factor still needs to be addressed with a great deal of care and sensitivity.

Illustrations of successful acquisition process

Siemens' acquisition of Plessey

Siemens of Germany, in a joint bid with GEC of the UK for the British company Plessey in 1989, acquired Plessey's electronic systems (PES) and air traffic control systems and management (ATM). According to the senior executives of these two Plessey companies, they had been starved of capital investment funds, equipment, and testing and design facilities by Plessey before the acquisition. Plessey also used to operate with a short payback of only two years.

Siemens handled the integration with great care. The Plessey companies were given a great deal of autonomy. ATM was made into a world centre. Initially, Siemens used a German consultant on a British cost-reduction project, causing some resentment among the UK managers. Subsequently, however, Siemens allowed the UK companies to choose their own consultants. UK managers were sent to Germany for intercultural training. The British senior executives feel that without Siemens their company would not have survived, and appreciate the greater autonomy and long-term financial support they have received from Siemens (*Financial Times*, 13.4.1994).

Nestlé's takeover of Rowntree

Nestlé, the Swiss food and confectionery giant, took over the much loved and respected Rowntree, the York-based confectioner, in a bitter hostile bid in 1988. This bid aroused a great deal of resistance from the Rowntree workforce, and a political storm, with calls for a reference to the Monopolies and Mergers Commission.

Nestlé approached the integration task with considerable care and sensitivity. Whereas it would normally take two to three years to integrate an acquisition fully, with Rowntree it took four years. Although Nestlé assured Rowntree at the time of the bid that its global confectionery strategy would be run from York, this assurance was not kept. However, York has become a global research centre for confectionery. There have been heavy capital investments in Rowntree since the takeover. There have been job losses, but there has also been increased productivity.

Nestlé, having neglected the confectionery side of its own business, needed Rowntree's expertise and brands. It has therefore left Rowntree under the charge of the UK managers. However, there has been a flow of managers between Rowntree and the rest of the Nestlé group, with some of the old Rowntree managers holding global positions in Zurich. This two-way flow of managers, the heavy investment, the higher profile of Rowntree in Nestlé's global strategy, and the degree of autonomy given to Rowntree have all combined to lessen the suspicion and hostility which accompanied the takeover in 1988 (*Financial Times*, 20.4.1994).

Hongkong & Shanghai Banking Corporation (HSBC) acquires Midland Bank

In 1992, HSBC acquired Midland, which had been experiencing declining profits and even losses in the previous ten years. Its international expansion effort had been disastrous. There were also problems with the top management of Midland. Thus Midland needed a strong rescue partner. HSBC was at the same time seeking expansion in Europe, following its successful expansion in Asia, the USA and Canada. Midland offered a strong retail banking base to HSBC in the UK. There were also size benefits in combining the two banks' foreign exchange and treasury operations. Together the banks would become a big global player.

There were cultural differences between the two banks. Although both had a fine heritage and proud history, HSBC was a very successful expanding bank, whereas Midland was in the doldrums. HSBC was also said to be more customer conscious and keenly aware of the bottom-line performance.

HSBC approached the integration with much sensitivity. In keeping with its customer-conscious approach, it raised the profile of the high street branch manager. Its approach to staff relations was that staff needed to be provided with good working conditions, so that the bank would have a cheerful workforce – again a customer-oriented approach. HSBC undertook a programme of branch refurbishment. There were many management changes, but there was also a two-way flow of managers between HSBC and Midland Bank (*Banking World*, May 1994).

Overview

This chapter has provided evidence on the success and failure of acquisitions based on surveys of managers who participated in acquisitions during planning, execution and post-acquisition integration. The survey evidence confirms the evidence from statistical studies presented in Chapter 13: namely, only about 50 per cent of acquisitions are regarded as successful by managers. The surveys also reveal the reasons which in managers' perceptions contributed to failure. Many critical success factors have been identified from the surveys. One of the most important factors in determining the success of an acquisition is the human factor. What do companies do when the acquisitions they have made have not lived up to expectations, or have outlived their original strategic purpose? Divestments have become an increasingly important solution to this problem and are examined in the next chapter.

References and further reading

Cartwright, S. and C. Cooper (1993) 'The psychological impact of merger and acquisition on the individual: a study of building society mergers', *Human Relations*, **46**, 3.

Coopers & Lybrand (1993) *Making a Success of Acquisitions*.

Hunt, J., S. Lees, J.J. Grumbar and P.D. Vivian (1987) *Acquisitions: The human factor*, London Business School.

Kitching, J. (1974) 'Why acquisitions are abortive', *Management Today*, November.

Newbould, G.D. (1970) *Management and Merger Activity*, Guthstead.

Haspeslagh, P. and D. Jemison (1991) *Managing Acquisitions*, Free Press.

15

Corporate divestments

The previous chapters dealt with the acquisition of one company by another. The result of an acquisition is to enlarge the size of the acquirer. The 1980s also witnessed, on a massive scale, the opposite of growth by acquisition: divestment. Many large firms in the USA and in the UK sold off parts of their businesses for a variety of reasons. While in most cases these sales were to other companies, in a large number of cases the buyers were the managers of the businesses being sold off. Such purchases by managers, called management buyouts (MBOs), have now become an established part of the M & A scene, with an impressive infrastructure of financial services.

In the 1980s many companies also pursued other methods of restructuring their business portfolios, aimed at enhancing share-holder value. These include spin-offs or demergers and equity carve-outs. Innovative methods of financing acquisitions of even very large firms, such as leveraged buyouts (LBOs), were introduced into the M & A scene. Together, these developments widened the scope and variety of transactions in the market for corporate control.

In this chapter, we describe the evolution of these new forms of corporate control transactions, and discuss the rationale behind them. The structure and characteristics of these different forms of corporate restructuring are examined and illustrated. The empirical evidence on the impact of corporate restructuring on shareholder wealth is presented.

Rationale for divestments

Table 15.1 provides a six-year comparison of M & A transactions involving UK companies. Divestments by UK companies form a substantial part of the total acquisitions of either independent UK companies or parts of UK companies. In 1989 they accounted for about 20 per cent of the total of acquisitions and divestments, whereas in 1993 they were nearly 50 per cent. Independent company acquisitions peaked in 1989 and divestments in 1988 in value terms. Whereas recession in the UK took a heavy toll of independent company acquisitions, divestments held their ground better, indicating that companies might have sustained their divestments as a way of coping with the recession.

That acquisitions and divestments rise and fall fairly in tandem is not surprising, since acquisitions and divestments may be part of the same strategy of firms in refocusing their portfolio of businesses. Often proceeds of divestments are used to finance the acquisitions. In a number of cases in the past, acquirers unbundled the acquired firms, retained those parts which made strategic sense, and sold off the ones which did not fit.

Why do companies divest? There are a number of factors which motivate divestments:

- The divested division or subsidiary may be underperforming in relation to its industry competitors, or in relation to the other businesses in the divestor's portfolio.

Table 15.1 Acquisitions and divestments in the UK, 1988–93

Year	Acquisitions		Divestments		Total	
	No.	Value (£m)	No.	Value (£m)	No.	Value (£m)
1993	745	8720	503	8640	1248	17 360
1992	684	14 428	468	5319	1152	19 747
1991	747	12 180	442	6001	1189	18 181
1990	912	17 457	612	10 221	1524	27 678
1989	1402	36 416	676	10 816	2078	47 232
1988	1633	24 369	608	13 254	2241	37 623

Note: Acquisitions include both private and public company targets.
Source: *Acquisitions Monthly Annuals.*

- The divested part may be performing reasonably well, but it may not be well positioned within its industry to give it long-term competitive advantage. The parent may judge that the prospect of gaining a strong competitive position is weak or may require excessive investment.

- The parent's strategic focus and priorities may have changed, and the divested part may have a poor fit with the new strategy. The parent may want to concentrate on areas with the greatest competitive strengths. This process is known as 'sticking to the knitting'.

- The divested part may have contributed negative synergy by absorbing a disproportionate amount of managerial resources, with loss of control and ineffective management.

- The parent may be too widely diversified, causing difficulties in monitoring the performance of divisional managers.

- The parent may be experiencing financial distress, and may need to raise cash to mitigate it and avoid eventual liquidation.

- The divested business may have been bought as part of an acquired company, and the parent may have no desire to keep it.

- The divested business may have been bought as part of an acquisition, and the parent may need to raise money to pay for the acquisition.

- The parent may feel that the divested part will be valued higher by the stock market if it is a 'stand-alone' entity, since more information about the divested company will be available to the stock market. This increases the ability of the stock market to value the company better, and may enhance the divestor shareholders' wealth.

- The divested part may have a better strategic fit with another company, enabling the latter to create value. The divestor may then share some of the added value for the benefit of its own shareholders.

- A divestment may also be used as a defence against a hostile takeover: for example, sale of 'crown jewels' (see Chapter 12).

The 'back to the core' strategy is a rebound from the poor performance of conglomeration, which happened on a large scale in the 1960s and 1970s. This conglomeration was itself an offspring of the strict antitrust regimes of those periods. With the more relaxed regimes of the 1980s in the USA under the Reagan administration, companies felt less inhibited about acquisitions that would enhance their market power, and had less need for diversifying into unrelated areas.

Forms of corporate divestment

Corporate divestments can be carried out in a variety of ways:

- Intercorporate sell-off: that is, sale to another company.
- Spin-off or demerger, where the divested part is floated on a stock exchange and the shares in that newly listed company are distributed to the shareholders of the parent.
- Equity carve-out, in which a subsidiary is floated on a stock exchange, but the parent retains the majority control.
- Management buyout (MBO) and its variants, such as management buyin (MBI).

Corporate sell-offs

A sell-off is a transaction between two independent companies. Such a transaction may be of benefit to both companies. The divestor may benefit from the cash flow proceeds, which could be put to more profitable use in other businesses within the group, or used to mitigate financial distress. Sell-off may also add value to the divestor by eliminating negative synergy, or by releasing managerial resources hitherto pre-empted by the divested business. It may also sharpen the strategic focus of the remaining businesses and enhance the divestor's competitive strengths.

For the buyer, the divested business may offer a better strategic fit than for the seller. Where the acquired business is related to any of its existing businesses, the buyer may enjoy increased market share and market power. This means that the business is more valuable to the buyer than to the seller. This added value may be creamed off by the buyer in full, or shared between the buyer and the seller. The sharing of the added value depends on the relative bargaining strength of the two parties, and this in turn depends upon the financial condition of the seller, the supply of divestments, the relative size of the two companies and the urgency of the divestor's need for cash.

If the divestor is in poor financial state, the divestment may be involuntary and thereby weaken its bargaining power. Nevertheless, the proceeds of sale may be used to regain financial strength. In that event, the company is likely to receive a better rating from the stock market than before the divestment.

Thus, for various reasons, a divestment may be good news for the divestor company shareholders. This is supported by empirical evidence for the UK and the USA. Afshar *et al.* (1992) examine, for a sample of 178 UK corporate sell-offs during 1985–6, whether the selling company shareholders earn risk-adjusted abnormal returns (see Chapter 13 for the abnormal return methodology). They find that, on the day before the press announcement of the sell-off event, divestor shareholders earn 0.85 per cent, which is statistically significant. Thus it appears that the stock market greets the sell-off announcement favourably.

In the same study, Afshar *et al.* (1992) also find that the stock market reaction is much more favourable – that is, divestor shareholders earn higher abnormal returns – the weaker the financial condition of the divestor. Financial condition is measured by the Z score, which is a weighted sum of four different financial ratios representing profitability, gearing, liquidity and operating resource. The Z score is derived as a measure of the bankruptcy potential of a company. Similar US evidence of the stock market reaction to sell-offs and other forms of divestment is discussed below.

Corporate spin-offs

In a corporate spin-off, a company floats off a subsidiary which may be a small part of the parent company. The newly floated company now has an independent existence and is separately valued in the stock market. Shares in the spun-off company are distributed to the shareholders of the parent company, and they own shares in two companies rather than just one. This increases the flexibility of the shareholders' portfolio decisions, since they now have the freedom to alter the proportion of their portfolios invested in each company. Previously, their investment was indivisible because they could invest in the subsidiary only by investing in the parent. A demerger is a variant of a spin-off, but the demerged company tends to be larger than in a spin-off.

From the parent's point of view, the spin-off may be preferable to a sell-off, since in the latter case the parent has to decide what to do with the sale proceeds when it does not have any investment opportunities to finance. Further, it appears that the stock market puts a higher value on two companies than on the parent prior to demerger because of the greater information about the separate companies after the flotation. The stock market, the argument goes, places a premium on corporate transparency.

Diversified companies may in the past have suffered a 'conglomerate discount' because of the lack of transparency. More fundamentally, such a discount is probably due to management control loss, discussed earlier. In a demerger, typically, the separating firms have little synergy in terms of production, technology or markets. When this discount is eliminated, the combined market value of the parent and its young offspring should be higher than the parent's alone before the demerger.

Demergers in the UK have been a few so far, and the major ones of recent years are listed in Table 15.2. In some cases, demerger was

Table 15.2 Corporate demergers in the UK

Year	Parent (activities)	Spun-off (activities)
1984	Bowater International (packaging, tissues, building products, paper, services)	Bowater North America (newsprint, paper and pulp)
1990	Courtaulds (chemicals, clothing and spinning)	Courtaulds Textiles (clothing, fabrics and fabrics spinning)
1990	BAT (tobacco, retailing, paper, financial services)	Argos (retailer)
1990	BAT (as above)	Wiggins Teape Appleton (pulp and paper)
1991	Racal Electronics (communications, cellular telephones, security systems)	Racal Telecom (cellular telephones)
1992	Racal Electronics (as above)	Chubb Group (security systems)
1993	ICI (explosives, industrial chemicals, materials, pharmaceuticals, agrochemicals and speciality chemicals)	Zeneca (pharmaceuticals, agrochemicals and specialities)
1994	Pearson (media, leisure, china)	Royal Doulton (china)

in response to a hostile takeover. For example, the conglomerate BAT was the target of a hostile bid by the Hoylake consortium for £13 billion in 1989. Hoylake aimed to create value from the takeover by unbundling BAT. BAT, after a vigorous defence campaign, thwarted the bid but promised to consider demerging on its own. This plan was followed by the spin-off of Argus and Wiggins Teape Appleton.

Similarly, Racal's demerger of Vodafone (Racal Telecom) and Chubb was triggered by Williams Holdings' hostile bid. In the case of ICI, although the demerger decision was already in contemplation, Hanson's acquisition of a 2.8 per cent stake in ICI in 1991, regarded by the ICI board as hostile, added to the urgency of the plan.

In the case of others, underperformance of the spun-off subsidiary and changed strategic priorities led to the demergers, as in Pearson's decision to demerge Royal Doulton. An important reason for a demerger is that it gives the management of the demerged parts greater freedom and focus. According to Sir Christopher Hogg, chairman of Courtaulds, the demerger released a great deal of energy among the managers of the separate companies.

If the above rationale for a demerger is true, the combined market value of the demerged firms must be greater than that of the pre-demerger parent. For example, prior to the demerger, Courtaulds was capitalised at £1025 million in March 1990. On the first day of dealings in the shares of the two demerged companies, Courtaulds and Courtaulds Textiles were valued at £1241 million and £248 million respectively, an increase in the combined value of £464 million. The effect of demerger on the market values of ICI and Zeneca is shown in Figure 15.1. We observe that the combined value of the demerged companies is higher than that of ICI alone prior to the demerger.

Structure and tax implications of demergers

A demerger involves the distribution of shares in the newly floated company to the parent company shareholders. The ratio of shares held by a shareholder in the demerged companies is likely to reflect the ratio of the assets or value of the two companies. In the Courtaulds case, shareholders received one Courtaulds Textiles share for every four parent shares. With ICI demerger, shareholders got one Zeneca share for each ICI share held. The allocation of assets and liabilities is often a complex process, and will affect the stock market valuation of the demerged companies. For example, if too much of the parent debt is loaded on to a demerged company, it

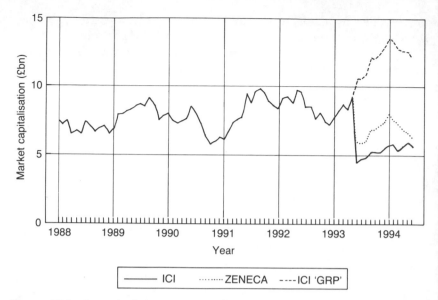

Figure 15.1 Impact of demerger on shareholder values for the ICI Group. Source: Datastream International.

may be seen as a more risky company and thus may be under-valued.

In the UK, the Finance Act 1980 made demerger much easier to undertake without heavy tax penalties, provided it is not construed by the Inland Revenue as a tax avoidance scheme. Since a demerger results in a distribution of shares to the parent company sharehol-ders, it has to be structured carefully to qualify as a tax-free arrangement for both the companies involved and the shareholders.

Tax benefits may arise in the form of deferred capital gains tax (CGT) and the absence of any advanced corporation tax (ACT) liability on the distribution of shares. However, the demerger must be justified on bona fide commercial grounds. The problems that arise in constructing a tax-free demerger are illustrated by the Courtaulds demerger (see Case Study 15.1).

Equity carve-outs

These are similar to spin-offs, but with only a minority of the shares in the floated subsidiary being offered to the public. Equity carve-out is thus a partial divestment. To the divestor, it has the advantage that cash is raised from the flotation. Moreover, it can gauge the market value of the subsidiary. However, the parent loses

CASE STUDY 15.1 Demerger raises tax problems for Courtaulds

The initial reaction of the Inland Revenue to the demerger proposal was one of suspicion. The main difficulty was with the company's £60 million of unrecovered ACT. The chemicals business generated 75 per cent of its turnover overseas, whereas the textiles were largely UK based. Thus for textiles to be assigned most of the unrecovered ACT would reduce the future tax liability of both companies. Courtaulds proposed splitting the ACT, £40 million going to textiles and £20 million to chemicals, but the Inland Revenue did not accept the division.

Source: *Financial Times*, 12.11.1990.

some control over the subsidiary, and if the disinvestment takes the parent's shareholding to below 75 per cent, group tax relief may cease to be available. Its ability to pass special resolutions could also be blocked. Since the parent continues to retain majority control, the minority stake may not be an attractive proposition to investors.

Management buyouts and buyins

In a management buyout (MBO), the parent sells a division or subsidiary to the incumbent management, or a private company is bought by incumbent management. In a management buyin (MBI), a new management team replaces the incumbent management. Where a public listed company is bought by its management, it is referred to as 'going private', since the company ceases to be listed. Table 15.3 shows that MBOs and MBIs have been significant in UK acquisitions in the last few years, accounting for about 11 per cent of them.

MBOs arise from a number of different sources. The vast majority of them are divestments by UK and foreign parents of subsidiaries. Private, family-owned companies are also often sold to managers. Companies in receivership, or parts of those companies, are also bought by managers as MBOs. Going-private deals are very few in number. In 1993/4 the sources of MBOs were as shown in Table 15.4.

Receivership as a source of MBOs is obviously related to the state of the economy, and becomes more important in a recession.

Table 15.3 Management buyouts (MBOs) and
buyins (MBIs) as a proportion of total acquisitions

Year	Number of MBOs/MBIs	Total value (£m)	% of total acquisitions[1]
1994[2]	243	1676	10.5
1993	252	1932	7.7
1992	339	2302	10.9
1991	340	2087	10.8
1990	383	2352	8.5
1989	361	5761	12.6
1988	297	4263	11.3
1987	290	3007	10.9

[1]Total acquisitions include independent company
acquisitions and divestments.
[2]Only nine months of the year covered.
Source: *Acquisitions Monthly*, MBO Supplement,
October 1994.

Table 15.4 Sources of management buyouts, 1993/4

Source	Number	Value (£m)
Corporate divestments	192	1614
Private companies	93	226
Receivership	18	117
Going private	4	65
Others	5	138

Source: *Acquisitions Monthly*, MBO Supplement,
October 1994.

Divestments in a recession tend to be defensive and driven by
rationalisation and cost cutting, whereas in boomtime they are
triggered more by strategic restructuring.

Managerial motivations for an MBO

What drives managers to become owners of the businesses they
have run under the direction and control of a parent? A survey of
MBO managers by Wright *et al.* (1991) revealed a number of reasons,
of which the most important was the desire to run one's own
business. In order of importance, managerial motivations in MBOs
were as follows:

* Opportunity to control own business.
* Long-term faith in company.

- Better financial rewards.
- Opportunity to develop own talents.
- Absence of head office constraints.
- Fear of redundancy.
- Fear of new owner after anticipated acquisition.

Financial and investment constraints imposed by the head office in a group may result in underexploitation of the full potential of a business, and may lead to frustration among the divisional managers.

Structure of an MBO

Since managers do not have the financial resources to buy out their companies on their own, the financial structure of an MBO depends on the capital supplied by specialist capital providers and banks. Management provides a small part of the equity. Institutions which specialise in MBO financing, such as venture capital firms, provide additional equity. Further funding is provided by debt, which falls into two types: senior debt and mezzanine debt.

In some MBOs, equity has also been raised from the employees by the formation of an employee share ownership plan (ESOP). Contribution from the company towards the purchase of its shares by an ESOP is corporation tax free. Moreover, the plan can borrow money to buy shares, and the contribution from the company can then be used to pay interest and repay the borrowing. Thus an ESOP is a tax-efficient method of raising funds to finance equity.

Senior debt has priority in payment of interest and repayment of principal. It is secured and, if it is a term loan, has a pre-arranged repayment schedule. The interest rate is normally a floating rate at a margin of 2–3 per cent over LIBOR (the London Inter-bank Offer Rate). Some part of the senior debt may be short term. Mezzanine debt, as the name suggests, is junior or subordinated to senior debt in terms of interest payment and capital repayment. It is not secured and is, therefore, more risky. Both debt components rank above equity.

The mezzanine layer is often in the form of preference shares or convertible loan stock or convertible preference shares. In the UK, some firms specialise in providing mezzanine or intermediate finance. The interest rate is generally 4–5 per cent above LIBOR. Interest rate margins for both senior and mezzanine debt depend on the general level of interest rates, the demand for debt and the competition among banks.

Institutional equity providers earn their reward from the return realised at the time of exit of the MBO. Exit is the process of realisation of the investments made in an MBO. Equity investors may expect an internal rate of return (IRR) of 25–30 per cent. Once again, this return depends on the riskiness of the MBO, demand for funds and competition among institutional equity providers, and the lead time to exit. Case Study 15.2 provides an example of such a structure.

In larger deals, the number of institutional equity and debt providers increases substantially as a mechanism for spreading risk. To the senior lenders, the mezzanine and equity provide a cushion. In Case Study 15.2, senior debt of £11.5 million is backed by £11.85 million of equity and mezzanine. However, the larger the mezzanine, the greater the cash outflow, the smaller the retained earnings on account of interest payment and the smaller the resulting net worth. Senior lenders are therefore wary of too much mezzanine, although it ranks behind senior debt.

Mezzanine lenders often demand an 'equity kicker' or 'sweetener' to compensate them for the high risk they run. An equity kicker is an equity warrant, and it enables the mezzanine holder to partake of

CASE STUDY 15.2   Financing the DRG Litho Supplies MBO, 1991

DRG Litho Supplies Ltd was bought out by the management team from DRG plc after it was taken over in a contested bid by Pembridge Investments in 1989. A new company, L. S. Holdings Ltd, was formed to acquire DRG. The total financing needed was:

Price payable to vendor	£20.70m
Working capital	1.65
Fees	1.00
	£23.35m

This was provided by:

Management equity	£0.50m
Institutions: Share capital	7.35
Mezzanine	4.00
Senior debt: Term loan	7.00
Overdraft and short term	4.50
	£23.35m

Source: Ernst & Young (1991), *MBO Guide*.

the upside potential of an MBO by exercising the warrants, and to receive shares in the company.

Where there is a financing gap after tapping all the above sources, sometimes the vendor agrees to fill the gap. Vendor financing can take the form of unsecured loan notes or preference shares or convertibles. Vendor financing also demonstrates goodwill towards the management. Where the MBO maintains some trading links with the erstwhile parent, such as a supplier, vendor financing may smooth such links.

The ratchet

MBOs have in the past been structured to include an incentive for the management to achieve or exceed agreed levels of performance after the buyout. Such an incentive is known as a ratchet. There are three types of ratchet related to targets based on:

- Profit level.
- Time of exit.
- Debt repayment.

The first two ratchets increase the amount or proportion of equity made available to the management when the targets are met. The last ratchet allows the interest margin on senior debt to be reduced if the MBO generates a sufficiently high level of cash flows. Reverse ratchets penalise management for failure to achieve targets. The operation of a ratchet is illustrated by the MBO of Mallinson-Denny (see Case Study 15.3).

Ratchets, though conceptually attractive as an incentive mechanism, may encounter severe problems in practice. First, profit-related ratchets require an agreed set of rules for measuring profits. Managements and the capital providers may disagree on interpretation of these rules. Second, management may be forced to adopt expedient policies which maximise short-term profits but endanger the long-term prospects of the company, such as cutting down on R & D. Third, the timing of exit is determined at the time of investment and may force an inopportune exit.

From the institutional investors' and lenders' perspective, a ratchet is a means of reducing valuation errors, since the management's share of equity depends upon future performance of the company. In this sense, a ratchet is similar to earn-out, discussed in Chapter 11. They both serve to mitigate the problems of information asymmetry and uncertainty in valuation.

CASE STUDY 15.3   Ratchet effect in Mallinson-Denny

Mallinson-Denny was bought out in 1985 by the management and was financed as follows:

Management equity:	
A ordinary shares of £1 each	£1.2m
Institutional equity:	
Convertible redeemable preferred ordinary shares (CRPO)	6.0
Cumulative redeemable first preference shares	15.6
Senior term loan + short-term debt + guarantees	70.5
	£93.3m

The terms of conversion of CRPO were that the holder would have 83.3 per cent of the company's equity if combined profits in the three years to 1988 were less than £13.6 million, whereas this would fall to 65 per cent assuming combined profits of £26 million. The management's share of equity is thus linked to profit performance.

Source: *Guide to Management Buy-outs*, Economist Publications, 1989: 168–71.

The exit

There are alternative ways of realising the investment made by the institutional investors and the management. These are: flotation on a stock market, trade sale, a second buyout, share repurchase or, if the MBO has failed, receivership. Of these, trade sale is the most popular method, followed by flotation. In the early 1980s, while 10 per cent of buyouts were floated, 15 per cent were sold to other companies (Houlden, 1990). Between 1985 and June 1990, 240 buyouts were sold to other groups compared to 145 flotations (Wright *et al.*, 1991). After the stock market crash of 1987, flotations became much more difficult.

Exits need to be carefully managed to maximise the returns to management and the investors. Timing of the exit is an important consideration, and also determines the exit mode. With the stock market in a bear phase, flotation is obviously not an attractive option. Exit policy may cause a conflict of interest between management and institutional investors, for whom exit crystallises their returns and allows them to finance other MBO opportunities. On the other hand, a flotation may subject management to unnecessary pressure from the stock market. But an exit allows management to realise their investment.

There is also a conflict of interest between equity investors and lenders who dislike early exits on good deals. So some senior lenders require early repayment fees or an incentive in the form of equity kickers.

Management buyins

An MBI requires the institutional investor to sponsor a new management team to take over the target company. This team is offered an equity stake to provide the right incentives. An MBI is probably inherently more hazardous than an MBO, since the new management team is unfamiliar with the target and its organisation structure and culture. However, where the incumbent management was lacklustre and a new management team with the right vision, strategy and experience is available, an MBI is an attractive option for the institutional sponsor. Case Study 15.4 exemplifies an MBI.

For the sponsor, management talent spotting is a fundamental part of an MBI. Institutions like 3i keep a register of over 200 would-be buyers-in. These managers have to assess the target from outside. Often they find skeletons very much in residence after the buyin. Further, vendors may have a sentimental preference for the incumbent management to lead a buyout. In order to overcome the problems of an MBI compared to an MBO, many institutional investors now prefer a combination of the two. One variant of this combination is called BIMBO (Buy-in management buyout). Another is CHIMBO (chairman in management buyout). These seek to blend the best of both worlds. Where the incumbent and incoming managers bring complementary strengths, the combined team is likely to enjoy greater cohesion and credibility.

Performance of MBOs

Performance of MBOs may be assessed over the short and the long term. Wright and Coyne (1985) found from a study of 111 MBOs up to 1983 that they showed improvement in profitability, trading relations, and cash and credit control systems, and also evidence of new product development. Thompson *et al.* (1989) studied 182 MBOs over 1983–6 and found support for the above results. Most respondents in their survey judged that trading profits and turnover were better than forecast in their business plans.

Over the long term, there is mixed evidence of MBO performance. A study by Houlden (1990) found that, in terms of return on capital

CASE STUDY 15.4   Management buyin of BP Nutrition Products

In May 1993, BP Nutrition's consumer products division was acquired in an MBI deal worth £273 million. The consumer products division was a leading supplier of own-label household detergents, cleaners and personal care products. Legal and General Ventures (LG), which won the mandate for the acquisition, had to put together a management team. The financing was made up of: £115 million of institutional equity, £115 million of senior debt, £30 million of mezzanine debt and £12 million of senior working capital loan. Following the deal, the new management were invited to become shareholders with up to 10 per cent equity stake.

LG lined up Mr Michael Handley, the former divisional director of RHM, a food manufacturer, to become managing director of the new company. Moreover, Sir Allen Sheppard, chairman and chief executive of Grand Metropolitan, a major international food and drinks company, was persuaded to become non-executive chairman of the new company formed to acquire the BP Nutrition division. LG was of the opinion that it had won the 'beauty parade' for the mandate thanks to the credible management team it had assembled.

Source: *Financial Times*, MBO survey, 8.12.1993.

and return on sales over the first three years after the MBO, company performance improved, but over the following three years it declined. 3i, the venture capital firm, however, contradicted this result and reported that its portfolio of MBOs was outperforming other companies it had invested in (Wright *et al.*, 1993).

Evidence on the performance of MBIs is mixed. A recent survey reported by Wright *et al.* (1993) of 58 buyins of private companies found that MBIs did more restructuring than MBOs. Operating profit was worse than forecast in 53 per cent of cases. Cost of finance and discovery of unexpected problems were the most serious problems faced by MBIs. However, BIMBOs appear to have been more successful. In a recent study of the 300 MBIs it had backed, 3i reported that BIMBOs had increased from less than 25 per cent of MBI deals in 1990 to 50 per cent in 1993. The study (3i, 1994) suggests that BIMBOs have become more effective than pure MBIs, since the involvement of the existing management provides the incoming manager with more reliable information, and the existing managers who remain part of the management team contribute equity and are, therefore, better motivated.

Divestments in the USA

The USA has witnessed massive restructuring over the last few years. This has taken the form of mergers, acquisitions and divestments. Divestments accounted for about 35–40 per cent of all mergers and acquisitions transactions in the 1980s. Divestments have manifested themselves in a variety of ways, including sell-offs, spin-offs, equity carve-outs and MBOs and MBIs. Many of them followed previous acquisitions. In some cases, they followed 'bust-up' takeovers in which unbundling the targets was one of the value creation strategies of the acquirers.

The reasons for divestments were similar to those which drive UK divestments. There have also been cases of involuntary divestments enforced by antitrust authorities. The break-up of AT&T, the telecommunication giant, into various 'Baby Bell' companies is an example of such an involuntary divestment. Several empirical studies of voluntary divestments of different types have shown that they create value for the divestor's shareholders.

The impact of sell-off announcements on divestor shareholders' wealth is generally positive and significant, as shown in Table 15.5. Thus a divestment is greeted favourably by the stock market. A company's spin-off decision is similarly treated. In a study of 59 spin-offs during 1963 and 1980, Miles and Rosenfeld (1983) found a positive and significant market reaction to spin-off announcements. When the divestment assumes the form of an MBO, the parent shareholders do not lose but actually gain according to Hite and Vetsuypens (1989) in their study of 151 such divestments.

Table 15.5   Abnormal returns (AR) on sell-off announcements

Study	Sample	Event window	% AR
Linn and Rozeff (1984)	77	(−1, 0) days	1.45
Jain (1985)	1064	(0)	0.09
Klein (1986)	202	(−2, 0)	1.12
Hite et al. (1987)	55	(−1, 0)	1.66
Hirschey et al. (1990)	170	(−1, 0)	1.46

Note: See Chapter 13 on abnormal returns methodology.
Announcement day is Day 0. All ARs except Jain's are statistically significant at the 5% level.

Leveraged buyouts in the USA

One particular type of acquisition which characterised the 1980s mergers and acquisitions scene is the leveraged buyout (LBO). As the name suggests, an LBO is an acquisition which is heavily financed by debt – either bank debt or securitised debt (i.e. bonds). Such a description, of course, fits many of the MBOs we have described above. Indeed, in 1989 many MBOs in the UK were financed with a debt to equity ratio of 6. Thus an MBO is a particular type of an LBO. In other types, an investing firm such as Kohlberg, Kravis and Roberts (KKR) collects a pool of equity, acts as a sponsor to a buyout, arranges the necessary debt finance and makes the takeover bid.

In its heyday in 1987, LBOs accounted for 7 per cent by number and 21 per cent by value of all acquisitions. The structure of an LBO is very similar to that of an MBO, with senior debt, subordinated debt and equity. Some of the LBOs relied on bust-up of the targets to bring down the high leverage after the buyout. The ideal targets for an LBO have stable cash flows, scope for cost reduction, low gearing, good management and separable non-core businesses which can be divested to raise cash and pay down debt.

Returns to shareholders in LBOs have generally been high. DeAngelo and DeAngelo (1986) found in their study of 72 going-private LBOs that the average premium was 56 per cent to target shareholders. Hite and Vetsuypens (1989) also provide evidence that leveraged MBOs generate positive returns to the divestor shareholders.

After an extensive study of the sources of gains from buyouts, Kaplan (1989) found that the MBOs had increased their operating margin and income, but had cut down inventories and capital expenditure in the first two years after the buyout. He also found that tax gains arose in LBOs, but they mainly accrued to target shareholders or the divestor.

Junk bonds and LBOs

The 1980s also witnessed the use of 'junk bonds' in financing LBOs. Junk bonds are corporate bonds which have not been accorded the investment grade ratings by Moody's or the S & P rating services. They are deemed risky enough for certain trust institutions to be prevented from investing in them. Hence the name 'junk bond' (JB). A more respectable name for these is high-yield bonds. JBs were not invented in the 1980s, but they were put to use in takeovers, especially hostile ones, during that period. Whereas in the 1970s, JBs accounted for 4 per cent of all corporate bond issues each year, by 1982 this proportion had climbed to 6 per cent and by 1985 it had reached 15 per cent or $15 billion (Gaughan, 1991).

There were several reasons for the growth of JBs:

- Decline of privately placed bonds with no secondary market and imposing onerous covenants on borrowers.
- Emergence of a market-maker, Drexel, Burnham and Lambert (DBL), which provided liquidity to the JB market.
- The perception that JBs were not after all high risk: that is, their default rates were not very much higher than that of investment grade bonds.
- Demand for funds to finance the burgeoning acquisition activity.

One of the earliest users of JBs was T. Boone Pickens, who raised JB funds to make a hostile bid for Gulf Oil. His Mesa petroleum was a comparatively small firm, yet it could make a presumptuous bid for Gulf because of the availability of JB funding. The most spectacular LBO in history was that of RJR Nabisco, the food and tobacco giant, for a staggering $25 billion in 1989. This LBO was orchestrated by KKR in the face of an MBO by the chief executive, Ross Johnson. The MBO raised considerable disquiet about the conflict of interest between top management and shareholders in a going-private MBO. KKR financed the LBO partly with loan notes which were subsequently replaced by JBs.

Use of JBs raised the gearing of many US companies and led to some high-profile bankruptcies. Moreover, many DBL executives were charged with and convicted of insider dealing, fraud and racketeering. The most famous of these was 'the king of junk', Michael Milken. With his downfall and that of other stars, DBL's fate was sealed and it went bankrupt.

At the height of its powers, DBL attempted to spread its junk gospel to Europe. In 1988, it set up a £200 million First Britannia fund to invest in JBs. However, this fad never caught on in the UK, although there have been examples of some very imprudent UK LBOs, such as Lowndes Queensway, Magnet and Gateway. Despite these dramatic developments surrounding their modern incarnation, JBs have shown a surprising resilience and have recently enjoyed a revival in the USA (*Financial Times*, 17.6.1993).

Divestments in Europe

In recent years, divestments, in particular MBOs and MBIs, have become part of corporate restructuring in Continental Europe, as shown in Table 15.6. But countries differ in the level of activity.

Intensity of MBO activity in a country depends on a number of factors:

- Supply of divestments by corporations, family companies and government privatisation programmes.
- Corporate finance infrastructure, which includes venture capital funds, and legal and accounting services.
- Concentration of family-owned firms and traditional reluctance to use institutional finance.
- Quality of financial and accounting information about companies.
- Reluctance to allow free due diligence audit by outsiders.
- Small and illiquid stock markets which prevent exit by flotation.
- Legal impediments to using the target's resources to finance buyouts.

Table 15.6   Buyouts and buyins in Europe,
1980–9

Country	Number	Total value ($m)
UK	2992	12 334
France	430	1358
Sweden	127	1332
Germany	111	654
Italy	53	523
Netherlands	245	310
Denmark	63	226
Finland	40	113
Belgium	52	107
Switzerland	46	107
Spain	35	85
Austria	15	69
Ireland	131	34
Norway	29	11

Source: Wright *et al.* (1993).

An example of the national differences in approach to MBOs is provided by the institutional preference for certain forms of exit (Wright and Robbie, *Acquisitions Monthly*, European MBO supplement, 1993). The three most preferred methods in the UK, France, Netherlands and Sweden are as follows:

UK: trade sale, flotation and secondary MBO.

France: full trade sale, partial trade sale, secondary MBO.

Netherlands: trade sale, sale to other investors, share repurchase.

Sweden: flotation, trade sale, sale to financial investor.

In France, Italy and Spain, the most important source of MBOs is the family-owned or private company. The vendors are keen to ensure management succession, preserve the firm they have built up and also reward the incumbent management for their loyalty. In Germany, Netherlands and Nordic countries, corporate divestments are the major source of MBOs (Wright *et al.*, 1993). Going-private deals are very rare in Continental Europe, with the most active after the UK being France.

The corporate finance infrastructure is slowly being strengthened with the cross-border activities of many venture capital firms and mezzanine providers from London into the Continent. With the increasing harmonisation of company law and accounting rules, Continental companies will become more transparent and easier to value for MBO purposes. There is also an evolving trend towards recognising shareholder interests, and a developing culture of share value maximisation as an important goal of corporate policy. This again is likely to increase the importance of stock markets and reduce the uncertainty about exit.

Overview

This chapter has provided an introduction to corporate divestments. The motivations behind divestments and their relationship to prior acquisitions by divestors have been examined. The variety of forms that a divestment can take have been described, and their characteristics discussed. The impact of divestments on divestor's shareholder wealth has been considered, and empirical evidence in support of a positive impact cited. It has been argued that divestments are an increasingly international phenomenon. Divestments in the USA and on Continental Europe have been highlighted to provide a contrast to the UK experience.

References and further reading

Afshar, K., R.J. Taffler and P.S. Sudarsanam (1992) 'The effect of corporate divestments on shareholder wealth: the UK experience', *Journal of Banking and Finance*, **16**, 115–35.

DeAngelo, H. and L. DeAngelo (1986) 'Going private: the effects of a change in ownership structure', in J.M. Stern and D.H. Chew (eds.), *The Revolution in Corporate Finance*, Blackwell.

Gaughan, P.A. (1991) *Mergers and Acquisitions*, HarperCollins.

Hirschey, M., M.B. Slovin and J.K. Zaima (1990) 'Bank debt, insider trading and the return to corporate sell-offs', *Journal of Banking and Finance*, **14**, 85–98.

Hite, G., J.E. Owers and R.C. Rogers (1987) 'The market for interfirm asset sales: partial sell-offs and total liquidations', *Journal of Financial Economics*, **18**, 229–52.

Hite, G. and M. Vetsuypens (1989) 'Management buyouts of divisions and shareholder wealth', *Journal of Finance*, **44**, 4, 953–70.

Houlden, B. (1990) 'Buy-outs and beyond: motivations, strategies and ownership changes', *Long Range Planning*, **23**, 4, 73–7.

Jain, P.C. (1985) 'The effect of voluntary sell-off announcements on shareholder wealth', *Journal of Finance*, **40**, 1, 209–24.

Kaplan, S. (1989) 'The effects of management buy-outs on operating performance and value', *Journal of Financial Economics*, **24**, 217–54.

Klein, A. (1986) 'The timing and substance of divestiture announcements: individual, simultaneous and cumulative effects', *Journal of Finance*, **41**, 3, 685–97.

Linn, S.C. and M.S. Rozeff (1984) 'The corporate sell-off', *Midland Corporate Finance Journal*, **2**, 2, 17–26.

Miles, J. and J. Rosenfeld (1983) 'The effect of voluntary spin-off announcements on shareholder wealth', *Journal of Finance*, **38**, 5, 1597–606.

Thompson, S., M. Wright and K. Robbie (1989) 'Buy-outs, debt and efficiency', *Journal of Applied Corporate Finance*, **2**, 1, 76–85.

3i (1994) *The Changing Face of Management Buy-ins*, 3i Group plc, London.

Wright, M. and J. Coyne (1985) *Management Buy-outs*, Croom Helm.

Wright, M., B. Chiplin and S. Thompson (1993) 'The market for corporate control, divestments and buyouts', in M. Bishop and J. Kay (eds.), *European Mergers and Merger Policy*, Oxford University Press.

Wright, M., S. Thompson, B. Chiplin and K. Robbie (1991) *Buy-ins and Buy-outs*, Graham & Trotman.

16

Cross-border acquisitions

In recent years the number of acquisitions made by companies in foreign countries has increased substantially. Such transnational or cross-border acquisitions (CBAs) have been motivated by a variety of strategic considerations, which often differ from those which drive purely domestic acquisitions. The approach to CBAs is not a straightforward extension of the approach to domestic acquisitions. CBAs are much more complex due to differences in political and economic environment, corporate organisation, culture, tradition, tax rules, law and accounting rules between the countries of the acquirer and the target company.

Acquirers need to have regard for these differences in considering, executing and managing overseas acquisitions. At first sight, the additional complexity of CBAs makes them very prone to failure, but this need not always be so. In this chapter, we examine the motivations behind CBAs, the differences in the political and economic environment among different countries and their impact on CBAs, problems in negotiating foreign acquisitions and the obstacles to efficient post-acquisition management.

This chapter provides some survey evidence on the success of CBAs and on the approaches taken by successful acquirers overseas. From the evidence we draw together those factors which seem to contribute to successful acquisitions. Some of these are common to those relevant to domestic acquisitions, but there are several which are of particular significance to CBAs.

Alternative overseas expansion strategies

Where a firm sees profitable opportunities in serving an overseas market with its own products or service goods, an acquisition is not the only vehicle for achieving that aim. The firm has the following options:

- Exporting from home to the overseas market.
- Licensing an overseas company to produce the goods.
- Greenfield investment in production facilities overseas.
- Acquisition or merger.
- Joint venture or other strategic alliance.

These alternative methods entail different costs, benefits and risks to the firm, and the choice has to be made by a trade-off among these. This book is concerned with the last two modes of entry into a foreign market, and this chapter discusses acquisitions and mergers. Chapter 17 deals with strategic alliances.

Recent trends in cross-border acquisitions

Recent years have witnessed an enormous spurt in cross-border acquisitions and mergers, minority interests and joint ventures. EC companies spent $9 billion in 1984, $64 billion in 1989 and $30 billion in 1991 on CBAs. In the same years, US companies spent $2.6 billion, $23.2 billion and $7.3 billion respectively. Japanese companies spent $0.2 billion, $14.7 billion and $3.7 billion. Thus 1989 represented the peak of CBAs. After a fall in 1991, these acquisitions have resumed an upward trend except in Japan, as shown in Table 16.1 for 1991–3. In 1992 the global CBAs amounted to $75.4 billion and in 1993 to $64.2 billion. Thus CBAs represent a massive shift of capital and corporate control around the world.

In 1991–3, the USA was a net seller of companies. So was the UK. France has been the most aggressive buyer of all countries with a net buy of $14.5 billion. Germany and Holland were also net buyers, but on a smaller scale. EC companies together were marginal net buyers of $5 billion, whereas the Rest of Europe were net sellers. Japan

Table 16.1 Cross-border acquisitions, 1991–3

Country/ region	Buying ($m)			Selling ($m)		
	1991	1992	1993	1991	1992	1993
USA	7267	14 455	15 309	17 926	10 396	18 651
UK	5909	6085	13 465	9181	15 078	7053
Germany	4679	4106	3249	2666	6742	1779
France	11 375	10 331	5926	2618	6678	3842
Holland	3754	1397	5738	1331	5129	4238
All EC	30 456	31 555	32 616	22 152	42 351	23 052
Rest of Europe	4067	5290	2794	3326	6416	7403
Japan	3696	4263	558	84	309	81

Source: KPMG (1994).

played a small role in cross-border acquisitions during 1991–3. The reason for low-level Japanese activity is discussed below.

While there are company-specific motives for undertaking CBAs, there are also massive economic forces which have acted to unleash the tide of CBAs we have seen. These include the following:

- The economic integration of the EC represented by the Single Market which began in 1992.

- Globalisation of the marketplace for many products, with the convergence of consumer needs, preferences and tastes.

- Increase in competition, which has assumed a global character with companies competing in several markets.

- Explosion of technology based on massive investments in R & D, design, marketing and distribution. To recover these costs, companies have to sell to the largest market possible, which means globalisation.

- Availability of capital to finance acquisitions and innovations in financial markets such as junk bonds (see Chapters 11 and 15).

- Privatisation of state enterprises, as in the former East Germany, which have become targets for foreign acquirers.

These economic forces have also brought about the restructuring of many industries. Cross-border acquisitions have played a part in such restructuring, as illustrated by the current insurance industry takeovers in the European Union and the pharmaceutical sector takeovers in the USA (see Case Study 16.1).

CASE STUDY 16.1   Industry restructuring and acquisitions

The UK's Commercial Union acquired the French insurer Groupe Victoire for £1.46 billion in June 1994. This was preceded by a string of cross-border mergers in the insurance industry driven by the Single European Market. In 1992 the European Union regulation allowing for a single licence for insurance companies to operate within the EU came into effect and triggered the takeover moves.

Drug companies' profits have been under pressure from governments, employers and insurance companies determined to drive down costs. President Clinton's health care reforms were aimed at reducing the cost of health care in the USA. Moreover, there was a trend towards generic substitution of branded drugs. Development costs were also escalating. To counter these pressures, many companies resorted to mergers as a means of spreading costs and increasing their negotiating strength vis-à-vis the buyers. Roche of Switzerland bought Syntex the US drugs company for $5.3 billion. Smith Kline Beecham, the Anglo–US company, bought the American Diversified Pharmaceutical Services for $2.3 billion.

Sources: *Guardian*, 11.6.1994; *Financial Times*, 4.5.1994.

Some industries have experienced more upheaval in the form of cross-border takeovers than others. The extent of acquisition activity in an industry reflects the nature of competition in that industry, the product life cycle, changes in regulations, the current level of concentration and technological changes. Chemicals and pharmaceuticals has been the most active sector in terms of cross-border takeovers in 1991–3, as shown in Table 16.2.

Table 16.2   Value of cross-border acquisitions in industries ($m)

Industry	1991	1992	1993
Chemicals and pharmaceuticals	5934	5284	12 337
Food, drinks and tobacco	3641	12 358	5388
Banking and finance	3237	11 472	5362
Electrical and electronics	5803	7309	4206
Oil and gas	2406	7093	3690
Insurance	5105	1152	3630
Total	49 730	75 382	64 242

Source: KPMG (1994).

Motivations behind cross-border acquisitions

Companies undertake international acquisitions for a number of strategic or tactical reasons:

- *Growth orientation*: to escape small home market, to extend markets served, to achieve economy of scale.

- *Access to inputs*: to access raw materials to ensure consistent supply, to access technology, to access latest innovations, to access cheap and productive labour.

- *Exploit unique advantages*: to exploit the company's brands, reputation, design, production and management capabilities.

- *Defensive*: to diversify across products and markets to reduce earnings volatility, to reduce dependence on exports, to avoid home country political and economic instability, to compete with foreign competitors in their own territory, to circumvent protective trade barriers in the host country.

- *Response to client needs*: to provide home country clients with service for their overseas subsidiaries, e.g. banks and accountancy firms.

- *Opportunism*: to exploit temporary advantages, e.g. a favourable exchange rate making foreign acquisition cheap.

Home country is the country of origin of the acquirer and host country is that of the acquired company. Many Swedish companies like Electrolux have been active cross-border acquirers, one of the reasons being the relatively small size of the Swedish market. Companies like Coca-Cola and Pepsi have expanded abroad to exploit their unique brands. Some companies have made US acquisitions in order to gain access to technology or be close to their customers. This is illustrated by UK company Dowty's acquisitions in the USA (see Case Study 16.2).

Barriers to takeovers

Takeovers, as we have seen in Chapter 12, face a variety of obstacles in different countries. Many of these are the same whether or not the bidder is a domestic or a foreign company. Some major barriers

CASE STUDY 16.2   Dowty's US acquisitions

Dowty was an international high-technology engineering company manufacturing advanced systems and products for aerospace, defence, maritime and information technology markets. Between 1976 and 1987 it acquired four US companies in aerospace, electronics and telecommunications for a total of $108 million.

Dowty used its US acquisitions to cross-sell its and the subsidiaries' products using each other's distribution channels in the USA and Europe. The acquisitions improved the company's international competitiveness, added new products, provided unique access to Boeing, the aircraft manufacturer, and enhanced the level and range of technology within the group. Moreover, the US subsidiaries were used to provide market intelligence on trends and new developments in the very important US market. The access to US collaborative agreements and technologically advanced products as a result of acquisitions was thought to give the company greater competitive advantage in Europe.

Source: J. Hamill and J. Crosbie, *Acquisitions Monthly*, October 1989.

are listed in Table 16.3. Use of many of these barriers by target companies to block takeover bids was discussed and illustrated in Chapter 12 on takeover defences. Countries differ from one another in terms of the level and effectiveness of these barriers.

In Continental Europe, family control of companies, even the listed ones, is a formidable obstacle to hostile takeovers. For example, in Italy, some of even the largest companies are family owned and controlled. Germany's industrial and commercial backbone is the Mittelstand, which is made up of family companies. Among these, the attitude to takeovers is one of reluctance and hostility, especially if any post-acquisition asset stripping is suspected. For this reason, British and American purchasers have gained a notoriety for their short-termism. For the owner-managers of Mittelstand companies, price is not everything, since they cherish their companies and wish them to be preserved (David Waller, *Financial Times*, 9.11.1993).

The importance of recognising the complexity of workers' rights, and the role of trade unions and politicians, is exemplified by the experience of the German detergents company Benckiser Group when it bought two Italian firms in 1987 (see Case Study 16.3).

The absence of reliable accounting information hinders a proper valuation of the target company. In many Continental countries like

Table 16.3 Barriers to takeovers in different countries

(a) Structural barriers

Statutory	Strong powers for supervisory boards to block mergers. Unions and workers' councils have say on takeovers and strong redundancy rights.
	Issue of bearer shares, double voting or non-voting shares. Absence of one share one vote (OSOV) principle.
	Discriminatory tax laws against foreign acquirers, e.g. withholding taxes on dividends.
Regulatory	Antitrust regulation, foreign investment review, rules of stock exchange and professional self-regulatory bodies.
	Absence of statutory or voluntary bodies to regulate takeovers.
Infrastructure	Absence of M & A services, e.g. legal, accounting, merchant banking services.

(b) Technical barriers

Management	Two-tier boards which cannot be removed or changed quickly. Families dominate share holding.
	Powers to issue shares with differential voting rights or to friendly persons. Powers to limit maximum voting rights. Powers to override shareholders in company's interest.

(c) Information barriers

Accounting	Accounting statements not available, quality of information poor. Low compliance with international accounting rules. Accounting practice biased to avoid tax liability, or conservative.
Shareholders	Due to issue of bearer shares, shareholding structure not known.
Regulation	Regulatory procedures not known or unpredictable.

(d) Culture and tradition

Attitude	'To sell is to admit failure' syndrome; dislike of hostile bids; dislike of institutional constraints on dividends or short-term profits. Xenophobia. Unwillingness to disclose information.
Value system	High premium on trust and confidence in negotiations rather than formal contracts.

Spain and Greece, accounts may not be publicly available. Where they are, they might not have been prepared rigorously in accordance with internationally accepted accounting principles. Moreover, in countries like Germany and Japan, accounts are prepared to

CASE STUDY 16.3   Benckiser's redundancy problems in Italy

Benckiser acquired two Italian companies, Mira Lanza and Panigal, in 1987, and planned redundancies in the companies as part of its rationalisation strategy. Italy has a state-assisted redundancy system, called Cassa Integrazione (CI), under which the central government pays a special unemployment benefit for a period of up to three years. The aim of the system is to help employees laid off as a result of short-term fluctuations in the market, in the belief that they would be reinstated when the business picked up.

Since CI's costs are borne by the state, redundancy plans need government approval and the decision is political. This increases the incentive for unions to call strikes to publicise the redundancy effects. Benckiser was therefore thrust into the public limelight and had to persuade the politicians of the merits of the redundancy plan. This atmosphere of confrontation and crisis was quite different from Benckiser's own experience in Germany, where there was much closer involvement between unions and management in resolving similar issues.

Source: Haig Simonian, *Financial Times*, 31.8.1990.

satisfy the tax rules and may tend to understate profits. In Germany, there has also been a traditional bias towards conservative valuation of assets and overprovisions which again understate profits.

In using the accounting information in those countries, the bidder therefore needs to adjust the profits, assets and liabilities to realistic levels. Although, within the European Union, many basic accounting rules have been harmonised, in practice there is a very wide variation in the availability and quality of accounting information. The problem created by accounting differences is illustrated by the case of T & N's German acquisition (see Case Study 16.4).

Cultural and political barriers to cross-border acquisitions often assume a high profile and can cause adverse publicity to the acquirer. Fear of foreign companies can arise even when the host and home countries have similar cultural profiles and speak the same language, as shown when the National Australia Bank (NAB) acquired the Bank of New Zealand (BNZ) for $787 million in 1992. Many New Zealanders harbour deepseated suspicions of their bigger neighbour. The acquisition was opposed by both politicians and shareholders, who even staged pickets outside BNZ branches (Terry Hall, *Financial Times*, 6.11.1992).

CASE STUDY 16.4   T & N faces up to German accounting complexity

T & N, the British automotive component manufacturer, agreed to buy Goetze Group (GG), a German company in the same line of business, in 1993. It needed to secure the approval of its UK shareholders, and for this purpose had to provide an accounting report on GG covering the previous three years. The London Stock Exchange (LSE) requirement was for such a report to conform to either UK or international accounting standards. Although GG's accounts had been prepared and audited in accordance with German accounting standards, they did not comply with the LSE requirement.

Differences between the accounting rules included accelerated depreciation, stock valuation without overheads, treatment of all leases as operating, and the unfunded nature of pensions in German accounts. These differences were so great that T & N obtained a waiver from the LSE, and T & N shareholders were warned that GG's net assets were understated in comparison with UK rules.

Source: N. Higgins and S. Roberts, *Acquisitions Monthly*, October 1993.

Post-acquisition integration

Integrating a foreign acquisition is generally much more complex and often presents formidable problems. Many of the approaches to integration of domestic acquisitions discussed in Chapters 4 and 14 are relevant to foreign acquisitions. However, with the latter, the lack of familiarity with the target's environment demands that the acquirer has a well-thought-out programme of integration. This does not mean there will be no surprises or that everything can be done according to this programme. Any expectation of that kind leads to the error of determinism discussed in Chapters 4 and 14.

Since the acquired company managers and staff tend to be unfamiliar with the language, managerial behaviour and corporate custom of the acquirer, they need to be reassured even more than in a domestic context of the intentions of the acquirer. The acquirer must develop a vision for the target under the new dispensation, and communicate this vision with clarity. The benefits to the acquired company, its managers and staff must be explicitly outlined. The interface between the two companies must be handled with extra sensitivity. Compensation arrangements for the acquired managers must be designed in accordance with the host country norms, and not transplanted from the acquirer.

In general, a foreign acquirer is likely to need the continued services of the incumbent management of the acquired company, since without them continuity may not be preserved. However, where the acquisition is based on a turnaround strategy, the management of the underperforming target will be dispensed with very quickly and a new management team put in its place. In carrying out rationalisation and redundancies, the local employment laws must be understood and complied with. Otherwise, as illustrated in the Benckiser case (see Case Study 16.3), the acquirer may be bogged down in a bitter and prolonged confrontation.

The application of these guidelines to a successful consummation of an acquisition is illustrated by Electrolux's acquisition of Zanussi in 1985 (see Case Study 16.5).

Survey evidence on international acquisitions

McKinsey, the management consultants, have examined the success of cross-border acquisitions (Bleeke *et al.*, 1993). Success is measured by (1) the improvement in the acquired company's return on equity and return on assets, and (2) whether the return on capital exceeded the acquirer's cost of capital. They report for a sample of 28 foreign acquisition programmes by 8 US, 9 Japanese and 11 European corporations. These programmes represented 319 deals valued at $68 billion.

The overall success rate for the sample was 57 per cent which is much better than for purely domestic acquisitions. Indeed, it compares favourably with the 55 per cent reported by Hunt *et al.* (1987) (see Chapter 14) and the much gloomier evidence from statistical studies (see Chapter 13). The McKinsey study identifies a number of critical success factors for this sample:

- Targets are in the core business of the acquirer.
- Targets are strong local performers in financial and capabilities terms.
- Acquirers focus on a few critical elements of the targets' business systems, especially those that are global.
- The acquirer and the acquired carry out significant mutual skill transfers.

- Acquirers integrate only the critical systems immediately.
- Acquirers learn from their experience (Bleeke *et al.*, 1993, ch. 6).

Acquisition programmes in core businesses have a high success rate, with 14 out of 22 regarded as successful. Where the targets had strong local performance 8 out of 9 programmes succeeded, whereas without such performance 7 out of 10 failed. Successful acquirers typically focused on critical global functions such as R & D in pharmaceuticals to give them worldwide competitive advantage. Skills transferred included product management, selling and distribution management, and product development. These skills were generally embedded in the organisation as a whole and not just in individuals.

The skill transfer mechanism was through moving a few senior managers between the acquirers and the acquired. In all 11 successful acquisitions skills transfer took place, whereas in 10 out of 13 unsuccessful programmes there was no transfer. Integration was done at a different pace depending upon how important the system element being integrated was. For example, a consumer products company rapidly patched its sales order entry system with the acquired, but delayed R & D integration.

Hoover (1993) focuses on the experience of Scandinavian acquirers in the USA. Out of 52 deals between 1970 and the mid-1980s, only 20 met the success criterion – that the return on capital exceeded the acquirer's cost of capital. Hoover undertook a detailed study of 11 leading Scandinavian companies' acquisition experience and distilled the characteristics which made a difference between success and failure. Successful acquirers had a predetermined strategic programme for the USA based on the following:

- The acquirers possessed a superior and transferable product or concept, focusing on a niche market to gain market share, targeting the relevant distribution channel and making a proper assessment of industry risk.
- The acquirers aimed to achieve tight financial objectives, and the acquisition teams were driven by these objectives. The acquired managers were given aggressive goals to achieve.
- The acquisition teams had managers with multiple skills and enjoyed the commitment of top management.
- Sources of synergy were estimated with due allowance for the tendency to overestimate.

CASE STUDY 16.5: Electrolux integrates Zanussi

Electrolux (E) of Sweden, the home appliance manufacturer, pursued a strategy of taking over underperforming target candidates in related lines of business and turning them around. In 1985, E acquired Zanussi (Z), also a manufacturer of home appliances, from Italy. After the acquisition, E took several steps to integrate Z and make it a profitable operation:

- New respected senior Italian managers were brought in.
- E communicated its objectives for Z clearly, and these held out good prospects for Z under E.
- Integration plans were quickly developed and implemented.
- The new senior management injected a new culture based on the Swedish work ethic.
- E first put Z on an even keel by providing competitive credit terms to its customers; the new management negotiated favourable terms from financiers and suppliers, helped by Z being now part of E.
- E discussed the plans with the unions and obtained their co-operation.
- Mutual transfer of strategic capabilities was initiated, e.g. technology and operational resources sharing.
- The implementation plan contained strong symbolic ingredients: negotiations were open; E's senior managers visited Z regularly; Z union leaders visited E and were impressed by the positive aspects of Swedish management.
- Z managers were given much autonomy; important functions were retained in Italy, contrary to pre-acquisition fears of Z management and staff.
- Z's new management also took tough decisions; middle management was told to 'play or quit'; the industrial relations manager of Z was sacked.
- Accounting and financial controls were put in place quickly. Task forces made up of both E and Z managers were set up to implement the plan to deadlines; tight financial targets, i.e. return on assets, were set.
- A positive integration atmosphere was created, with mutual understanding between E and Z. Capabilities transfer took place in this atmosphere.

Source: Adapted from Ghoshal and Haspeslagh (1993).

- Negotiations were hard-nosed with a 'walk-away' price.
- Expectations and needs of US target managements were considered sensitively, with incentive-based compensation to retain them.

- A pre-planned integration programme was applied swiftly (Hoover, 1993).

The above success characteristics of Scandinavian acquirers are similar to those observed by Hunt *et al.* (1987) in their study of British acquirers in the USA. They emphasise the need to mix with US managers at both business and social levels, to be tolerant of difference in management styles, to build trust and confidence, and to introduce executive share options. Such a compensation arrangement is particularly important for US managers.

Overview

This chapter has described the increasing trend towards cross-border acquisitions and mergers. It has examined the industry-related factors which have contributed to this trend, and the corporate motivations behind cross-border acquisitions. The barriers to takeovers in many European countries have been highlighted. The problems of post-acquisition integration are more complex in cross-border acquisitions than in purely domestic ones. Survey evidence has been provided that cross-border acquisitions are successful in more than half the cases. Critical success factors in cross-border acquisitions have been identified from the survey evidence. Acquisition is only one of several alternatives to service an overseas market. Strategic alliance is another. It is to this that we now turn in Chapter 17.

References and further reading

Bleeke, J., D. Ernst, J.A. Isono and D.D. Weinberg (1993) 'Succeeding at cross-border mergers and acquisitions' (chapter 6) and 'The new shape of cross-border mergers and acquisitions' (chapter 7) in J. Bleeke and D. Ernst (eds.), *Collaborating to Compete*, John Wiley.

Coopers & Lybrand (1989) *Barriers to Takeovers in the European Community*, Department of Trade and Industry, London.

Ghoshal, S. and P. Haspeslagh (1993) 'Electrolux: the acquisition and integration of Zanussi' in J. Henry and A. Eccles (eds.), *European Cases in Strategic Management*, Chapman Hall.

Hoover, W.E., Jr (1993) 'Making successful acquisitions: United States' in J. Bleeke and D. Ernst (eds.) *Collaborating to Compete*, chapter 12, McKinsey & Co, John Wiley.

Hunt, J., S. Lees, J.J. Grumbar and P.D. Vivian (1987) *Acquisitions: The human factor*, London Business School.

KPMG (1994) *Dealwatch: The KPMG Corporate Finance Network Report*, 1.

17

Strategic alliances

We have seen that acquisitions and mergers often fail to live up to their expectations and objectives. Companies therefore need to explore alternative means of achieving the same objectives. In recent years, there has been a surge of strategic alliances among companies across the globe. These strategic alliances fall short of outright acquisitions and take a variety of forms, from simple agreements between firms to buy or sell each other's goods, to the creation of separate and legally distinct entities.

Strategic alliances are motivated by considerations such as cost reduction, technology sharing, product development, market access or access to capital. Their objectives are not dissimilar to those in conventional acquisitions. Properly structured strategic alliances can be a less expensive alternative to acquisitions. The logic is that, if two or more companies pool their resources, their joint objectives can be secured more easily and economically. Despite the attractions of strategic alliances, their track record is not very good. Some estimates suggest that more than two-thirds of strategic alliances fail.

In this chapter, we describe the different types of strategic alliance and their characteristics. The recent trend towards such alliances in different industries and different global regions is examined. The basic structure of an alliance and the motivations of partners to an alliance are delineated. The reasons for instability in alliances are explored. The chapter concludes with a summary of research findings on the performance of strategic alliances and some guidelines for avoiding failure.

Types of strategic alliance

Any arrangement or agreement under which two or more firms co-operate in order to achieve certain commercial objectives may be called a strategic alliance. The various types of strategic alliance are as follows:

- Supply or purchase agreement.
- Marketing or distribution agreement.
- Agreement to provide technical services.
- Management contract.
- Licensing of know-how, technology, design or patent.
- Franchising.
- Joint venture.

These co-operative arrangements differ in the following respects:

- The scope for joint decision making.
- Capital commitment.
- The way the risks and rewards are shared.
- Organisational structure.

Capital commitment often arises in the form of an equity investment.

While joint ventures may be equity or non-equity ventures, the other types of co-operative arrangement are generally non-equity. For example, with a licence or a management contract, the partner giving the licence or providing the management service will receive a royalty or management fee. The royalty may in some cases be based on the profits accruing to the licensee. Non-equity arrangements do not normally create jointly owned entities distinct from the alliance partners. The scope for joint decision making is also limited.

Equity and non-equity joint ventures

In this book we concentrate on joint ventures. An equity joint venture (EJV) involves two or more legally distinct firms (the parents) investing in the venture and participating in the venture's management. The venture itself is constituted as a separate entity distinct from the parents. A venture may come into being as a new activity, or may be created by transferring and pooling some or all of the existing interests of parents. An EJV is very similar to a merger, and an example is given in Case Study 17.1. A non-equity joint venture (NEJV) may also involve the pooling of resources, but no separate entity is created. The purpose of equity investment is twofold: first, to finance the operations of the joint venture (JV); second, to enhance the commitment of the parents to the venture.

CASE STUDY 17.1   Advanced Micro Devices (AMD) and Fujitsu venture together

AMD, a US semiconductor manufacturer with a turnover of $1.2 billion, entered into a production joint venture with Fujitsu, Japan's biggest computer company, in July 1992. The venture was formed to build a $700 million factory to manufacture flash memory devices. AMD had the flash technology, but needed a big partner to finance the investment and also bear the large risk involved. Fujitsu needed the technology.

A JV company in which AMD and Fujitsu owned equal shares was to be set up. In addition, each parent was to take about 5 per cent equity stake in the other. From AMD's point of view, this would ensure Fujitsu's interest in the financial success of AMD. The agreement forbade either parent from producing the devices outside the JV.

Source: *Financial Times*, 15.7.1992.

The operations of the JV may sometimes overlap with those of the parents. For example, they may be targeting the same markets and selling the same or similar products. Such an overlap creates inevitable friction between the JV and the parent concerned. A parent may transfer some of its activities to the venture, but it may also enter into similar ventures with other parents. Again this may lead to a conflict of interest. Since the management of a venture is often shared between the parents, further conflicts may arise if the two parents are not compatible in terms of organisational objectives and culture. A joint venture has to be negotiated and structured in such a way as to minimise these conflicts. The sources of these frictions and conflicts and how they may be guarded against are discussed below.

Since a joint venture is a co-operative enterprise, the line between co-operation and a cartel may often be blurred. Thus JVs may give rise to concerns about their competitive implications, and are hence subject to the antitrust regulations in the UK, the European Union and other countries, such as the USA. The tax implications of different structures and locations of the JV must also be taken into account in formulating a JV, in order to maximise the benefits to the parents. How the JVs will be accounted for in the parents' published accounts also needs to be considered in structuring a JV.

International joint ventures

While JVs between companies operating within the same country (domestic JVs) are important, some of the largest JVs of recent years have been international, involving companies from different countries. The reasons for international joint ventures (IJVs) are many:

- Globalisation of product markets.
- Globalisation of competition.
- Rapid technological change and short product life cycle.
- Huge costs of research and development.
- High fixed costs of brand development, distribution networks and information technology.
- Diffusion of technological capabilities and resources.
- Relatively high cost of acquisitions and mergers.

Increasing globalisation of product markets has resulted from the convergence of consumer tastes, preferences and life styles. This means that competition among companies to serve those product markets is also global. This has given opportunities for companies from one part of the world to market their products in another part. However, such global marketing and distribution cannot be undertaken by any company on its own. Hence the strategic alliances aimed at marketing and distribution. For example, Allied-Lyons of Britain entered into an alliance with Suntory of Japan in 1989 to distribute each other's drinks products in the UK, USA and Japan. The two partners also entered into a joint sales and manufacturing operation for food products in Australia.

Many of today's products are based on complex technologies, some of them cutting edge. Competition has increasingly been shaped by technological innovations, which themselves are subject to intense competition. The cost of research and development leading to these innovations has mounted beyond the technical and material resources of any single company. Hence the need for alliances aimed at technology sharing and development.

Technological competition has also meant that product life cycles have become shorter, thus escalating the pressure for new technologies and new products. Very few companies on their own can keep up with such a technological spiral. Therefore, companies have to share and pool their resources.

Technological capabilities are now much more diffused than in the past, with many more companies from many more countries being repositories of pockets of technological expertise and excellence. There is, therefore, an incentive for these companies to pool their expertise and achieve technological synergy. An example of this fragmentation of technological capabilities is in semiconductors. IBM's alliance with Toshiba of Japan and Siemens of Germany to develop a 256-megabit chip illustrates the alliance approach to overcoming this fragmentation.

The so-called multimedia products, combining voice, visual and information technologies demonstrate that technology can no longer be neatly pigeon-holed, and that boundaries between technologies are becoming irrelevant. This again demands that companies with capabilities in different areas come together by mergers or alliances to create these new products. This explains the scramble among telecommunications and computer companies to form alliances or to merge. The attempted merger of Sprint, the American telecommunications group, and Electronic Data Services is an example of this trend (*The Guardian*, 17.5.1994). British Telecom's alliance with MCI of the USA, and the alliance between Sprint of the USA and French Telecom and Deutsche Telecom, are recent examples of this trend.

The cost of cutting-edge technological research and development, of producing products for far-flung international markets, of distributing them and of information technology has led to very high fixed costs. One way of spreading these costs is to form alliances for research and development, production, distribution, etc. Thus alliances have become a commonsense method of spreading huge fixed costs.

Although many of the market access and cost reduction goals can be achieved by mergers and acquisitions, in many cases the cost and risks of mergers and acquisitions may be greater than with strategic alliances, although they could also avoid some of the problems of management control, conflict of interest and so on, which have plagued joint ventures.

Trends in international joint ventures

Glaister and Buckley (1994) examine the patterns of international joint ventures formed by UK companies with companies from Western Europe, the USA and Japan during 1980 to 1989. The 520 IJVs in their sample are those reported in the *Financial Times*. The regional distribution of the sample IJVs is shown in Table 17.1.

Thus Western Europe was the most important destination for UK IJVs. In general, IJVs increased in popularity in 1985–9 compared to 1980–4, with 60 per cent of the sample IJVs being formed in the second period and 40 per cent in the first. Much of the increase occurred in Western Europe, no doubt in response to the increasing economic integration of the European Union countries and the impending Single European Market in 1992.

Glaister and Buckley (1994) also report several other interesting findings:

- *Industry pattern*: about 60 per cent of the IJVs were in financial services, telecommunications, aerospace, automobiles, chemicals, distribution, computers, and food and drink.

- *Purpose*: 45 per cent of the IJVs were related to a non-marketing purpose such as production or R & D, 27 per cent to marketing and 28 per cent to provision of a service such as insurance or design consultancy. The purpose varied between regions, with marketing dominating in the USA and Japan, and non-marketing dominating in Western Europe.

- *Partners*: about 85 per cent of the IJVs were with just one partner.

Table 17.1 International joint ventures of UK firms, 1980–9

Region	Number	% of total
Western Europe	213	41
USA	188	36
Japan	90	17
Other	29	6
Total	520	100

Note: Other includes partners from more than one region or from outside the three regions.

- *Equity interest*: equity JVs slightly outnumbered the non-equity JVs. In two-thirds of cases, the UK partner had 50 per cent or more of equity interest.

Models of a joint venture

Co-operative model

The above analysis of IJVs reveals definite patterns in terms of industry, purpose and equity interest. This suggests that JVs are more appropriate in certain industries than in others. They can secure some purposes more effectively than others. Further, the existence of equity interest is deemed necessary in certain cases, but not in others. How do we explain these choices which JV partners make?

The choices are determined by the basic structure of a JV, which is a co-operative enterprise in which the motivations and payoffs of the partners may not always be congruent. In the case of JVs among companies who are also actual or potential competitors in the same markets or in related markets, JVs can give rise to opportunistic behaviour: that is, cheating. Whether any partner in a JV can get away with cheating depends upon the negative payoff – the punitive sanction to such behaviour.

The incentives to co-operation and the sanction against cheating are captured by a famous model in game theory known as the Prisoner's Dilemma (PD). This dilemma arises when two prisoners jointly charged with an offence face different payoffs to confessing and not confessing to the offence, as shown in Figure 17.1. In this game, if both prisoners refrain from confessing, they are *collectively* better off than if one confesses and the other does not. In the latter case, the confessor is rewarded with freedom, while the non-confessing partner gets a seven-year prison sentence. Thus the incentive to cheat on the partner is greater than the incentive to co-operate.

Each prisoner's decision problem is complicated by (1) lack of communication between them and (2) the possibility of getting away with 'squealing'. If each partner can trust the other – that is, if there is a form of non-verbal communication born of years of working together – then the chances of both prisoners not confessing are improved. Alternatively, if squealing does not lead to a happy ending in blissful freedom, but leads to sanctions from the non-

PRISONER 2

	Confess	Not confess
Confess	Both get 5 years	P1 goes free P2 gets 7 years
Not confess	P1 gets 7 years P2 goes free	Both get 1 year

PRISONER 1

Note: P1 and P2 are prisoners 1 and 2.

Figure 17.1   The Prisoner's Dilemma.

confessing prisoner's friends or worse, again a co-operative behaviour will ensue.

Many joint ventures have built-in opportunities for cheating and
for one partner to gain at the expense of the other. For example, one
partner can assiduously learn all the other can teach while withhold-
ing its own contribution. Early JVs between American and Japanese
firms were often cited as examples of such behaviour, with the
Japanese as the offending party. The JV then becomes a zero-sum,
rather than a positive-sum, game.

The real trick in constructing a successful JV is therefore to
increase the payoffs to co-operative behaviour and the sanctions to
the 'beggar my partner' behaviour. Careful selection of a partner
with a reputation for honest behaviour, and good communication
between partners, will help. Further, mutual dependency between
the partners is important. Such a mutual dependency in a JV context
means that the partners bring complementary strengths to the
venture. Where they have the same strengths and weaknesses, the

tendency will be for them to gain from each other rather than by working together.

Mutual dependency in a single, one-off venture may not, however, prevent a partner from learning as much as possible of the other partner's skills, technology and management systems, and making use of this learning subsequently to gain competitive advantage over the former partner. This is less likely to happen if the venture is of a long or indefinite duration, or where it is accepted by both partners as the beginning of a series of future ventures. In the latter case, the expectation that the venture is a repetitive game dilutes the incentive to cheat the first time round. The aim, therefore, is to maximise the benefits to both parties from a long-term commitment.

One way of increasing the long-term mutual commitment is to provide for equity investment in the venture by both parties. In the alliance between Advanced Micro Devices and Fujitsu, the mutual minority equity investment was clearly motivated by this consideration (see Case Study 17.1 above).

Transaction cost model

A joint venture requires an agreement between two or more parties, and leads to transaction costs which include contracting, monitoring and enforcement costs. The venture partners must draw up a sufficiently detailed contract to cover the structure, mutual rights and responsibilities, performance measurement, and enforcement of contractual obligations and remedies. These transaction costs depend on the nature of the venture and the relationship between the venture partners. A complex venture such as in high-technology research and development needs a more elaborate contract than a service provision venture, since the future outcome of the R & D is less predictable and the attendant risk much greater.

Transaction costs can be reduced if the venture is based on trust and commitment of the parties. Since, in a joint venture, a successful outcome depends on the interactions between people from the two parents, a relational contract based on trust and commitment is much more important than a formal, legally enforceable contract. An ideal venture is one in which the partners sign a contract and then put it away never to be referred to again. A frequent reading of the contract signals lack of trust and commitment.

Structuring a joint venture

A joint venture operation involves four stages (Zahra and Elhagrasey, 1994):

1. Choice of joint venture as a strategic alternative.
2. Partner selection.
3. Negotiation and selection of contractual form.
4. Management of the venture.

At the first stage, the firm has to evaluate carefully whether a joint venture is the appropriate mechanism for achieving its strategic objectives. A joint venture should be compared with alternative modes, such as a greenfield operation, an acquisition or a merger. In making the choice, the costs, benefits and risks of the alternatives must be considered.

Partner selection for a JV is a very important step, and partners should be evaluated on several criteria: the partner's objectives in a JV, the compatibility of these objectives between partners, the potential partner's commitment, resources, management style and organisational systems, and corporate culture. The track record of the potential partner in JVs must also be examined.

Negotiating a JV agreement should be done with the utmost care. The objectives of the JV must be stated with clarity. The assumptions behind the expected performance must be explicitly articulated. Benchmarks for measuring performance and formulae for sharing the costs and profits of the venture must be agreed. Negotiation must also cover the arrangements for the management of the venture, the contribution each partner will make to the management, who will assume the leadership, and what will be the relationship between the parents and the venture as well as between the parents.

Each partner will be concerned to ensure that access to its core technology is carefully regulated. It may be necessary to ring-fence such technology. Case Study 17.2 highlights this problem in the joint venture between GE and Snecma. In other cases, ring-fencing is necessary in order to prevent your partner emerging as a latter-day competitor. Otherwise the venture will be reduced to a meaningless and 'hollowed-out' shell.

Duration of the venture and the exit must be agreed between the

CASE STUDY 17.2   GE ring-fences its core technology

American company GE and the French company Snecma formed a joint venture called CFM in 1974 to design and produce an engine for small civilian aircraft. The US government was reluctant to allow GE to use the top-secret design of the B1 engine core for the new engine development. However, after direct talks between Presidents Nixon and Pompidou, the US government agreed that the gas turbine core could be used, but GE could not give Snecma the technology. GE then built the gas turbine core and Snecma the low-pressure outer parts of the engine. Thus within the JV there were still significant proprietary technologies which the partners did not reveal to each other.

Source: *Financial Times*, 1.2.1989.

partners. How the assets, the technology and the profits and losses at the time of exit will be shared must form part of the agreement. The majority of JVs are terminated by the strong partner buying out the weak partner. Of course, such an end may be engineered by the buyer in an opportunistic way.

As with acquisitions, it is people who make joint ventures succeed. A venture normally involves managers and technical staff working together to achieve its common goals. The interface between the people from the two parents who come together in a venture therefore needs to be carefully managed. It may be necessary to evolve a new organisation with its own value system and culture appropriate for the venture. However, evolving it is an extremely arduous task, as illustrated by CMB Packaging (see Case Study 17.3).

Regulatory issues in joint ventures

Joint ventures, like mergers, raise competition issues, since their potential impact may be to restrict competition in the markets in which the parents are operating. JVs are therefore regulated in many countries. In the UK, JVs and co-operative agreements are regulated under different laws:

- General common law against restraint of trade.

CASE STUDY 17.3   The French and the British fall out over packaging

CMB Packaging (CMB) was formed in 1989 through the merger of the French Carnaud and the British Metal Box to make the largest packaging company in Europe and the third largest in the world. The ownership of CMB was divided between Metal Box (25.5 per cent), CGIP (the French holding company of the erstwhile Carnaud, 25.5 per cent) and institutional shareholders in the UK and France.

Mr Jean Marie Descarpentries became the chairman and managing director of CMB, and proceeded to create a new organisational culture and management style for CMB distinct from its British and French parents. However, this did not succeed, partly due to Mr Descarpentries' own style of management, which was regarded by many British managers assigned to CMB as autocratic. The clash of management styles led to many senior British personnel leaving CMB, and the British presence on the board of CMB also declined. Thus, despite his lofty aim to blend the best of British and French management styles to produce a new style for CMB, Mr Descarpentries failed and he quit the company in September 1991.

Source: *Financial Times*, 12.9.1991.

- The Fair Trading Act 1973 (FTA) and the procedures of the Monopolies and Mergers Commission (MMC).
- The Restrictive Trade Practices Act (RTPA).
- The Resale Prices Act 1976 (RPA).
- Articles 85 and 86 of the Treaty of Rome. Merger Regulation 1990.

In other countries, such as Germany and the USA, the antitrust and anticartel laws may apply.

The operation of the FTA and the role of the Office of Fair Trading (OFT) and the MMC were discussed in Chapter 5. The RTPA prevents enforcement of any agreement between two or more persons who carry on business in the UK containing restrictions as to prices, terms and conditions, quantities, processes of manufacture or persons from whom or to whom goods are to be supplied. The RPA prohibits maintenance of resale prices at the behest of suppliers.

European Union regulation of joint ventures

As noted in Chapter 5, the EU rules distinguish between a 'concentrative venture' and a 'co-operative venture'. A venture is concentrative if:

- it is a permanent autonomous economic entity; and
- there is no co-ordination of the competitive behaviour either between the parents or between the parents and the venture.

Thus the creation of a concentrative joint venture signifies a structural change in the marketplace. Such ventures are regulated under the Merger Regulation rules discussed in Chapter 5.

A co-operative venture falls outside the Merger Regulation and is governed by Article 85, the anti-cartel rule, and Article 86, the anti-dominance abuse rule (see Chapter 5 for details). Clearance procedures under either article are not as clear cut or time bound as those under the Merger Regulation. There is thus an incentive for parents to structure their joint ventures to fall within the latter.

In practice, the distinction between the two types of JV is not easy to make. Hence it is worthwhile approaching the European Commission for confidential guidance before structuring a JV. Article 85 prohibits agreements between undertakings which may affect trade between member states, and which aim to restrict competition within the Common Market. Any JV contrary to that article is void.

Article 85 provides for individual or block exemption of certain agreements from its prohibitory effect. To qualify for individual exemption, the JV must contribute to improving the production or distribution of goods, or promoting technical or economic progress within the Common Market. The block exemptions relate to Specialisation Agreements and Research and Development Agreements. Under these exemptions, certain agreements containing restrictions on production or distribution, or restrictive agreements on joint research, will not be prohibited. The circumstances under which individual exemption may be granted are illustrated in the case of Eirpage (see Case Study 17.4).

Article 86, which prohibits abuse of dominance by undertakings, may also apply to the JV if it leads to a dominant position and that position is then abused. If the parents have joint dominance, the formation of the JV may be construed as an abuse of that dominance.

CASE STUDY 17.4   Eirpage wins individual exemption

Bord Telecom Eireann (BTE) and Motorola Ireland Limited (MIL) formed
a JV for a paging system connected to the Irish telecommunications
network. The two parents exercised joint control of the JV. Both BTE and
MIL had the necessary expertise to provide the paging service each on its
own. If they had entered the market separately, they would have been
competitors. The European Commission declared that the JV was
restrictive of competition.

The Commission then considered whether the JV should be given
exemption, and concluded that the system could not have been achieved
rapidly without the JV. This was of benefit to Irish consumers. The JV
was therefore given individual exemption.

Source: Wheaton (1993).

Performance evaluation of joint ventures

How do we assess the success or failure of a strategic alliance? One
possible yardstick is their mortality rate: that is, how soon after their
formation they get dissolved or taken over. Dissolution or takeover
per se does not signify failure, since an alliance which has served its
purpose may be dissolved to the satisfaction of the partners or sold
to one of them. Where dissolution or takeover is premature, failure
may be inferred.

McKinsey & Co., the strategy consultants, examined a sample of
49 cross-border strategic alliances (CBSAs) made by companies in
the top 150 in Europe, the USA and Japan (Bleeke and Ernst, 1993).
These CBSAs were motivated by the desire to speed entry into new
markets, to develop and commercialise new products, to gain skills
or to share costs. Success was measured in terms of return on assets
or on equity, and whether the return exceeded the cost of capital.

The survey revealed that 51 per cent of the CBSAs were regarded
as successful and 33 per cent as failures by both partners. The
remainder failed for at least one of the partners. Further, 67 per cent
of the CBSAs ran into trouble in the first two years. Some 78 per
cent of all the alliances which were terminated ended in acquisition
by a partner, and 5 per cent by a third party; 17 per cent were
dissolved.

Bleeke and Ernst (1993) identified characteristics which distinguished successful CBSAs. One of them is the geographical overlap
in the operations of the partners. Whereas 62 per cent of CBSAs

with minimal overlap succeeded, only 25 per cent of those with moderate or high overlap did so, and 37 per cent of the latter failed. This result is consistent with our argument that complementarity is conducive to a successful relationship between partners.

Alliances which provided for flexibility to broaden their scope were also more successful. Further, equal ownership reduced the scope for opportunism between partners and enhanced co-operative behaviour, as suggested by the Prisoner's Dilemma model described earlier. For a sample of 20 CBSAs with a 50:50 ownership interest, 60 per cent were successful, whereas for a sample of 13 with an uneven split of equity interest, only 31 per cent were successful and 61 per cent failed.

Critical success factors in alliances

From the theoretical models of joint ventures as well as the survey evidence presented, we may draw up a list of factors potentially conducive to successful alliances:

- Partners should bring complementary skills, capabilities and market positions to the alliance;
- Market overlap between partners should be minimal to avoid conflict of interest;
- Partnership should be based on a balance of business strength and ownership interest among partners;
- The alliance must have a degree of autonomy with strong leadership and continual commitment and support from the parents;
- The alliance must build up trust and confidence between the partners and not depend only on the contractual rights and obligations;
- Divergence of management styles and corporate cultures must be handled with sensitivity, and a new common style and culture distinct from the parents' must be evolved.

Even longstanding strategic alliances can break down because of the divergence of strategies which the partners want to pursue. Thus the potential for rivalry and distrust between partners always exists in strategic alliances, as illustrated by the rift between Compaq and Intel (see Case Study 17.5).

CASE STUDY 17.5   Compaq and Intel fall out over strategy

Compaq, the US personal computer manufacturer, had a longstanding strategic relationship with Intel, the US microchip manufacturer. Compaq was the largest customer for the Intel chips. Compaq's revenues in 1993 were $7.1 billion, and Intel's were $8.78 billion. In September 1994, the alliance between the two companies came under strain when Intel started a multimillion dollar advertising campaign, 'Intel inside', to promote its semiconductor. Intel's aim was to ensure that personal computer makers using the Intel chips carried an 'Intel inside' sticker on their products.

Compaq considered that Intel's campaign was undermining the Compaq brand name, and alleged that Intel was trying to promote itself at the expense of Compaq. Compaq also complained that Intel was not rewarding it for being the company's largest customer, and that Intel was making personal computers in direct competition with Compaq.

Source: *Financial Times*, 12.9.1994.

Overview

This chapter has provided an introduction to strategic alliances, which are under certain circumstances preferable to conventional acquisitions and mergers. Information has been provided on the recent and increasing trend towards strategic alliances, and different types of strategic alliance have been described. Strategic alliances, however, have their own problems, such as opportunism, inappropriate structure, and unsuitable or unreliable partners. These problems have caused many strategic alliances to fail. We have examined the survey evidence on strategic alliances formed by top companies in Europe, the USA and Japan. From this survey evidence and the theoretical models of strategic alliances, a list of critical success factors has been provided.

References and further reading

Bleeke, J. and D. Ernst (1993) 'The way to win in cross-border alliances', in J. Bleeke and D. Ernst (eds.) *Collaborating to Compete*, John Wiley.

Glaister, K.W. and P. Buckley (1994) 'UK international joint ventures: an analysis of patterns of activity and distribution', *British Journal of Management*, **5**, 33–51.

Jarillo, J. Carlos and H.H. Stevenson (1991) 'Cooperative strategies, the payoffs and pitfalls', *Long Range Planning*, **24**, 1, 64–70.

Kay, J. (1993) *Foundation of Corporate Success*, Oxford University Press, chs 3 and 10.

Lei, D. (1993) 'Offensive and defensive uses of alliances', *Long Range Planning*, **26**, 4, 32–41.

Wheaton, J.B. (1993) 'EEA and EC competition law: application to joint ventures', IIR Conference, Helsinki.

Zahra, S. and G. Elhagrasey (1994) 'Strategic management of international joint ventures', *European Management Journal*, **12**, 1, 83–93.

Author index

Subject index

Note: Case study references to companies are shown in **bold** type; companies listed in tables are shown in *italics*.